5 STEPS TO A 5™

AP English Language and Composition

2024

Barbara L. Murphy
Estelle M. Rankin

McGraw Hill

New York   Chicago   San Francisco   Athens   London   Madrid
Mexico City   Milan   New Delhi   Singapore   Sydney   Toronto

1 2 3 4 5 6 7 8 9   LHS   28 27 26 25 24 23
1 2 3 4 5 6 7 8 9   LHS   28 27 26 25 24 23   (Elite Student Edition)

ISBN   978-1-265-28863-1
MHID   1-265-28863-1

e-ISBN   978-1-265-28938-6
e-MHID   1-265-28938-7

ISBN   978-1-265-29074-0 (Elite Student Edition)
MHID   1-265-29074-1

e-ISBN   978-1-265-29187-7 (Elite Student Edition)
e-MHID   1-265-29187-X

Trademarks: McGraw Hill, the McGraw Hill logo, 5 Steps to a 5 and related trade dress are trademarks or registered trademarks of McGraw Hill and/or its affiliates in the United States and other countries and may not be used without written permission. All other trademarks are the property of their respective owners. McGraw Hill is not associated with any product or vendor mentioned in this book.

The series editor for this book was Grace Freedson and the project editor was Del Franz.

AP, Advanced Placement Program, and College Board are registered trademarks of the College Board, which was not involved in the production of, and does not endorse, this product.

McGraw Hill products are available at special quantity discounts to use as premiums and sales promotions or for use in corporate training programs. To contact a representative, please visit the Contact Us pages at www.mhprofessional.com.

McGraw Hill is committed to making our products accessible to all learners. To learn more about the available support and accommodations we offer, please contact us at accessibility@mheducation.com. We also participate in the Access Text Network (www.accesstext.org), and ATN members may submit requests through ATN.

CONTENTS

STEP 4 Review the Knowledge You Need to Score High

STEP 5 Build Your Test-Taking Confidence

Appendixes

PREFACE

Welcome to our latest revised AP English Language class. As we said in the earlier versions of this book, we are, first and foremost, teachers who have taught Advanced Placement to literally thousands of students who successfully took the AP exam. There you can test how well you have internalized the skill and material presented in a specific chapter.

We see you as a student in our class—only quieter! Our philosophy has always been NOT to teach only for the AP test. Instead, our goal is to develop those insights, appreciations, and skills that lead to advanced levels of facility with a wide range of texts. These are the same skills that will enable you to do well on the AP English Language exam. Our aim is to remove your anxiety and to improve your comfort level with the test. We believe that you are already motivated to succeed; otherwise, you would not have come this far. And, obviously, you would not have purchased this prep book.

Because you are already in an AP English class, this book is going to supplement your course readings, analysis, and writing. We are going to give you the opportunity to practice processes and techniques that we know from experience REALLY WORK! If you apply the techniques and processes presented in this book, we are confident you can succeed both in the course and on the exam.

We have listened to comments and suggestions from both instructors and students of AP English Language. Keeping their thoughts in mind, this revised text has more interactive activities and practice to help hone those skills needed to do well in class and on the AP English Language exam. In addition, there are special review questions and activities related to specific chapters that McGraw Hill has available on its website devoted to the *5 Steps* series.

Let's begin.

ACKNOWLEDGMENTS

Our love and appreciation to Leah and Allan for their constant support and encouragement. Special thanks to our professional mentors who have guided us throughout our careers: Steven Piorkowski and Howard Damon. To the following for their support and suggestions: Diane Antonucci, Jodi Rice, Margaret Cross Rice, Pat Kelley, Stephanie Tidwell, Sandi Forsythe, Arthurine Dunn, Dominic Constanzi, Virginia DeFrancisci, Christine Scharf—thank you.

A special thank you and appreciation to Molly Little for her review, comments, and suggestions that will better allow clear access to the concepts, goals, and skills addressed in this text. A Yale graduate, Molly teaches AP English Language and Composition at Arundel High School in Gambrills, Maryland. She has taught all levels of high school English and is active in the school's equity work and student leadership initiatives.

The authors want to acknowledge the participation, insights, and feedback provided us by the following colleagues and students:

East Islip High School:
   Teacher: Marge Grossgold
   Students: Kyle Hill, Jamie Ray

Freeport High School:
   Teacher: Virginia DeFrancisci
   Students: Nicole Bailey, Raymond Cowan, Shyanne Gardner, Mia Sorrentino

Garden City High School:
   Teachers: Mary Watts, Ed Schmeider
   Students: Alexandra Wertis, Michael Marino

Jericho High School:
   Teachers: Diane Antonucci, Patricia Gulitti
   Students: Vikas Anand, Jenna Butner, Shinae Lee, Josh Levine, Boyang Li, Anish Mashettiwar, Erica Ross, Sherli Yeroushalmi, Qi Yu

Kings Park High School:
   Teacher: Jeanne Palm
   Students: Fred Langer, Stephanie Kersling, Janet Lee

Moro Bay High School:
   Teacher: Michelle Dowell
   Students: Katey Maruska, Heather Spellacy

Roslyn High School:
   Student: Jenna Kahn

Wellington High School:
   Teacher: Margaret Cross Rice
   Student: Annaliesa Copan

Also, our thanks to Yale University students Danielle Tumminio and Jilian Cabot Fletcher. We'd also like to acknowledge the collaborative and inventive participants in the recent AP English Language Institutes held at Goucher College, Molloy College, in Lewes, Delaware; and in Philadelphia, Pennsylvania, for their contributions and constructive comments.

ABOUT THE AUTHORS

Barbara L. Murphy taught AP Language and other college-level courses at Jericho High School for more than 26 years. She has been a reader of the AP Language and Composition exam for many years and is a consultant for the College Board's AP Language and Composition, for which she has conducted workshops, conferences, and Summer Institutes.

After earning her BA from Duquesne University and her MA from the University of Pittsburgh, Ms. Murphy did her doctoral course work at Columbia University. She also holds professional certifications in still photography and motion picture production and is one of the founding members of the women's film company Ishtar Films.

Estelle M. Rankin taught AP Literature at Jericho High School for more than 25 years. She was honored as an AP Literature Teacher of the Year and as a Long Island Teacher of the Year. A recipient of the Cornell University Presidential Scholars' Award, she was also recognized by the C.W. Post Master Teachers Program.

Ms. Rankin earned her BA from Adelphi University and her MA from Hofstra University. She pursued further graduate work in the field of creative studies at Queens College and Brooklyn College.

She did extensive work in the research and development of film, drama, and creative writing curricula, SAT prep, and the new NYS Regents benchmarks for English, and participated in numerous AP Literature conferences and workshops, and was a College Board consultant for pre-AP and AP English.

Ms. Murphy and Ms. Rankin are also the coauthors of McGraw Hill's *5 Steps to a 5: AP English Literature*, *Writing the AP English Essay*, and *Writing an Outstanding College Application Essay*.

Special acknowledgement to Caity Gladstone-Mueller for her much appreciated and careful review, comments, and suggestions that will better allow clear access to the AP English Language and Composition concepts, goals, and skills addressed in this text.

Caity Gladstone-Mueller has taught secondary English in central Virginia for ten years. Currently teaching AP English Language and Composition and Dual Enrollment English, she has also taught every level of English in grades 6–12. Caity earned her BA in English from Sweet Briar College, an MA in English from Longwood University, and an MFA in the study and writing of Children's and YA Literature from Hollins University. Ms. Gladstone-Mueller is also a professor in the Focused Inquiry Department at VCU.

Pitts, Leonard. "Warning: Beware of Idiot Warning Labels." *Baltimore Sun*, May 30, 2000, https://www.baltimoresun.com/news/bs-xpm-2000-05-30-0005270015-story.html.

Ramos, Wendy. "Prose Analysis Flow Chart."

Rosenblatt, Roger. "Tell Me a Story." From the November 22, 2005, broadcast of *The PBS Newshour*, pbs.org/newshour/show/tell-me-a-story.

Sekula, Allen. "Reading an Archive." From *Blasted Allegories*. Copyright © 1987 by MIT. Used by permission of the publisher, MIT Press.

"The Voice of the Story, the Story as Voice," an excerpt from "Reading Blind"; first appeared in *The Best American Short Stories 1989* © 1989 O.W. Toad, Ltd.

Thurnberg, Greta. Speech to the United Nations Climate Action Summit, September 23, 2019.

Urban, Dennis. "History Evolves as Scholars Learn More." *Newsday* "Letters to the Editor," August 23, 2019.

INTRODUCTION: THE FIVE-STEP PROGRAM

Some Basics

Reading

We believe that reading should be an exciting interaction between you and the writer. You must bring your own context to the experience, and you must feel comfortable reaching for and exploring ideas. You are an adventurer on a journey of exploration, and we act as your guides. We set the itinerary, but you will set your own pace. You can feel free to "stop and smell the roses" or to explore new territory.

The Journey

On any journey, each traveler sees something different on new horizons. So, too, each student is free to personalize their own literary experience, provided they try at all times to strive for excellence and accuracy.

Critical Thinking

There are no tricks to critical thinking. Those who claim to guarantee you a 5 by using gimmicks are doing you a disservice. No one can guarantee a 5. However, the reading and writing skills you will review, practice, and master will give you the very best chance to do your very best. You will have the opportunity to learn, to practice, and to master the critical thinking processes that can empower you to achieve your highest score.

Philosophy of This Book: In the Beginning . . .

This is an important concept for us, because we believe that if you focus on the beginning, the rest will fall into place. When you purchased this book and decided to work your way through it, you were beginning your journey to the AP English Language and Composition exam. We will be with you every step of the way.

Why This Book?

We believe we have something unique to offer you. For more than 25 years we have addressed the needs of AP students just like you, and we have been fortunate to learn from these students. Therefore, the contents of this book reflect genuine student concerns and needs. This is a student-oriented book. We will not overwhelm you with pompous language, mislead you with inaccurate information and tasks, or lull you into a false sense of confidence through cutesy shortcuts. We stand behind every suggestion, process, and question we present. There is no "busywork" in this book.

We know you will not do every activity we suggest. Therefore, think of this text as a resource and guide to accompany you on your AP English Language and Composition exam journey throughout the year. This book is designed to serve many purposes. It will:

- clarify requirements for the AP English Language and Composition exam;
- provide you with test practice;
- show you models and rubrics on which you can model and evaluate your own work;
- anticipate and answer your questions;
- enrich your understanding and appreciation of the writing process;
- help you pace yourself; and
- make you aware of the Five Steps to Mastering the AP English Language and Composition exam.

Organization of the Book

We know that your primary concern is information about the AP English Language and Composition exam; therefore, we begin with an overview of the AP exam in general. We then introduce you to the Diagnostic/Master exam we use throughout the book to show you the "ins and outs" of an AP test. In separate chapters, you will become familiar with both sections of the exam. We lead you through the multiple-choice questions and how to go about answering them, and we take you through the essay questions and approaches to writing these essays.

Because you must be fluent in the language and the process of composition, synthesis, and analysis, we provide a full comprehensive review part in analysis, synthesis, and argument. This review is not a mere listing of terms and concepts. Rather, it is a series of practices that will hone your analytical and writing skills. However, do not fear. You will find terms and concepts clearly delineated within their contexts. We will also provide you with annotated suggestions for high-interest readings for analysis, synthesis, and argument.

After carefully working your way through Chapters 4 through 10, you may wish to go to McGraw Hill's *5 Step* series website which provides review, reinforcement, and enrichment questions that refer to the skills covered in each chapter. You can compare your response(s) with what we provide on the website for this book: **www.mhpracticeplus.com**

A separate section of this book contains the practice exams. Here is where you will test your own skills. You may be sure that the selections included in each exam are on an AP level. The multiple-choice questions provide practice with types of questions asked on AP exams. The essay questions are designed to cover the techniques and terms required by the AP exam. The free-response essays are both challenging and specific, but broad enough to suit all curricula. After taking each exam, you can check yourself against the explanations of every multiple-choice question and the ratings of the sample student essays.

The final part is one you should not pass over. It contains a glossary of terms, a bibliography of works that may be of importance to you, and a list of websites related to the AP English Language and Composition exam.

Introduction to the Five-Step Preparation Program

The Five-Step Preparation Program is a powerful tool designed to provide you with the best possible skills, strategies, and practice to help lead you to that perfect 5 on the AP English Language and Composition exam administered each May to more than 250,000 high school students. Each of the five steps will provide you with the opportunity to get closer and closer to the 5, which is the "Holy Grail" to all AP students.

Step 1: Set Up Your Study Program

- Month-by-month: September through May
- The calendar year: January through May
- Basic training: the 4 to 6 weeks before the exam

Step 2: Determine Your Test Readiness

- A comprehensive review of the exam
- One "Diagnostic/Master exam" you will go through step by step and question by question to build your confidence level
- Explanation of multiple-choice answers

Step 3: Develop Strategies for Success

- Learn about the test itself
- Learn to read multiple-choice questions
- Learn how to answer multiple-choice questions, including whether or not to guess
- Learn how to deconstruct the essay prompts
- Learn how to plan the essay

Step 4: Review the Knowledge You Need to Score High

- A comprehensive review of analysis and argument
- Practice activities that will hone your skills in close reading
- Practice activities in critical thinking
- Practice activities in critical/analytical/argumentative writing

Step 5: Build Your Test-Taking Confidence

- The opportunity to take a Diagnostic/Master exam
- Time management techniques/skills
- Two practice exams that test how well-honed your skills are
- Rubrics for self-evaluation

Finally, at the back of the book you'll find additional resources to aid your preparation. These include:

- Glossary of terms
- Bibliography for further reading
- Websites related to the AP English Language exam

The Graphics Used in This Book

To emphasize particular skills and strategies, we use several icons throughout this book. An icon in the margin will alert you that you should pay particular attention to the accompanying text. We use three icons:

 This icon points out a very important concept or fact that you should not pass over.

 This icon calls your attention to a problem-solving strategy that you may want to try.

 This icon indicates a tip that you might find useful.

In addition, **bold** and **<u>bold underlined</u>** words indicate terms included in the Glossary.

Scattered throughout the book are marginal notes and numerous shaded boxes. We urge you to pay close attention to them because they can provide tips, hints, strategies, and further explanations to help you reach your full potential.

Use of the Personal Pronoun in This Book

We strive to respect each other's humanity and to honor how we all identify. We are also aware of the continuing controversy about the use of personal pronouns and are aware that language is flexible and evolving. With that in mind, *5 Steps to a 5: English Language and Composition* will use a variety of these personal pronouns throughout the text: he/his, she/her, and they/their until a neutral pronoun is developed that is accepted by the MLA, APA, etc.

Set Up Your Study Program

CHAPTER 1

What You Need to Know About the AP English Language and Composition Exam

IN THIS CHAPTER

Summary: Information about the AP English Language and Composition exam and its scoring.

Key Ideas

✪ Learn answers to frequently asked questions.

✪ Learn how your final score is calculated.

✪ Learn tips for successfully taking the exam.

BASIC INFORMATION ABOUT THE AP ENGLISH LANGUAGE EXAM

The 3 hour 15 minute AP English Language exam is comprised of TWO sections: Multiple Choice and Essays.

- Part 1 of the exam is *multiple choice*.
  - You have 1 hour to complete this section.
  - There are 45 questions related to both close reading and composition.
  - Multiple choice is 45% of the final score.
- Part 2 of the exam has 3 essay prompts: synthesis, rhetorical analysis, argument.
  - The three essays are scored using a 6 point rubric:
    - 1 point for thesis/claim
    - 4 points for appropriate evidence and commentary
    - 1 point for sophistication (complexity)

Background on the AP English Language and Composition Exam

What Is the AP Program?

The Advanced Placement program was begun by the College Board in 1955 to construct standard achievement exams that would allow highly motivated high school students the opportunity to be awarded advanced placement as freshmen in colleges and universities in the United States. Today, there are more than 39 courses and exams with over 2.7 million students from every state in the nation, and from foreign countries, taking the annual exams in May.

As is obvious, the AP programs are designed for high school students who want to take college-level courses. In our case, the AP English Language and Composition course and exam are designed to involve high school students in college-level English studies in both the use and structure of language and composition.

Who Writes the AP English Language and Composition Exam?

According to the College Board, the AP Comp exam is created by a group of college and high school English instructors called the "AP Test Development Committees." Their job is to ensure that the annual AP Comp exam reflects what is being taught and studied in college-level English classes at the high schools.

This committee writes a large number of multiple-choice questions that are pretested and evaluated for clarity, appropriateness, and range of possible answers. The committee also generates a pool of essay questions, pretests them, and chooses those questions that best represent the full range of the scoring scale to allow the AP readers to evaluate the essays equitably.

It is important to remember that the AP English Language and Composition exam is thoroughly evaluated after it is administered each year. This way, the College Board can use the results to make course suggestions and to plan future tests.

What Are the AP Scores and Who Receives Them?

Once you have taken the exam and it has been scored, your test will be given one of five numbers by the College Board.

- 5 indicates you are extremely well qualified.
- 4 indicates you are well qualified.
- 3 indicates you are qualified.
- 2 indicates you are possibly qualified.
- 1 indicates you are not qualified to receive college credit.

Your score is reported first to your college or university, second to your high school, and third to you. All the reporting is usually completed by the middle to end of July.

Answers to Frequently Asked Questions About the Exam

If I Don't Take an AP Composition Course, Can I Still Take the AP English Language and Composition Exam?

Yes. Although the AP English Language and Composition exam is designed for the student who has had a year's course in AP English Language and Composition, there are high schools that do not offer this type of course, and the students in these high schools have also done well on the exam. However, if your high school does offer an AP Composition course, by all means take advantage of it and the structured background it will provide you.

How Is the AP English Language and Composition Exam Organized?

The exam has two parts and is scheduled to last 3 hours and 15 minutes. The first section is a set of multiple-choice questions based on a series of prose passages. You will have 1 hour to complete this part of the test. The second section of the exam is a 2-hour and 15-minute essay writing segment consisting of three different essays: analysis, argument, and synthesis. According to the College Board's **AP English Language and Composition Exam Instructions**, the 15-minute reading period in Section II is recommended, not required. Students are strongly encouraged to use the reading period to read the questions and sources and plan their responses. They may begin writing their responses during that time if they choose to do so. However, our advice is to use this time for careful reading.

After you complete the multiple-choice section, you will hand in your test booklet and scan sheet, and you will be given a brief break. Note that you will not be able to return to the multiple-choice questions when you return to the examination room.

Must I Check the Box at the End of the Essay Booklet That Allows the AP People to Use My Essays as Samples for Research?

No. This is simply a way for the College Board to make certain that it has your permission if it decides to use one or more of your essays as a model. The readers of your essays pay no attention to whether or not that box is checked. Checking the box will not affect your grade either.

How Is My AP English Language and Composition Exam Scored?

Let's look at the basics first. The multiple-choice section counts for 45% of your total score, and the essay section counts for 55%. Next comes a four-part calculation: the raw scoring of the multiple-choice section, the raw scoring of the essay section, the calculation of the composite score, and the conversion of the composite score into the AP grade of 5, 4, 3, 2, or 1.

How Is the Multiple-Choice Section Scored?

The scan sheet with your answers is run through a computer that counts the number of correct answers. Questions left blank and questions answered incorrectly are treated the same and get no points. There is no longer a "guessing penalty," which formerly involved the deduction of a fraction of a point for answering a question but getting it wrong.

How Is My Essay Section Scored?

Each of your essays is read by a different, trained AP reader called a "faculty consultant." The AP/College Board people have developed a highly successful training program for its readers, together with many opportunities for checks and double checks of essays to ensure a fair and equitable reading of each essay.

The scoring guides are carefully developed by the chief faculty consultant, question leader, table leaders, and content experts. All faculty consultants are then trained to read and score just **one** essay question on the exam. They become experts in that one essay question. No one knows the identity of any writer. The identification numbers and names are covered, and the exam booklets are randomly distributed to the readers in packets of 25 randomly chosen essays. Table leaders and the question leader review samples of each reader's scores to ensure quality standards are constant.

Each essay is scored as 6, 5, 4, 3, 2, 1, plus 0, with 6 the highest possible score. Once your essay is given a number from 6 to 1, the next set of calculations is completed using a formula developed to account for the score of each essay. This is the raw score for the essay section of the exam.

$$(\text{pts.} \times 3.055) + (\text{pts.} \times 3.055) + (\text{pts.} \times 3.055) = \text{essay raw score}$$

$$\text{Essay 1} \qquad\qquad \text{Essay 2} \qquad\qquad \text{Essay 3}$$

How Do They Calculate My Composite Score?

You need to do a little math here: 150 is the total composite score for the AP English Language and Composition test. Fifty-five percent of this score is the essay section; that equals 82.5 points. Forty-five percent of the composite score is the multiple-choice section, which equals 67.5 points. Each of your three essays is scored on a 6-point scale; therefore, each point is worth 4.58. You would divide the number of multiple-choice questions by 67.5. For example, if there were 45 questions, each point of the raw score would be multiplied by 1.5. If you add together the raw scores of each of the two sections, you will have a composite score.

How Is My Composite Data Turned into the Score Reported to My College?

Remember that the total composite scores needed to earn a 5, 4, 3, 2, or 1 differ each year. This is determined by a committee of AP/College Board/ETS directors, experts, and statisticians. The score is based on such items as:

- AP distribution over the past three years
- Comparability studies
- Observations of the chief faculty consultant
- Frequency distributions of scores on each section and the essays
- Average scores on each exam section and essays

However, over the years a trend can be observed that indicates the number of points required to achieve a specific score.

- 150–100 points = 5
- 99–86 = 4
- 85–67 = 3

2 and 1 fall below this range.

What Should I Bring to the Exam?

- Several pencils
- A good eraser
- Several BLACK pens (black ink is easier on the eyes)
- A watch
- Something to drink—water is best
- A quiet snack, such as Life Savers
- Tissues

Are There Additional Recommendations?

- Allow plenty of time to get to the test site.
- Wear comfortable clothing.
- Eat a light breakfast or lunch.
- Remind yourself that you are well prepared and that the test is an enjoyable challenge and a chance to share your knowledge. Be proud of yourself! You worked hard all year. Now is your time to shine.

Is There Anything Special I Should Do the Night Before the Exam?

We certainly don't advocate last-minute cramming, and, if you've been following the guidelines, you won't have to. However, there may be a slight value to some last minute review. Spend the night before the exam relaxing with family or friends. Watch a movie; play a game; talk with friends, blog, or use Twitter; and then find a quiet spot. While you're unwinding, flip through your own notebook and review sheets. By now, you're bound to be ready to drift off to sleep. Pleasant dreams.

CHAPTER 2

How to Plan Your Time

IN THIS CHAPTER

Summary: Assess your own study patterns and preparation plans.

Key Ideas

✪ Explore three approaches.

✪ Choose a calendar that works for you.

Three Approaches to Prepare for the AP English Language and Composition Exam

No one knows your study habits, likes, and dislikes better than you. You are the only one who can decide which approach you want and/or need to adopt to prepare for the AP English Language and Composition exam. Look at the brief profiles below. These may help you to place yourself in a particular prep mode.

You are a full-year prep student (Approach A) if:

1. You like to plan for a vacation or the prom a year in advance.
2. You never think of missing a practice session, whether it's for your favorite sport, musical instrument, or activity.
3. You like detailed planning and everything in its place.
4. You feel you must be thoroughly prepared.
5. You hate surprises.
6. You are always early for appointments.

You are a one-semester prep student (Approach B) if:

1. You choose your outfit about a week before the Prom.
2. You are willing to plan ahead to feel comfortable in stressful situations, but are okay with skipping some details.
3. You feel more comfortable when you know what to expect, but a surprise or two does not floor you.
4. You are always on time for appointments.

You are a 4- to 6-week prep student (Approach C) if:

1. You accept or find a date for the prom a week before the big day.
2. You work best under pressure and close deadlines.
3. You feel very confident with the skills and background you've learned in your AP English Language and Composition class.
4. You decided late in the year to take the exam.
5. You like surprises.
6. You feel okay if you arrive 10 to 15 minutes late for an appointment.

CALENDARS FOR PREPARING FOR THE AP ENGLISH LANGUAGE AND COMPOSITION EXAM

Calendar for Approach A:
Yearlong Preparation for the AP English Language and Composition Exam

Although its primary purpose is to prepare you for the AP English Language and Composition exam you will take in May, this book can enrich your study of language and composition, your analytical skills, and your writing skills.

SEPTEMBER–OCTOBER (Check off the activities as you complete them.)

_____ Determine into which student mode you would place yourself.

_____ Carefully read the Introduction and Chapter 1.

_____ Pay very close attention to the "Walk Through" the Diagnostic/Master exam.

_____ Use the internet to take a look at the AP website(s).

_____ Skim the Comprehensive Review section. (These areas will be part of your yearlong preparation.)

_____ Buy a highlighter.

_____ Flip through the entire book. Break the book in. Write in it. Highlight it.

_____ Get a clear picture of what your own school's AP English Language curriculum is.

_____ Review the Bibliography and establish a pattern of outside reading.

_____ Begin to use this book as a resource.

NOVEMBER (The first 10 weeks have elapsed.)

_____ Write the argument essay in the Diagnostic/Master exam.

_____ Compare your essay with the sample student essays.

_____ Refer to Chapters 6 and 9 on the argument essay.

_____ Take five of our prompts and write solid opening paragraphs.

DECEMBER

_____ Maintain notes on literary works studied in and out of class.

_____ Refine analytical skills (see Chapters 5 and 8).

_____ Write one of the two analytical essays in the Diagnostic/Master exam. (This will depend on the organization of your own curriculum.)

_____ Compare your essay with the sample student essays.

JANUARY (20 weeks have now elapsed.)

_____ Write the synthesis essay in the Diagnostic/Master exam. (This will depend on your previous choice.)

_____ Compare your essay with the sample student essays.

_____ Refer to Chapters 7 and 10 on the synthesis essay.

FEBRUARY

_____ Take the multiple-choice section of the Diagnostic/Master exam.

_____ Carefully go over the explanations of the answers to the questions.

_____ Score yourself honestly.

_____ Make a note of terms and concepts and types of questions that give you trouble.

_____ Review troublesome terms by checking the Glossary.

MARCH (30 weeks have now elapsed.)

_____ Form a study group.

_____ Choose a selection you have studied in class and create an essay question to go with it, or you can use one of our suggested prompts.

_____ Choose a passage from a current editorial and create an essay question to go with it, or you can choose one of our suggested prompts.

_____ Write one of the analytical essays.

_____ Write one of the synthesis essays.

_____ Compare essays and rate them with your study group. (Use our rubrics.)

APRIL

_____ Take Practice Exam 1 in the first week of April.

_____ Evaluate your strengths and weaknesses.

_____ Study appropriate chapters to correct weaknesses.

_____ Practice creating multiple-choice questions of different types with your study group.

_____ Develop and review worksheets for and with your study group.

MAY—First two weeks (THIS IS IT!)

_____ Highlight only those things in the Glossary about which you are still unsure. Ask your teacher for clarification. Study!

_____ Write at least three times a week under timed conditions.

_____ Take Practice Exam 2.

_____ Score yourself.

_____ Give yourself a pat on the back for how much you have learned and improved over the past nine months.

_____ Go to the movies. Call a friend.

_____ Get a good night's sleep. Fall asleep knowing you are well prepared.

GOOD LUCK ON THE TEST!

Calendar for Approach B:
Semester-Long Preparation for the AP English Language and Composition Exam

The following calendar assumes that you have completed one semester of language and composition and will use those skills you have been practicing to prepare you for the May exam. You still have plenty of time to supplement your course work by taking our study recommendations, maintaining literary notations, doing outside readings, and so forth. We divide the next 16 weeks into a workable program of preparation for you.

JANUARY–FEBRUARY (Check off the activities as you complete them.)

_____ Carefully read the Introduction and Chapter 1.

_____ Write the three essays on the Diagnostic/Master exam.

_____ Compare your essays with the sample student essays.

_____ Complete the multiple-choice section of the Diagnostic/Master exam.

_____ Carefully go over the answers and explanations of the answers.

_____ Take a close look at the Bibliography for suggestions regarding possible outside readings.

MARCH (10 weeks to go)

_____ Form a study group.

_____ Choose a favorite essay or excerpt from a book and create an essay question to go with it, or you can use one of our suggested prompts.

_____ Choose a prose passage or essay and create an essay question to go with it, or you can choose one of our suggested prompts.

_____ Write one of the analytical essays.

_____ Write one of the synthesis essays.

_____ Compare essays and rate them with your study group. (Use our rubrics.)

APRIL

_____ Take Practice Exam 1 in the first week of April.

_____ Evaluate your strengths and weaknesses.

_____ Study appropriate chapters to correct weaknesses.

_____ Practice creating multiple-choice questions of different types with your study group.

_____ Develop and review worksheets for and with your study group.

MAY—First two weeks (THIS IS IT!)

_____ Highlight only those things in the Glossary about which you are still unsure. Ask your teacher for clarification. Study!

_____ Write at least three times a week under timed conditions.

_____ Take Practice Exam 2.

_____ Score yourself.

_____ Give yourself a pat on the back for how much you have learned and improved over the past nine months.

_____ Go to the movies. Call a friend.

_____ Get a good night's sleep. Fall asleep knowing you are well prepared.

GOOD LUCK ON THE TEST!

Calendar for Approach C:
4- to 6-Week Preparation for the AP English Language and Composition Exam

At this point, we assume that you have been developing your argumentative, analytical, and writing skills in your English class for more than six months. You will, therefore, use this book primarily as a specific guide to the AP English Language and Composition exam. Remember, there is a solid review section in this book, to which you should refer.

Given the time constraints, now is not the time to try to expand your AP curriculum. Rather, it is the time to limit and refine what you already do know.

APRIL

_____ Skim the Introduction and Chapter 1.
_____ Carefully go over the "Rapid Review" sections of Chapters 5 through 10.
_____ Strengthen, clarify, and correct your weak areas after taking the Diagnostic/Master exam.
_____ Write a minimum of three sample opening paragraphs for each of the three types of essays.
_____ Write a minimum of two timed essays for each type of essay on the exam.
_____ Complete Practice Exam 1.
_____ Score yourself and analyze your errors.
_____ Refer to the appropriate chapters to correct weaknesses.
_____ Refer to the Bibliography.

_____ If you feel unfamiliar with specific forms of discourse, refer to the list of suggested appropriate works.
_____ Develop a weekly study group to hear each other's essays and discuss writing.
_____ Skim and highlight the Glossary.

MAY—First two weeks (THIS IS IT!)

_____ Complete Practice Exam 2.
_____ Score yourself and analyze your errors.
_____ Refer to the appropriate chapters to correct weaknesses.
_____ Go to the movies. Call a friend.
_____ Get a good night's sleep. Fall asleep knowing you are well prepared.

GOOD LUCK ON THE TEST!

"One of the first steps to success on the AP exam is knowing your own study habits."
—Margaret R., AP Language teacher

STEP 2

Determine Your Test Readiness

CHAPTER 3

A First Look at the Diagnostic/Master Exam

IN THIS CHAPTER

Summary: Familiarize yourself with the diagnostic exam.

Key Ideas

✪ Examine the multiple-choice section in Section I of the exam.
✪ Peruse the essay questions in Section II.

What follows is our version of an AP English Language and Composition exam we use throughout this book to demonstrate processes, examples, terms, and so forth. We call this our Diagnostic/Master exam. You will not be taking this exam at this point, but we would like you to "walk through" the exam with us, now.

The first part of this 3¼-hour exam is always going to be the multiple-choice section, which lasts 1 hour. It comprises primarily nonfiction. The multiple-choice section of the Diagnostic/Master exam contains several passages from different time periods and of different styles and purposes. It may include letters, essays, journal entries, editorials, speeches, and excerpts from longer works. The multiple-choice questions for each selection were developed to provide you with a wide range of question types and terminology that have been used in the actual AP English Language and Composition exams over the years.

To begin to know how the exam is structured, take some time now to look through the multiple-choice section of the Diagnostic/Master exam. Do not try to answer questions; just peruse the types of passages and questions.

- Review all of the pages of the test and familiarize yourself with their format.
- See where the long and short readings are.

"You know, from my experience with AP exams, I've learned never to assume anything."
— Jeremy G.,
   AP student

- Check the total number of questions and know what you are facing.
- Check out the essay prompts.

A Word About Our Sample Student Essays

We field-tested each of the essay questions in a variety of high schools, both public and private. We could have chosen to present essays that would have "knocked your socks off"; however, we chose to present samples we feel are truly representative of the essays usually written within the time constraints of the exam.

These essays are indicative of a wide range of styles and levels of acceptability. We want you to recognize that there is not one model to which all essays must conform.

"To Thine Own Self Be True" (Polonius–*Hamlet*)

This well-known caveat is always the very best advice and especially appropriate for the writer. Listen to your teacher's advice; listen to our advice; listen to your own voice. That's the voice we want to "hear" in your writing. Use natural vocabulary and present honest observations. It is wonderful to read professional criticism, but you cannot adopt another's ideas and remain true to your own thoughts. Trust your brain—if you've prepared well, you'll do well.

DIAGNOSTIC/MASTER EXAM
ADVANCED PLACEMENT ENGLISH LANGUAGE AND COMPOSITION
Section I

> The multiple-choice section of the exam will have 45 questions.
> - 20–25 will be related to close reading/analysis.
> - 20–25 will be related to the rhetorical situation.

Total Time—1 hour

Carefully read the following passages and answer the accompanying questions.

Questions 1–12 are based on the following passage from "Samuel Johnson on Pope," which appeared in *The Lives of the English Poets* (1779–1781).

The person of Pope is well known not to have been formed by the nicest model. He has compared himself to a spider and, by another, is described as protuberant behind and before. He is said to have been beautiful in his infancy, but he was of a constitution feeble and weak. As bodies of a tender frame are easily distorted, his deformity was probably in part the effect of his application. But his face was not displeasing, and his eyes were animated and vivid.   5

By natural deformity, or accidental distortion, his vital functions were so much disordered, that his life was a "long disease."

He sometimes condescended to be jocular with servants or inferiors; but by no merriment, either of others or his own, was he ever seen excited to laughter.   10

Of his domestic character frugality was a part eminently remarkable. Having determined not to be dependent, he determined not to be in want, and, therefore, wisely and magnanimously rejected all temptations to expense unsuitable to his fortune.

The great topic of his ridicule is poverty; the crimes with which he reproaches his antagonists are their debts and their want of a dinner. He seems to be of an opinion not   15 very uncommon in the world, that to want money is to want everything.

He professed to have learned his poetry from Dryden, whom he praised through his whole life with unvaried liberality; and perhaps his character may receive some illustration, if he be compared with his master.

Integrity of understanding and nicety of discernment were not allotted in a less   20 proportion to Dryden than to Pope. But Dryden never desired to apply all the judgment that he had. He wrote merely for the people. When he pleased others, he contented himself. He never attempted to mend what he must have known to be faulty. He wrote with little consideration and, once it had passed the press, ejected it from his mind.

Pope was not content to satisfy; he desired to excel, and, therefore, always endeavored   25 to do his best. Pope did not court the candor, but dared the judgment of his reader, and, expecting no indulgence from others, he showed none to himself. He examined lines and words with minute and punctilious observation, and he retouched every part with diligence, until he had nothing left to be forgiven.

Poetry was not the sole praise of either; for both excelled likewise in prose. The   30 style of Dryden is capricious and varied; that of Pope is cautious and uniform. Dryden observes the motions of his own mind; Pope constrains his mind to his own rules of composition. Dryden's page is a natural field, diversified by the exuberance of abundant vegetation. Pope's is a velvet lawn, shaven by the scythe, and leveled by the roller.

If the flights of Dryden are higher, Pope continues longer on the wing. If of Dryden's   35 fire the blaze is brighter, of Pope's the heat is more regular and constant. Dryden is read with frequent astonishment, and Pope with perpetual delight.

1. The primary purpose of the passage is to
   A. provide a character sketch of Pope
   B. examine the principles of poetic style
   C. criticize Dryden
   D. present a model for future poets
   E. create an opportunity for the writer to show off his own skills

2. The passage discusses a contrast among all of the following except:
   A. prose and poetry
   B. Pope and Dryden
   C. body and mind
   D. poverty and wealth
   E. body and soul

3. The thesis is located in line(s)
   A. 1
   B. 7–8
   C. 11
   D. 20–21
   E. 36–37

4. The character of Pope is developed by all of the following except:
   A. examples
   B. comparison
   C. contrast
   D. satire
   E. description

5. According to the passage, Pope and Dryden are
   A. rivals
   B. equally intelligent
   C. outdated
   D. equally physically attractive
   E. in debt

6. From the passage, the reader may infer that Pope
   A. was extravagant
   B. was a man of the people
   C. was jealous of Dryden
   D. had a desire to be popular
   E. had a bitter, satirical nature

7. "If the flights" (35) means
   A. Pope's writing will outlive Dryden's
   B. both Pope and Dryden are equal
   C. Pope is not idealistic
   D. Pope is more wordy
   E. Pope is not as bright as Dryden

8. Lines 20–24 indicate that Dryden was what type of writer?
   A. one who labored over his thoughts
   B. one who wrote only for himself
   C. one who wrote only for the critics
   D. one who wrote to please Pope
   E. one who did not revise

9. The tone of the passage is
   A. informal and affectionate
   B. formal and objective
   C. condescending and paternalistic
   D. laudatory and reverent
   E. critical and negative

10. In the context of the passage, "until he had nothing left to be forgiven" (29) means
    A. Pope outraged his readers
    B. Pope suffered from writer's block
    C. Pope exhausted his subject matter
    D. Pope's prose was revised to perfection
    E. Pope cared about the opinions of his readers

11. "Shaven" and "leveled" in line 34 indicate that Pope's style of writing was
    A. natural
    B. richly ornamented
    C. highly controlled
    D. mechanical
    E. analytical

12. Based on a close reading of the final paragraph of the passage, the reader could infer that the author
    A. looks on both writers equally
    B. prefers the work of Pope
    C. sees the two writers as inferior to his own writing style
    D. indicates no preference
    E. prefers the work of Dryden

Questions 13–23 are based on the following excerpt from Charlotte Perkins Gilman's "Politics and Warfare," which appears in *The Man-Made World: Our Androcentric Culture* (1911).

There are many today who hold that politics need not be at all connected with warfare; and others who hold that politics is warfare from start to finish.

The inextricable confusion of politics and warfare is part of the stumbling block in the minds of men. As they see it, a nation is primarily a fighting organization; and its principal business is offensive and defensive warfare; therefore the ultimatum with which they oppose the demand for political equality—"women cannot fight, therefore they cannot vote."

Fighting, when all is said, is to them the real business of life; not to be able to fight is to be quite out of the running; and ability to solve our growing mass of public problems; questions of health, of education, of morals, of economics; weighs naught against the ability to kill.

This naïve assumption of supreme value in a process never of the first importance; and increasingly injurious as society progresses, would be laughable if it were not for its evil effects. It acts and reacts upon us to our hurt. Positively, we see the ill effects already touched on; the evils not only of active war, but of the spirit and methods of war; idealized, inculcated, and practiced in other social processes. It tends to make each man-managed nation an actual or potential fighting organization, and to give us, instead of civilized peace, that "balance of power" which is like the counted time in the prize ring—only a rest between combats.

It leaves the weaker nations to be "conquered" and "annexed" just as they used to be; with "preferential tariffs" instead of tribute. It forces upon each the burden of armament; upon many the dreaded conscription; and continually lowers the world's resources in money and in life.

Similarly in politics, it adds to the legitimate expenses of governing the illegitimate expenses of fighting; and must needs have a "spoils system" by which to pay its mercenaries.

In carrying out the public policies the wheels of state are continually clogged by the "opposition"; always an opposition on one side or the other; and this slow wiggling uneven progress, through shorn victories and haggling concessions, is held to be the proper and only political method.

"Women do not understand politics," we are told; "Women do not care for politics"; "Women are unfitted for politics."

It is frankly inconceivable, from the androcentric viewpoint, that nations can live in peace together, and be friendly and serviceable as persons are. It is inconceivable also, that, in the management of a nation, honesty, efficiency, wisdom, experience and love could work out good results without any element of combat.

The "ultimate resort" is still to arms. "The will of the majority" is only respected on account of the guns of the majority. We have but a partial civilization, heavily modified to sex—the male sex.

13. The author's main purpose in the passage is to
   A. argue for women being drafted
   B. criticize colonialism
   C. present a pacifist philosophy
   D. criticize the male-dominated society
   E. protest tariffs

14. In paragraph 2, the author maintains that men support their position on equality for women based upon which of the following approaches?
   A. begging the question
   B. a syllogism using a faulty premise
   C. an appeal to emotion
   D. circular reasoning
   E. an *ad hoc* argument

15. Using textual clues, one can conclude that "androcentric" most probably means
   A. robot-centered
   B. world-centered
   C. female-centered
   D. self-centered
   E. male-centered

16. In paragraph 4, "increasingly injurious as society progresses" is reinforced by all of the following <u>except</u>:
   A. "ill effects already touched on" [paragraph 4]
   B. "active war" [paragraph 4]
   C. "weaker nations to be 'conquered' and 'annexed'" [paragraph 5]
   D. "illegitimate expenses of fighting" [paragraph 6]
   E. "Women do not understand politics" [paragraph 8]

17. In addition to indicating a direct quotation, the author uses quotation marks to indicate
   A. the jargon of politics and warfare
   B. the coining of a phrase
   C. a definition
   D. the author's scholarship
   E. that the author does not take responsibility for her words

18. According to the author, men view the primary purpose of government to be
   A. educating the people
   B. solving the "mass of public problems"
   C. obtaining as much power as possible
   D. economics
   E. health

19. The argument shifts from a discussion of warfare to a discussion of politics in the first sentence of which of the following paragraphs?
   A. paragraph 4
   B. paragraph 5
   C. paragraph 6
   D. paragraph 7
   E. paragraph 9

20. The tone of the passage is best described as
   A. ambivalent
   B. reverent
   C. condescending
   D. accusatory
   E. indifferent

21. To present her argument, Gilman primarily uses which of the following rhetorical strategies?
   A. process
   B. definition
   C. cause and effect
   D. narration
   E. description

Questions 22–30 are based on author Ernest J. Gaines's introduction to his 2000 short film titled *An Obsession*, which is about a cemetery on the Riverlake plantation that he bought and is dedicated to preserving.

An Obsession by Ernest Gaines

An obsession of mine concerns a half-acre of land in south-central Louisiana. This plot of land is surrounded by sugarcane fields on all sides, some of the rows coming within twenty feet of it. This plot of land is where my ancestors have been buried the past hundred years, where most of the people I knew as a child are now buried. This is Riverlake plantation, Point Coupee Parish, Oscar, Louisiana. 1

The first fifteen and a half years of my life were spent on this place. My ancestors for over a hundred years planted the sugarcane here, hoed the sugarcane, plowed it, cut it and, when it was time, hauled it to the mills. They, like too many others who worked this land, are buried here in unmarked graves because they could not afford the headstones. 2

A hundred years ago, the land was owned by one man who designated that the land would be a cemetery for the people on that plantation, but he did not give it to them, nor would he let them buy it. Today the land is owned by sixteen people who live all over the country and probably different parts of the world, some of whom I'm sure have never visited the plantation or know anything about the cemetery which lies there. Yet it is their land, and those who are buried there do not own even six feet of the ground. 3

Many rural cemeteries have been destroyed all over this country, and day and night I worry that the same fate may happen to this one. There is no law in the state of Louisiana that I am aware of that says it cannot be done. My wife and I and several friends from my childhood are trying to find a way to get control of the land. We have contacted lawyers to work with us and presently we are keeping the place clean of overgrowth, because that is one excuse landowners and developers use to plow under cemeteries. "We didn't know that one was there." 4

At a recent interview, I was asked where would I like to be buried and I answered that I'd like to be in the same place where my ancestors are. The interviewer asked me what would I like on my headstone and I said, "To lie with those who have no marks." These are the people for whom I wrote letters as a child, read their letters because many of them could not read nor could they write. Many of them had to go into the fields before they had a chance to go to school. Yet they're the ones responsible for my being here tonight. Not only did they encourage me to stay in school, but they, and only they, have been the source of all of my writings. I've said many times before that my novels, my short stories, are just continuations of the letters that I started writing for them some fifty years ago, and since I've tried to say something about their lives on paper— their joy, their sorrows, their love, their fears, their pride, their compassion—I think it is only my duty now to do as much as I can to see that they lie in peace forever. 5

22. The exigence for Gaines's passage is
    A. the need for funding to further the author's cause
    B. the possibility that the author may lose his plantation
    C. the growing possibility that the unmarked graves of slaves and other plantation workers may be lost to developers and farmers
    D. a protest movement to save unmarked graves of slaves
    E. the 400th anniversary of the first slave being brought into the Virginia colony

23. The function of the first paragraph is to
    A. establish the setting of the issue Gaines wishes to address
    B. begin developing the historical background of the location
    C. build a contrast between the accepted importance of the plantation to the lack of care paid to the cemetery
    D. emphasize that the cemetery has no name that might protect it
    E. develop the personal connection the author has with the location

24. Which item could most appropriately be added to end the series in paragraph 2 beginning with, *My ancestors for over a hundred years planted the sugarcane here . . .*
    A. and, when it was time, profited nothing from it
    B. and, when it was time, left the plantation to pursue new lives
    C. and, when it was time, were buried next to those fields
    D. and, when it was time, bought their freedom
    E. and, when it was time, reseeded the land for new crops

25. The thesis is located in which paragraph?
    A. 1
    B. 2
    C. 3
    D. 4
    E. 5

26. Which of the following is the major rhetorical strategy the author uses to support his thesis?
    A. appeal to emotions through historical anecdotes
    B. appeal to the audience's sense of guilt
    C. appeal to author's credibility through personal anecdotes
    D. appeal to reason through an overview of legal issues
    E. appeal to the audience's sense of historical precedence

27. Which of the following sentences could best be added to the end of paragraph 4?
    A. The destruction of these cemeteries across the nation is an example of systematic racism.
    B. It is urgent that we continue to speak up for the people buried in these cemeteries until we can find a lasting way to protect them.
    C. The lack of empathy on the part of these landowners needs to be punished in the civil court system.
    D. I speak to all of you today in the hopes that you will support our efforts to save these sites by contacting your local states representatives.
    E. It is necessary that permanent monuments are erected in these rural cemeteries to acknowledge the forgotten.

28. Which of the following best describes the author's purpose in including the following direct quotation in paragraph 5?

The interviewer asked me what would I like on my headstone and I said,
"To lie with those who have no marks."

A. adds needed pacing
B. presents an ironic counterbalance to the direct quotation in paragraph 4
C. presents an illustration of the thesis
D. appeals to the emotions of the audience
E. emphasizes the author's reportorial approach to his subject

29. The rhetorical purpose of the set of dashes used in the last sentence is to
A. supply an aside to the audience
B. provide an overview of the author's literary works
C. provide a continuation of the list begun at the start of this sentence
D. emphasize what is stated in the sentence in the last paragraph beginning with *Not only did they encourage me . . .*
E. enumerate what *their lives* consisted of

30. Carefully read the following two sentences:

I've said many times before that my novels, my short stories, are just continuations of the letters that I started writing for them some fifty years ago, and since I've tried to say something about their lives on paper—their joy, their sorrows, their love, their fears, their pride, their compassion—I think it is only my duty now to do as much as I can to see that they lie in peace forever. (Original sentence)

I've said many times before that my novels, my short stories, are just continuations of the letters that I started writing for them some fifty years ago, and since I've tried to say something about their lives on paper—their joy, their sorrows, their love, their fears, their pride, their compassion—It is my duty to see that they lie in peace forever. (A second version)

What does the original imply that the second version does not?
A. The author will continue to write as much and as often as he can to benefit his ancestor's memories.
B. The author will take his story to audiences across the Nation.
C. The author is thinking about running for public office to secure the rights of his Louisiana ancestors.
D. Instead of writing for and about his ancestors, the author will act on their behalf.
E. The author is retiring from writing and will work solely to support the Riverlake Plantation cemetery.

Questions 31–41 are connected to the following essay written in response to a 2015 article concerned with what constitutes healthy eating.

To Eat or Not to Eat Healthy Foods

My friends and I are like the folks surveyed in a recent Reuters/Ipsos online poll. The majority favored limiting advertising of unhealthy food and soda. But, this majority also said a big NO to banning fast food restaurants. We want our drive-in burgers and tacos. How do we say "yes" to healthy foods and a healthy planet while still craving our Big Macs and fries? Several recommendations have already been made.   1

There are those who see our planet suffering from our love of beef. The carbon footprint left by our increasing "food production, processing, consumption, and waste disposal" (Hamerschlag) results in a huge amount of greenhouse gases released into our atmosphere and the pollution of our water. Our health is being adversely affected by our continued consumption of beef and processed meats. (Hamerschlag) For these groups, one possible solution would be to have everyone in the U.S. give up meat or cheese one day a week. Not counting the health benefits, they calculate the effects on emissions to be like "taking 7.6 million cars off the road." (Ewing)   2

Groups concerned about world hunger maintain that eating meat increases the number of hungry people. Why? Ezra Klein says that it takes 16 pounds of grain to produce one pound of meat—grain that hungry people can't eat because the grain is being sold and fed to livestock. The remaining grain is more expensive because there is less of it. What to do? For Klein and others: make meat more expensive. More expensive meat = less* meat consumption = more grain available = less hunger.   3

And, what about those who want us to eat a healthier diet? The research shows that "eating green is good for you." (Walsh)* As previously mentioned, red meat, processed food, etc., have a high carbon footprint, and they are also high in fat and calories. A "green diet of vegetables, fruits, whole grains, fish and lean meat like chicken" is also friendly to both our own health and the health of our planet. (Walsh) Mark Bittman and many other food experts would like to see high-fat, high-calorie processed foods taxed. He sees it as a way of saving billions of dollars in health care costs and saving "millions of lives." (Bittman)   4

It's hard to deny the findings of recent research. It's also hard to say "no" to burgers and fries or to that steak on the grill. Going "cold-turkey" and becoming a total vegan is not going to happen for me and not for most people in our country. Forcing it on us with high taxes and restrictive laws will only turn us into a nation of liars, sneaks, and criminals. Perhaps we can learn something from the way cigarettes have been treated in the past several decades: taxation, advertising, education, and ultimately self-interest. Right now, I'm listening to Jonathan Kaplan of the Natural Resource Defense Council who has said, "If you can't buy a Prius, you can certainly eat like one."   5

31. The writer wants to add the following sentence to the fourth paragraph to provide further information.

    For instance, Thomas Walsh, the CEO of the Eat Healthy; Live Longer Institute, travels throughout the United States advocating for healthy eating.

    Where would this sentence best be placed?
    A. before the first sentence
    B. after the second sentence
    C. before the fourth sentence
    D. after the fourth sentence
    E. after the last sentence

32. The author uses which major rhetorical appeal to support and develop the thesis?
    A. appeal of reason
    B. appeal to emotions
    C. appeal to authority
    D. appeal to timeliness and opportunity
    E. appeal to commonality

33. What is the rhetorical effect of using equal signs in the last sentence of paragraph 3?
    A. continuation of the "mathematical" image
    B. appeal to those who are convinced when confronted with cause and effect
    C. a sense of irony
    D. a sense of inevitability
    E. a sense of balance

34. The author's purpose can best be stated as
    A. advocating for a limit on the consumption of red meat
    B. highlighting some of the difficulties related to food and the environment
    C. criticizing those who recommend limiting meat production
    D. reviewing the current state of research about food production and its effect on the environment
    E. defending those who favor high taxes on both those who produce meat and those who consume it.

35. In context, which choice best combines the last two sentences in paragraph 4?
    A. No change
    B. To save billions of dollars and "millions of lives," Mark Bittman recommends taxing high-fat and high-calorie processed foods.
    C. According to Mark Bittman and many other food experts, one way to save billions of dollars and "millions of lives" is to tax high-fat and high-calorie processed food.
    D. Saving billions of dollars and saving "millions of lives," would be the major result of taxing high-fat and high-calorie processed food, argues Mark Bittman and many other food experts.
    E. To encourage people to avoid high-fat, and high-calorie processed foods, Mark Bittman and other healthy food advocate taxing these foods, which will save billions of dollars in health care and save "millions of lives."

36. The logic of the fourth paragraph would be better served if the sentence beginning with *As previously mentioned, red meat . . .* were placed
    A. at the beginning of the paragraph, before the sentence beginning with *And, . . .*
    B. before the last sentence beginning with *He sees it . . .*
    C. after the first sentence
    D. before the next to last sentence beginning with *Mark Bittman . . .*
    E. after the last sentence

37. The writer wants to more clearly introduce the thesis of the essay in the first paragraph. Which of the following versions of the first sentence beginning with *My friends and I . . .* would best serve that purpose?

A. No change

B. My friends and I recently saw a Reuters/ Ipsos online poll.

C. My friends and I are like most Americans when it comes to eating healthy.

D. A recent Reuters/Ipsos poll indicates Americans are looking to government to solve the questions revolving around healthy eating.

E. The results of a recent Reuters/Ipsos online poll about attitudes toward eating healthy should be of interest to us all.

38. In the last sentence of the first paragraph, the writer hopes to lead the reader into an examination of some of the recent research and recommendations of experts and organizations connected to healthy eating and to the environment. Which version of this last sentence best accomplishes this goal?

A. No change

B. This question and others related to healthy eating and the environment have been the subject of many research projects and recommendations.

C. Here is what some of the experts in healthy eating recommend.

D. It's difficult to come to any conclusion about healthy eating and the environment.

E. Research seems to favor the government solving this problem.

39. The obvious exigence for this essay is

A. an assigned writing prompt

B. a concern for the environment

C. fear of eating the wrong foods

D. anger with climate change

E. desire to change people's attitude toward healthy eating

40. Which of the following does the writer NOT assume about the audience?

A. They have eaten fast food.

B. They have had experience with paying taxes.

C. They have a working knowledge of environmental science.

D. They have an interest in protecting the environment.

E. They have an interest in eating healthy.

41. The last sentence of the essay beginning with *Right now, I'm . . .* indicates to the reader that the writer most probably

A. will find a compromise when dealing with food choices and their effects on the environment

B. is confused about what to do about food choices and the environment

C. will keep in mind the relationship between food choices and their effects on the environment when grocery shopping or eating out

D. will advocate for corporations to become more active in protecting the environment

E. will advocate for government taking a larger role in addressing this situation

Questions 42–45 are based on the following letter to the editor published in *Newsday* on August 23, 2019.

History Evolves as Scholars Learn More

When the *New York Times* published "The 1619 Project" on Aug. 18, 2019, there was a backlash from conservative critics about the integrity and accuracy of the project, which aims to reframe U.S. history with slavery as its foundation. 1

Newsday columnist Cathy Young writes that "The 1619" project is "revisionist," a common pejorative used to discredit histories that highlight negative aspects of America's past ["A revisionist narrative of slavery," Opinion, Aug. 20, 2019]. In Young's view, "Increasingly, the prevailing view among progressives . . . is that the United States was founded on slavery and built on the backs of the enslaved." 2

But all history is revisionist, as it is based on newly uncovered primary sources, scholarship, and contributions from groups—like enslaved Africans and African-Americans—excluded from previous accounts. The editors and authors of "The 1619 Project" would likely embrace the claim that theirs is a revisionist history that tells "the unvarnished truth," in the words of historian John Hope Franklin. 3

While praising some parts of the "1619" study, Young maintains that the scholarship was questionable regarding the assertion that slavery was the cornerstone of the founding of this country and which still affects our American culture today. She writes that "we risk replacing one mythology with another that demonizes America and its achievements" and could make "ordinary Americans feel that patriotism is being made politically incorrect." This is a false dichotomy; history isn't a zero-sum endeavor, either patriotic or critical. It's both, because uncovering negative aspects from the past pushes us toward a brighter future. 4

As a teacher of history, I must teach about the good, the bad and the ugly to help students think critically to understand the devastating impact of slavery and racism on our country. 5

Dennis Urban,
History teacher

This is a letter to the editor, and by definition it is brief. If the author wished to further develop this into an essay of around 500–800 words, he might consider the following:

42. The location of the thesis of this letter is
   A. all of paragraph one
   B. the last sentence of paragraph 2
   C. the first sentence of paragraph 3
   D. he last sentence of paragraph 4
   E. all of the last paragraph

43. The writer is considering placing the last sentence someplace else in the letter. Considering the rhetorical situation, including the exigence, what would be the best placement?
   A. as is
   B. at the very beginning
   C. before paragraph 2
   D. before paragraph 3
   E. before paragraph 4

44. The writer wants an effective transition from the introductory paragraph to the main idea of the text. Which of the following would best achieve this goal?

A. Leave as is.

B. One critic is a contributing editor to *Reason* magazine.

C. A recent edition of this newspaper published one of these conservative opinions.

D. One of these conservative writers is *Newsday* columnist Cathy Young who writes that . . . [sentence continues as in the original].

E. I read one of these opinions in a recent edition of this newspaper.

45. The writer wants to add the following sentence to the text to provide additional information.

It should be noted that "1619 Project" was published to correspond with the 400th anniversary of the arrival of the first African slaves in Jamestown, the first English settlement in North America.

Where would the sentence best be placed?

A. the beginning of the first paragraph

B. the end of the first paragraph

C. the beginning of the second paragraph

D. the end of the second paragraph

E. the end of the last paragraph

END OF SECTION I

The second part of the test is the 2¼-hour essay writing section. This is taken after the break following completion of the multiple-choice section of the exam. You will be required to write three different essays: analysis, synthesis, and argument.

Because The College Board wants to make certain that directions and expectations are clear to those taking the exam, each type of essay prompt will have a stable (standard) wording. Only the specifics related to the text and/or context will change. At the end of each prompt will be a list of instructions prescribed by The College Board as printed in the *AP English Language and Composition Course and Exam Description*, pp. 11–113.

The analysis prompt asks you to analyze the author's purpose and how he achieves it. The argument question requires you to take a position on an issue and develop it with appropriate evidence. The synthesis prompt directs you to carefully read several sources related to a specific topic and to cite at least three of these sources to support and/or illustrate your position.

The additional 15 minutes is to allow time for careful reading and annotation of each of the prompts and all of the resources provided for the synthesis essay. You are not required to spend this time only reading prompts and sources. But, we recommend that you do so.

You may begin once you feel you have an understanding of the demands of each prompt. Remember: READ THE PROMPT.

Section II

Total Time—2¼ hours

Question 1

(Suggested time—45 minutes. This question counts as one-third of the total score for Section II.)

English Language and Composition

Reading Time: 15 minutes
Suggested Writing Time: 40 minutes

A recent Supreme Court decision has provoked much debate about private property rights. In it, the court ruled that the city of New London was within the bounds of the *U.S. Constitution* when it condemned private property for use in a redevelopment plan. This ruling is an example of the classic debate between individual rights versus the greater good.

Carefully read the following sources, including any introductory information. **Then, in an essay that synthesizes at least three of the sources for support, take a position that adddresses the government's right to take property from one private owner to give to another to further economic development constitutes a permissible "public use" under the Fifth Amendment.**

Make certain that you take a position and that the essay centers on your argument. Use the sources to support your reasoning; avoid simply summarizing the sources. You may refer to the sources by their letters (Source A, Source B, etc.) or by the identifiers in the parentheses below.

- Source A (*U.S. Constitution*)
- Source B (*60 Minutes*)
- Source C (*Kelo* decision)
- Source D (Koterba, editorial/political cartoon)
- Source E (Broder)
- Source F (Britt, editorial/political cartoon)
- Source G (CNN and American Survey)

- Respond to the prompt with a thesis that may establish a line of reasoning.
- Provide evidence from at least three of the provided sources to support the thesis. Indicate clearly the sources used through direct quotation, paraphrase, or summary. Sources may be cited as Source A, Source B, etc., or by using the description in parentheses.
- Explain the relationship between the evidence and the thesis.
- Demonstrate an understanding of the rhetorical situation.
- Use appropriate grammar and punctuation in communicating the argument.

Source A

"Amendments." The United States Constitution, 1787.
The following is a section from the Fifth Amendment to the *U.S. Constitution*.

"nor shall private property be taken for public use, without just compensation."

Note: This is known as *eminent domain*, which refers to the power of government to take private property for "public use" if the owner is fairly compensated. Eminent domain has been used to build roads, schools, and utility lines. Cities also have used it to transfer property from unwilling sellers to developers who want to build shopping malls, offices, or other projects.

Source B

Adapted from the July 4, 2004, edition of *60 Minutes*. Available at http://www.cbsnews
      .com/stories/2003/09/26/60minutes/main575343.shtml.
The following is part of an interview conducted for the CBS news magazine *60 Minutes*. In it, the audience is introduced to a couple whose house had been taken by the local government for development of condos.

Jim and Joanne Saleet are refusing to sell the home they've lived in for 38 years. They live in a quiet neighborhood of single-family houses in Lakewood, Ohio, just outside Cleveland. The City of Lakewood is trying to use eminent domain to force the Saleets out to make way for more expensive condominiums. But the Saleets are telling the town, "Hell no! They won't go."

"The bottom line is this is morally wrong, what they're doing here. This is our home. And we're going to stay here. And I'm gonna fight them tooth and nail. I've just begun to fight," says Jim Saleet. "We talked about this when we were dating. I used to point to the houses and say, 'Joanne, one of these days, we're going to have one of these houses.' And I meant it. And I worked hard."

Jim Saleet worked in the pharmaceutical industry, paid off his house, and then retired. Now, he and his wife plan to spend the rest of their days there, and pass their house on to their children.

But Lakewood's mayor, Madeleine Cain, has other plans. She wants to tear down the Saleets' home, plus 55 homes around it, along with four apartment buildings and more than a dozen businesses.

Why? So that private developers can build high-priced condos, and a high-end shopping mall, and, thus, raise Lakewood's property tax base.

The mayor told 60 Minutes *that she sought out a developer for the project because Lakewood's aging tax base has been shrinking, and the city simply needs more money.*

"This is about Lakewood's future. Lakewood cannot survive without a strengthened tax base. Is it right to consider this a public good? Absolutely," says the mayor, who admits that it's difficult and unfortunate that the Saleets are being asked to give up their home.

The Saleets live in an area called Scenic Park, and because it is so scenic, it's a prime place to build upscale condominiums. With great views, over the Rocky River, those condos will be a cinch to sell. But the condos can't go up unless the city can remove the Saleets and their neighbors through eminent domain. And, to legally invoke eminent domain, the city had to certify that this scenic park area is, really, "blighted."

"We're not blighted. This is an area that we absolutely love. This is a close-knit, beautiful neighborhood. It's what America's all about," says Jim Saleet. "And, Mike, you don't know how humiliating this is to have people tell you, 'You live in a blighted area,' and how degrading this is."

"The term 'blighted' is a statutory word," says Mayor Cain. "It is, it really doesn't have a lot to do with whether or not your home is painted. . . . A statutory term is used to describe an area. The question is whether or not that area can be used for a higher and better use."

Source C

Kelo v. New London. U.S. Supreme Court 125 S. Ct. 2655.

The following is a brief overview of a decision by the U.S. Supreme Court in 2005.

> Susette Kelo, et al. v. City of New London, et al., *125 S. Ct. 2655 (2005), more commonly* Kelo v. New London, *is a land-use law case argued before the United States Supreme Court on February 22, 2005. The case arose from a city's use of eminent domain to condemn privately owned real property so that it could be used as part of a comprehensive redevelopment plan.*
>
> *The owners sued the city in Connecticut courts, arguing that the city had misused its eminent domain power. The power of eminent domain is limited by the Fifth and Fourteenth Amendments to the United States Constitution. The Fifth Amendment, which restricts the actions of the federal government, says, in part, that "private property [shall not] be taken for public use, without just compensation"; under Section 1 of the Fourteenth Amendment, this limitation is also imposed on the actions of U.S. state and local governments. Kelo and the other appellants argued that economic development, the stated purpose of the Development Corporation, did not qualify as public use.*
>
> *The Supreme Court's Ruling: This 5:4 decision holds that the governmental taking of property from one private owner to give to another in furtherance of economic development constitutes a permissible "public use" under the Fifth Amendment.*

Source D

Koterba, Jeff, *Omaha World Herald.* Available at http://cagle.msnbc.com/news/
    EminentDomain/4.asp.

The following editorial/political cartoon appeared in an Omaha, Nebraska, newspaper.

Jeff Koterba, *Omaha World Herald*, NE

Source E

Broder, John M, "States Curbing Right to Seize Private Homes." *New York Times*,
February 21, 2006.

The following passage is excerpted from an article published in the *New York Times*.

*"Our opposition to eminent domain is not across the board," he [Scott G. Bullock of the
Institute for Justice] said. "It has an important but limited role in government planning and the building of roads, parks, and public buildings. What we oppose is eminent
domain abuse for private development, and we are encouraging legislators to curtail it."*

*More neutral observers expressed concern that state officials, in their zeal to protect
homeowners and small businesses, would handcuff local governments that are trying to
revitalize dying cities and fill in blighted areas with projects that produce tax revenues
and jobs.*

*"It's fair to say that many states are on the verge of seriously overreacting to the
Kelo decision," said John D. Echeverria, executive director of the Georgetown Environmental Law and Policy Institute and an authority on land-use policy. "The danger
is that some legislators are going to attempt to destroy what is a significant and sometimes painful but essential government power. The extremist position is a prescription
for economic decline for many metropolitan areas around the country."*

Source F

Britt, Chris, *The State Journal-Register*. Available at http://cagle.msnbc.com/news/
EminentDomain/4.asp.

The following editorial cartoon appeared in a Springfield, Illinois, newspaper.

Chris Britt, Springfield, IL — *The State Journal-Register*

Source G

Andres, Gary J., "The Kelo Backlash." *Washington Times*, August 29, 2005.

CNN Pollserver, "Local governments should be able to seize homes and businesses." *Quick Vote*, June 23, 2005. Available at http://www.cnn.com/POLLSERVER/ results/18442.exclude.html.

The following are the results of two surveys/polls. The first appeared in a *Washington Times* article, and the second was commissioned by CNN.

American Survey | July 14–17, 2005

An American Survey of 800 registered voters nationwide shows 68 percent favoring legislative limits on the government's ability to take private property away from owners, with 62 percent of Democrats, 74 percent of independents and 70 percent of Republicans supporting such limits.

Created: Thursday, June 23, 2005 at 11:48:12 EDT

Local governments should be able to seize homes and businesses:

For public use	33%	58481 votes
For private economic development	1%	2445 votes
Never	66%	117061 votes

Total: 177987 votes

This QuickVote is not scientific and reflects the opinions of only those Internet users who have chosen to participate. The results cannot be assumed to represent the opinions of Internet users in general, nor the public as a whole.

Question 2

(Suggested time—45 minutes. This question counts as one-third of the total score for Section II.)

The following paragraphs are from the opening of Truman Capote's *In Cold Blood* (1966). Compose a well-written essay analyzing the rhetorical choices Capote makes to convey his characterization of Holcomb and its citizens. In your response you should do the following:

- Respond to the prompt with a thesis that analyzes the writer's rhetorical choices.
- Select and use evidence to develop and support your line of reasoning.
- Explain the relationship between the evidence and your thesis.
- Demonstrate an understanding of the rhetorical situation.
- Use appropriate grammar and punctuation in communicating your argument.

The village of Holcomb stands on the high wheat plains of western Kansas, a 1
lonesome area that other Kansans call "out there." Some seventy miles east of the
Colorado border, the countryside, with its hard blue skies and desert-clear air, has an
atmosphere that is rather more Far Western than Middle West. The local accent is
barbed with a prairie twang, a ranch-hand nasalness, and the men, many of them, wear
narrow frontier trousers, Stetsons, and high-heeled boots with pointed toes. The land
is flat, and the views are awesomely extensive; horses, herds of cattle, a white cluster
of grain elevators rising as gracefully as Greek temples are visible long before a traveler
reaches them.

Holcomb, too, can be seen from great distances. Not that there is much to see— 2
simply an aimless congregation of buildings divided in the center by the main-line
tracks of the Santa Fe Railroad, a haphazard hamlet bounded on the south by a brown
stretch of the Arkansas (pronounced "Ar-kan-sas") River, on the north by a highway,
Route 50, and on the east and west by prairie lands and wheat fields. After rain, or
when snowfalls thaw, the streets, unnamed, unshaded, unpaved, turn from the thickest
dust into the direst mud. At one end of the town stands a stark old stucco structure,
the roof of which supports an electric sign—Dance—but the dancing has ceased and
the advertisement has been dark for several years. Nearby is another building with an
irrelevant sign, this one in flaking gold on a dirty window—HOLCOMB BANK. The
bank closed in 1933, and it is one of the town's two "apartment houses," the second
being a ramshackle mansion known, because a good part of the local school's faculty
lives there, as the Teacherage. But the majority of Holcomb's homes are one-story
frame affairs, with front porches.

Down by the depot, the postmistress, a gaunt woman who wears a rawhide jacket 3
and denims and cowboy boots, presides over a falling-apart post office. The depot,
itself, with its peeling sulphur-colored paint, is equally melancholy; the Chief, the
Super Chief, the El Capitan go by every day, but these celebrated expresses never pause
there. No passenger trains do—only an occasional freight. Up on the highway, there
are two filling stations, one of which doubles as a meagerly supplied grocery store,
while the other does extra duty as a cafe—Hartman's Cafe, where Mrs. Hartman, the
proprietress, dispenses sandwiches, coffee, soft drinks, and 3.2 beer. (Holcomb, like all
the rest of Kansas, is "dry.")

And that, really, is all. Unless you include, as one must, the Holcomb School, a 4
good-looking establishment, which reveals a circumstance that the appearance of the
community otherwise camouflages: that the parents who send their children to this
modern and ably staffed "consolidated" school—the grades go from kindergarten
through senior high, and a fleet of buses transport the students, of which there are
usually around three hundred and sixty, from as far as sixteen miles away—are, in
general, a prosperous people. . . . The farm ranchers in Finney County, of which
Holcomb is a part, have done well; money has been made not from farming alone
but also from the exploitation of plentiful natural-gas resources, and its acquisition is
reflected in the new school, the comfortable interiors of the farmhouses, the steep and
swollen grain elevators.

Until one morning in mid-November of 1959, few Americans—in fact, few 5
Kansans—had ever heard of Holcomb. Like the waters of the river, like the motorists
on the highway, and like the yellow trains streaking down the Santa Fe tracks, drama,
in the shape of exceptional happenings, had never stopped there. The inhabitants of the
village, numbering two hundred and seventy, were satisfied that this should be so, quite
content to exist inside ordinary life . . .

Question 3

(Suggested time—45 minutes. This question counts
as one-third of the total score for Section II.)

In his famous "Vast Wasteland" address to the National Association of Broadcasters in May of 1961, Newton Minow, the Chairman of the Federal Communications Commission, spoke about the power of television to influence the taste, knowledge, and opinions of its viewers around the world. Carefully read the following, paying close attention to how timely it is today, especially in light of the Internet, smartphones, social media, and digital games, etc.

Minow ended his speech warning that "The power of instantaneous sight and sound is without precedent in mankind's history. This is an awesome power. It has limitless capabilities for good—and for evil. And it carries with it awesome responsibilities— responsibilities which you and [the government] cannot escape . . ."

Using your own knowledge and your own experiences or reading, write a carefully constructed essay in which you present your position on Minnow's ideas about mass media and technology.

In your response you should do the following:

- Respond to the prompt with a thesis that may establish a line of reasoning.
- Explain the relationship between the evidence and your thesis.
- Select and use evidence to develop and support your line of reasoning.
- Demonstrate an understanding of the rhetorical situation.
- Use appropriate grammar and punctuation in communicating your argument.

END OF SECTION II

"Even though I was 'turned off' by the thought of having to read old-fashioned writing, I was really proud of myself once I found out that I could make sense out of it when I concentrated and focused the way my teacher showed us."
—Sean V.S.,
 AP student

So, that's what the Advanced Placement English Language exam looks like.

If you're being honest with yourself, you're probably feeling a bit overwhelmed at this point. DON'T BE AFRAID TO ADMIT IT. This is primarily why we are going to deconstruct this entire Diagnostic/Master exam for you and with you throughout this book. By the time you reach Practice Exams 1 and 2, you should be feeling much more confident and comfortable about doing well on the AP English Language and Composition exam.

As you progress through this book, you will:

- take each section of the Diagnostic/Master exam;
- read the explanations for the answers to the multiple-choice questions;
- read sample student essays written in response to each of the three prompts;
- read the rubrics and ratings of the student essays; and
- evaluate your own performance in light of this information.

STEP **3**

Develop Strategies for Success

Section I of the Exam—
The Multiple-Choice Questions

IN THIS CHAPTER

Summary: Become comfortable with the multiple-choice section of the exam. If you know what to expect, you can prepare.

Key Ideas

✪ Prepare yourself for the multiple-choice section of the exam.
✪ Review the types of multiple-choice questions asked on the exam.
✪ Learn strategies for approaching the multiple-choice questions.
✪ Score yourself by checking the answer key and explanations for the multiple-choice section of the Diagnostic/Master exam.

The multiple-choice section of the exam will be constructed to address each of the following categories among the 45 questions:

CATEGORY	WEIGHTING OF QUESTIONS
Reading: rhetorical situation	11%–15%
Writing: rhetorical situation	11%–13%
Reading: claim and support	13%–15%
Writing: claim and support	11%–13%
Reading: clarity of organization	11%–15%
Writing: clarity of organization	13%–15%
Reading: style	11%–13%
Writing: style	11%–13%

Introduction to the Multiple-Choice Section of the Exam

Multiple choice? Multiple guess? Multiple anxiety? It's been our experience that the day after the exam finds students bemoaning the difficulties and uncertainties of Section I of the AP English Language and Composition exam.

"It's unfair."

"I didn't understand a word of the third reading."

"Was that in English?"

"Did you get four Ds in a row for the last reading?"

"I just closed my eyes and pointed."

Is it really possible to avoid these and other exam woes? We hope that by following along with us in this chapter, you will begin to feel a bit more familiar with the world of multiple-choice questions and, thereby, become a little more comfortable with the multiple-choice section of the exam.

What Is It About the Multiple-Choice Questions That Causes Such Anxiety?

Basically, a multiple-choice question is a familiar, and sometimes stressful, method of gauging understanding. Why? Because, by its very nature, a multiple-choice question forces you to determine specifically what the test maker sees as the correct choice. You must concentrate on choosing the correct answer among a group of incorrect choices. However, we know that complex literary works have a richness that allows for ambiguity. In the exam mode, you are expected to match someone else's reading of a work with your own reading of the text. This is what often causes the student to feel that the multiple-choice section is a kind of "gotcha" situation. But it's a part of the exam you will have to face head-on. So our advice is to be aware of the multiple-choice difficulties and limitations and practice using the exams in this book and the exams provided by The College Board.

This said, it's wise to develop a strategy for success. Once again, practice is the key to this success.

You've answered all types of multiple-choice questions during your career as a student. The test-taking skills you have learned in your social studies, math, and science classes may also apply to this specific situation.

A word in defense of the test makers is in order here. The test is designed to allow you to shine, NOT to be humiliated. To that end, the people who design the multiple-choice questions take their job seriously and take pride in their product. You will not find "cutesy" questions, and they will not play games with you. What they will do is present several valid options in response to a challenging and appropriate question. These questions are designed to separate the knowledgeable, perceptive, and thoughtful reader from the superficial and impulsive one.

What Should I Expect in Section I?

For this first section of the AP English Language and Composition exam, you are allotted 1 hour to answer 45 objective questions on three to five prose passages. The selections come from works of nonfiction and are from different time periods, of different styles, and of different purposes. In other words, you will not find two essays by Thoreau in the multiple-choice section of the same test.

These are NOT easy readings. They are representative of the college-level work you have been doing throughout the year.

"You know, when my teacher required us to make up multiple-choice questions that came from the AP prompts we wrote essays on, I really became more confident about how to answer these types of questions on the exam."
—Samantha T., AP student

> The multiple choice section of the exam is constructed around major two categories: Reading and Writing. Each of these two categories will include questions related to the rhetorical situation, claims and evidence, reasoning and organization, and style.
>
> **Reading questions will expect you to:**
>
> - Clarify how choices relate to the rhetorical situation
> - Interpret claims and evidence as related to the thesis
> - Interpret the line of reasoning presented in the argument
> - Infer/conclude how stylistic elements relate to the argument's purpose
>
> **Writing questions will expect you to:**
>
> - Demonstrate your ability to make choices in a text in response to the rhetorical situation
> - Choose relevant evidence in developing a line of reasoning
> - Evaluate organization and commentary when trying to strengthen the line of reasoning
> - Decide which words and/or composition elements can be used to strengthen an argument

You will be expected to:

- follow sophisticated syntax;
- respond to diction;
- be comfortable with upper-level vocabulary;
- be familiar with rhetorical terminology;
- make inferences;
- be sensitive to irony and tone;
- recognize components of organization and style;
- be familiar with modes of discourse and rhetorical strategies; and
- recognize how information contained in citations contributes to the author's purpose.

THE GOOD NEWS IS . . . the selection is self-contained. If it is about the Irish Potato Famine, you will NOT be at a disadvantage if you know nothing about Irish history. Frequently, there will be biblical references in a selection. This is especially true of works from an earlier time period. You are expected to be aware of basic allusions to biblical and mythological works often found in literary texts, but the passage will never require you to have any particular religious background.

DO NOT LET THE SUBJECT MATTER OF A PASSAGE THROW YOU. Strong analytical skills will work on any passage.

How Should I Begin to Work with Section I?

Take no more than a minute and thumb through the exam, looking for the following:

- The length of the selections
- The time periods or writing styles, if you can recognize them
- The number of questions asked
- A quick idea of the type of questions

This brief skimming of the test will put your mind into gear, because you will be aware of what is expected of you.

"Even though it's time-consuming, I find it invaluable to take class time to accurately simulate exam conditions."
—Cynthia N.,
    AP teacher

How Should I Proceed Through This Section of the Exam?

Timing is important. Always maintain an awareness of the time. Wear a watch. (Some students like to put it directly in front of them on the desk.) Remember, this is not your first encounter with the multiple-choice section of the test. You've probably been practicing timed exams in class; in addition, this book provides you with three timed experiences. We're sure you will notice improvements as you progress through the timed practice activities.

Depending on the particular passage, you may take less or more time on a particular passage, but know when to move on. The test DOES NOT become more difficult as it progresses; therefore, you will want to give yourself the opportunity to answer each set of questions.

Work at a pace of about one question per minute. Every question is worth the same number of points, so don't get bogged down on those that involve multiple tasks. Don't panic if a question is beyond you. Remember, it will probably be beyond a great number of the other students taking the exam. There has to be a bar that determines the 5s and 4s for this exam. Just do your best.

Reading the text carefully is a must. Begin at the beginning and work your way through.

Most people read just with their eyes. We want you to slow down and to read with your senses of sight, sound, and touch.

- Underline, circle, and annotate the text. (You might want to keep SOAPStone or SPACE CAT in mind as you read. See the glossary if you need a review of these two acronyms.)
- Read closely, paying attention to punctuation, syntax, diction, pacing, and organization.
- Read as if you were reading the passage aloud to an audience, emphasizing meaning and intent.
- This technique may seem childish, but it works. Using your finger as a pointer, underscore the line as you are reading it aloud in your head. This forces you to slow down and to really notice the text. This will be helpful when you have to refer to the passage.
- Use all of the information given to you about the passage, such as title, author, date of publication, and footnotes.
- Be aware of organizational and rhetorical devices and techniques.
- Quickly skim the questions stems, ignoring the choices. This will give you an idea as to what is expected of you as a reader of the given text.
- Be aware of thematic lines and be sensitive to details that could be material for multiple-choice questions.

> You can practice these techniques anytime. Take any work and read it aloud. Time yourself. A good rate is about 1½ minutes per page.

Types of Multiple-Choice Questions

Is the Structure the Same for All of the Multiple-Choice Questions?

No. There are several basic patterns that the AP test makers employ. These include:

1. The *straightforward question.*
   - The passage is an example of
     C. a contrast/comparison essay
   - The pronoun "it" refers to
     B. his gait

2. The question that refers you to specific lines and asks you to *draw a conclusion* or *interpret.*
   - Lines 52–57 serve to
     A. reinforce the author's thesis

3. The ALL . . . <u>EXCEPT</u> *question* requires more time, because it demands that you consider every possibility.
   - The AP English Language and Composition exam is all of the following <u>except</u>
     A. It is given in May of each year.
     B. It is open to high school seniors.
     C. It is published in the *New York Times*.
     D. It is used as a qualifier for college credit.
     E. It is a 3-hour test.

4. The question that asks you to *make an inference or to abstract a concept not directly stated in the passage.*
   - In "Letter from a Birmingham Jail," the reader can infer that the speaker is
     E. religious

5. The question related to the rhetorical situation: This question deals with context, purpose, audience.
   - Which of the following is the major strategy the author uses to support the thesis of this passage?
     This is the type of question that requires you to consider the rhetorical situation of the passage and HOW the writer addresses it. For example: Which of the following is not an assumption the author makes about the audience?

6. The question that asks you to act in the role of the writer during the writing process.
   - The writer is considering adding the following sentence to the end of paragraph 5:

     Driving more defensively, I move from the fast lane into the middle lane.

     Should the writer make this revision?
     A. Yes, because the reader wants to know what the driver does next.
     B. No, because it is off topic.
     C. No, because it doesn't really relate to the topic sentence of the paragraph.
     D. Yes. This sentence adds to the reader's understanding of the writer.
     E. No. This sentence adds nothing to the information in the paragraph and begs for an answer to what happens when the driver moves into the middle lane.

7. The question that asks you to become involved in the revision process.
   - Which item could most appropriately be added to end the series in paragraph 2 beginning with, *My ancestors for over a hundred planted the sugarcane here . . .*
     A. and, when it was time, profited nothing from it.
     B. and, when it was time, left the plantation to pursue new lives.
     C. and, when it was time, were buried next to those fields.
     D. and, when it was time, bought their freedom.
     E. and, when it was time, reseeded the land for new crops.

What Kinds of Questions Should I Expect on the Exam?

The multiple-choice questions center on form and content. Naturally, the test makers are assessing your understanding of the meaning of the selection as well as your ability to draw inferences and perceive implications based on the given work. They also want to know if you understand HOW an author develops his or her ideas, and CHOICES the author could make when revising the text.

The questions, therefore, will be *factual*, *technical*, *analytical*, and *inferential*. The brief chart below illustrates the types of key words/phrases in these four categories you can expect to encounter.

Note: THERE IS NO NEED TO MEMORIZE THIS CHART. Likewise, do not panic if a word or phrase is not familiar to you. You may or may not encounter any or all of these words or phrases on any given exam. You can, however, count on meeting up with many of these in our practice exams in this book.

FACTUAL	TECHNICAL	ANALYTICAL	INFERENTIAL
Words refer to	Sentence structure	Rhetorical strategy	Effect of diction
Allusions	Style	Shift in development	Tone
Antecedents	Grammatical purpose	Rhetorical stance	Inferences
Pronoun referents	Dominant technique	Style	Effect of description
	Imagery	Metaphor	Effect of last paragraph
	Point of view	Contrast	Effect on reader
	Organization of passage	Comparison	Narrator's attitude
		Cause/effect	Image suggests
	Narrative progress of passage	Argument	Effect of detail
		Description	Author implies
	Conflict	Narration	Author most concerned with
	Irony	Specific–general	Symbol
	Function of . . .	General–specific	Purpose
		How something is characterized	Intended audience
		Imagery	Exigence
		Passage is primarily concerned with	
		Function of . . .	

A WORD ABOUT JARGON: Jargon refers to words unique to a specific subject. A common language is important for communication, and there must be agreement on the basic meanings of terms. Although it is important to know the universal language of a subject, it is also important that you NOT limit the scope of your thinking to a brief definition. All of the terms used in the above chart are categorized only for easy reference. They also work in many other contexts. In other words, THINK OUTSIDE OF THE BOX.

Scoring the Multiple-Choice Section

How Does the Scoring of the Multiple-Choice Section Work?

Multiple-choice scores are based solely on the number of questions answered correctly. Therefore, it is to your advantage to answer ALL of the multiple-choice questions. Your chances of guessing the correct answer improve if you skillfully apply the process of elimination to narrow the choices.

Strategies for Answering the Multiple-Choice Questions

"One of my biggest challenges in preparing for the exam was to learn not to jump to conclusions when I was doing the multiple-choice questions."
—Samantha S., AP student

As observed earlier, you've been answering multiple-choice questions most of your academic life, and you've probably figured out ways to deal with them. There may, however, be some points you have not considered that will be helpful for this particular exam.

General Guidelines

- Work in order. We like this approach for several reasons:
  — It's clear.
  — You will not lose your place on the scan sheet.
  — There may be a logic to working sequentially which will help you to answer previous questions. BUT, this is your call. If you are more comfortable moving around the exam, do so.
- Write on the exam booklet. Mark it up. Make it yours. Interact with the test.
- Do not spend too much time on any one question.
- Do not be misled by the length or appearance of a selection. There is no correlation between this and the difficulty of the questions.
- Don't fight the question or the passage. You may know other information about the subject of the text or a question. It's irrelevant. Work within the given context.
- Consider all the choices in a given question. This will guard against your jumping to a false conclusion. It helps you to slow down and to look closely at each possibility. You may find that your first choice was not the best or most appropriate one.
- Maintain an open mind as you answer subsequent questions in a series. Sometimes a later question will contradict an answer to a previous one. Reconsider both. Likewise, even the phrasing of a question may point to an answer in a previous question.
- Remember that all parts of an answer must be correct.
- When in doubt, go back to the text.

Specific Techniques

- <u>Process of Elimination</u>—This is the primary tool, except for direct knowledge of the answer.
  1. Read the five choices.
  2. If no choice immediately strikes you as correct, you can
     — eliminate any which are obviously wrong;
     — eliminate those choices which are too narrow or too broad;
     — eliminate illogical choices;
     — eliminate answers which are synonymous;
     — eliminate answers which cancel each other out.
  3. If two answers are close,
     — find the one general enough to contain all aspects of the question
     OR
     — find the one limited enough to be the detail the question is seeking.

- <u>Substitution/Fill In the Blank</u>
  1. Rephrase the question, leaving a blank where the answer should go.
  2. Use each of the choices to fill in the blank until you find the one that is the best fit.

- <u>Using Context</u>
  1. Use this technique when the question directs you to specific lines, words, or phrases.
  2. Locate the given word, phrase, or sentence and read the sentence before and after the section of the text to which the question refers. Often this provides the information or clues you need to make your choice.

- <u>Anticipation</u>
  As you read the passage for the first time, mark any details and ideas that you would ask a question about. You may second-guess the test makers this way. (Again, you might want to keep SOAPStone or SPACE CAT in mind as you read. See the glossary if you need a review of these two acronyms.)

- <u>Intuition/The Educated Guess</u>
  You have a wealth of skills and knowledge in your language and composition subconscious. A question or a choice may trigger a "remembrance of things past." This can be the basis for your educated guess. Have the confidence to use the educated guess as a valid technique. Trust your own resources.

> ## A Survival Plan
>
> If time is running out and you haven't finished the last selection,
>
> 1. Scan the remaining questions and look for:
>   — the shortest questions; and/or
>   — the questions that point you to a line.
>
> These two types of questions are relatively easy to work with and to verify.
>
> 2. Look for specific detail/definition questions.
>
> 3. Look for self-contained questions.
>   "The jail sentence was a bitter winter for his plan" is an example of
>   C. an analogy.
>
> You did not have to go to the passage to answer this question.

Some Thoughts About Guessing

You can't be hurt by making educated guesses based on a careful reading of the selection. Be smart. Understand that you need to come to this exam well prepared. You must have a foundation of knowledge and skills. You cannot guess through the entire exam and expect to do well.

This is not the lotto. This book is not about how to "beat the exam." We want to maximize the skills you already have. There is an inherent integrity in this exam and your participation in it. With this in mind, when there is no other direction open to you, it is perfectly fine to make an educated guess.

Is There Anything Special I Should Know About Preparing for the Multiple-Choice Questions?

After you have finished with the Diagnostic/Master exam, you will be familiar with the format and types of questions asked on the AP English Language and Composition exam.

However, just practicing answering multiple-choice questions on specific works will not give you a complete understanding of this questioning process. We suggest the following to hone your general multiple-choice skills with AP Lang multiple-choice skills.

- Choose a passage from a full-length prose work that you have read before or a self-contained essay, plus choose another that contains documentation/citations. (Take a close look at your science and social studies texts for examples.)
- Read the selection a couple of times and create several multiple-choice questions about specific sections of the selection.
  — Make certain the section is self-contained and complex.
  — Choose a speech, a philosophical passage, an essay, an editorial, a letter, a preface or epilogue, a significant passage from a chapter, or a news article.
- Refer to the chart given earlier in this chapter for suggested language and type.
- Administer your miniquiz to a classmate, study group, or class.
- Evaluate your results.
- Repeat this process through several different works during your preparation for the exam. The selections can certainly come from those you are studying in class.
- Create a variety of question types.

Here's What Should Happen as a Result of Your Using This Process

- Your expectation level for the selections in the actual test will be more realistic.
- You will become familiar with the language of multiple-choice questions.
- Your understanding of the process of choosing answers will be heightened.
- Questions you write that you find less than satisfactory will trigger your analytical skills as you attempt to figure out "what went wrong."
- Your understanding of terminology will become more accurate.
- BONUS: If you continue to do this work throughout your preparation for the AP exam, you will have created a mental storehouse of literary and analytical information. So, when you are presented with an analytical or argument essay in Section II, you will have an extra resource at your disposal.

You might want to utilize this process throughout the year with selections studied in and out of class and keep track of your progress. See the Bibliography at the back of this book.

A Note on Timing Yourself

It is now your turn to try the Diagnostic/Master exam, Section I.

Do this section in ONE sitting. Time yourself!

Be honest with yourself when you score your answers.

Note: If the 1 hour passes before you have a chance to finish all of the questions, stop where you are and score what you have done up to this point. Afterward, complete the remaining parts of the section, but do not count it as part of your score.

When you have completed all of the multiple-choice questions in this diagnostic exam, carefully look at the explanations of the answers. Spend time here and assess which types of questions are giving you trouble. Use this book to learn from your mistakes.

ANSWER SHEET FOR DIAGNOSTIC MULTIPLE-CHOICE QUESTIONS

1. _____   13. _____   25. _____   37. _____

2. _____   14. _____   26. _____   38. _____

3. _____   15. _____   27. _____   39. _____

4. _____   16. _____   28. _____   40. _____

5. _____   17. _____   29. _____   41. _____

6. _____   18. _____   30. _____   42. _____

7. _____   19. _____   31. _____   43. _____

8. _____   20. _____   32. _____   44. _____

9. _____   21. _____   33. _____   45. _____

10. _____   22. _____   34. _____

11. _____   23. _____   35. _____

12. _____   24. _____   36. _____

I did ☐ did not ☐ finish all the questions in the allotted 1 hour.

I had _____ correct answers. I had _____ incorrect answers. I left _____ blank.

I have carefully reviewed the explanations of the answers, and I think I need to work on the following types of questions:

The current AP English Language exam divides the multiple choice section of the exam into "Reading" and "Writing" categories with separate texts for each type. However, for our purposes, each of the texts in the practice exam contains both "Reading" and "Writing" questions.

DIAGNOSTIC/MASTER EXAM
ADVANCED PLACEMENT ENGLISH LANGUAGE AND COMPOSITION
Section I

The multiple-choice section of the exam will have 45 questions.
- 20–25 will be related to close reading/analysis.
- 20–25 will be related to the rhetorical situation.

Total Time—1 hour

Carefully read the following passages and answer the accompanying questions.

Questions 1–12 are based on the following passage from "Samuel Johnson on Pope," which appeared in *The Lives of the English Poets* (1779–1781).

The person of Pope is well known not to have been formed by the nicest model. He has compared himself to a spider and, by another, is described as protuberant behind and before. He is said to have been beautiful in his infancy, but he was of a constitution feeble and weak. As bodies of a tender frame are easily distorted, his deformity was probably in part the effect of his application. But his face was not displeasing, and his eyes were animated and vivid.   5

By natural deformity, or accidental distortion, his vital functions were so much disordered, that his life was a "long disease."

He sometimes condescended to be jocular with servants or inferiors; but by no merriment, either of others or his own, was he ever seen excited to laughter.   10

Of his domestic character frugality was a part eminently remarkable. Having determined not to be dependent, he determined not to be in want, and, therefore, wisely and magnanimously rejected all temptations to expense unsuitable to his fortune.

The great topic of his ridicule is poverty; the crimes with which he reproaches his antagonists are their debts and their want of a dinner. He seems to be of an opinion not   15 very uncommon in the world, that to want money is to want everything.

He professed to have learned his poetry from Dryden, whom he praised through his whole life with unvaried liberality; and perhaps his character may receive some illustration, if he be compared with his master.

Integrity of understanding and nicety of discernment were not allotted in a less   20 proportion to Dryden than to Pope. But Dryden never desired to apply all the judgment that he had. He wrote merely for the people. When he pleased others, he contented himself. He never attempted to mend what he must have known to be faulty. He wrote with little consideration and, once it had passed the press, ejected it from his mind.

Pope was not content to satisfy; he desired to excel, and, therefore, always endeavored   25 to do his best. Pope did not court the candor, but dared the judgment of his reader, and, expecting no indulgence from others, he showed none to himself. He examined lines and words with minute and punctilious observation, and he retouched every part with diligence, until he had nothing left to be forgiven.

Poetry was not the sole praise of either; for both excelled likewise in prose. The   30 style of Dryden is capricious and varied; that of Pope is cautious and uniform. Dryden observes the motions of his own mind; Pope constrains his mind to his own rules of composition. Dryden's page is a natural field, diversified by the exuberance of abundant vegetation. Pope's is a velvet lawn, shaven by the scythe, and leveled by the roller.

If the flights of Dryden are higher, Pope continues longer on the wing. If of Dryden's   35 fire the blaze is brighter, of Pope's the heat is more regular and constant. Dryden is read with frequent astonishment, and Pope with perpetual delight.

1. The primary purpose of the passage is to
   A. provide a character sketch of Pope
   B. examine the principles of poetic style
   C. criticize Dryden
   D. present a model for future poets
   E. create an opportunity for the writer to show off his own skills

2. The passage discusses a contrast among all of the following except:
   A. prose and poetry
   B. Pope and Dryden
   C. body and mind
   D. poverty and wealth
   E. body and soul

3. The thesis is located in line(s)
   A. 1
   B. 7–8
   C. 11
   D. 20–21
   E. 36–37

4. The character of Pope is developed by all of the following except:
   A. examples
   B. comparison
   C. contrast
   D. satire
   E. description

5. According to the passage, Pope and Dryden are
   A. rivals
   B. equally intelligent
   C. outdated
   D. equally physically attractive
   E. in debt

6. From the passage, the reader may infer that Pope
   A. was extravagant
   B. was a man of the people
   C. was jealous of Dryden
   D. had a desire to be popular
   E. had a bitter, satirical nature

7. "If the flights" (35) means
   A. Pope's writing will outlive Dryden's
   B. both Pope and Dryden are equal
   C. Pope is not idealistic
   D. Pope is more wordy
   E. Pope is not as bright as Dryden

8. Lines 20–24 indicate that Dryden was what type of writer?
   A. one who labored over his thoughts
   B. one who wrote only for himself
   C. one who wrote only for the critics
   D. one who wrote to please Pope
   E. one who did not revise

9. The tone of the passage is
   A. informal and affectionate
   B. formal and objective
   C. condescending and paternalistic
   D. laudatory and reverent
   E. critical and negative

10. In the context of the passage, "until he had nothing left to be forgiven" (29) means
    A. Pope outraged his readers
    B. Pope suffered from writer's block
    C. Pope exhausted his subject matter
    D. Pope's prose was revised to perfection
    E. Pope cared about the opinions of his readers

11. "Shaven" and "leveled" in line 34 indicate that Pope's style of writing was
    A. natural
    B. richly ornamented
    C. highly controlled
    D. mechanical
    E. analytical

12. Based on a close reading of the final paragraph of the passage, the reader could infer that the author
    A. looks on both writers equally
    B. prefers the work of Pope
    C. sees the two writers as inferior to his own writing style
    D. indicates no preference
    E. prefers the work of Dryden

Questions 13–23 are based on the following excerpt from Charlotte Perkins Gilman's "Politics and Warfare," which appears in *The Man-Made World: Our Androcentric Culture* (1911).

There are many today who hold that politics need not be at all connected with 1
warfare; and others who hold that politics is warfare from start to finish.

The inextricable confusion of politics and warfare is part of the stumbling block 2
in the minds of men. As they see it, a nation is primarily a fighting organization; and
its principal business is offensive and defensive warfare; therefore the ultimatum with
which they oppose the demand for political equality—"women cannot fight, therefore
they cannot vote."

Fighting, when all is said, is to them the real business of life; not to be able to fight 3
is to be quite out of the running; and ability to solve our growing mass of public
problems; questions of health, of education, of morals, of economics; weighs naught
against the ability to kill.

This naïve assumption of supreme value in a process never of the first importance; 4
and increasingly injurious as society progresses, would be laughable if it were not for
its evil effects. It acts and reacts upon us to our hurt. Positively, we see the ill effects
already touched on; the evils not only of active war, but of the spirit and methods of
war; idealized, inculcated, and practiced in other social processes. It tends to make
each man-managed nation an actual or potential fighting organization, and to give us,
instead of civilized peace, that "balance of power" which is like the counted time in the
prize ring—only a rest between combats.

It leaves the weaker nations to be "conquered" and "annexed" just as they used 5
to be; with "preferential tariffs" instead of tribute. It forces upon each the burden of
armament; upon many the dreaded conscription; and continually lowers the world's
resources in money and in life.

Similarly in politics, it adds to the legitimate expenses of governing the illegitimate 6
expenses of fighting; and must needs have a "spoils system" by which to pay its
mercenaries.

In carrying out the public policies the wheels of state are continually clogged by the 7
"opposition"; always an opposition on one side or the other; and this slow wiggling
uneven progress, through shorn victories and haggling concessions, is held to be the
proper and only political method.

"Women do not understand politics," we are told; "Women do not care for politics"; 8
"Women are unfitted for politics."

It is frankly inconceivable, from the androcentric viewpoint, that nations can live in 9
peace together, and be friendly and serviceable as persons are. It is inconceivable also,
that, in the management of a nation, honesty, efficiency, wisdom, experience and love
could work out good results without any element of combat.

The "ultimate resort" is still to arms. "The will of the majority" is only respected on 10
account of the guns of the majority. We have but a partial civilization, heavily modified
to sex—the male sex.

13. The author's main purpose in the passage is to
    A. argue for women being drafted
    B. criticize colonialism
    C. present a pacifist philosophy
    D. criticize the male-dominated society
    E. protest tariffs

14. In paragraph 2, the author maintains that men support their position on equality for women based upon which of the following approaches?
    A. begging the question
    B. a syllogism using a faulty premise
    C. an appeal to emotion
    D. circular reasoning
    E. an *ad hoc* argument

15. Using textual clues, one can conclude that *androcentric* (9th paragraph) most probably means
    A. robot-centered
    B. world-centered
    C. female-centered
    D. self-centered
    E. male-centered

16. In paragraph 4, "increasingly injurious as society progresses" is reinforced by all of the following except:
    A. "ill effects already touched on" [paragraph 4]
    B. "active war" [paragraph 4]
    C. "weaker nations to be 'conquered' and 'annexed'" [paragraph 5]
    D. "illegitimate expenses of fighting" [paragraph 6]
    E. "Women do not understand politics" [paragraph 8]

17. In addition to indicating a direct quotation, the author uses quotation marks to indicate
    A. the jargon of politics and warfare
    B. the coining of a phrase
    C. a definition
    D. the author's scholarship
    E. that the author does not take responsibility for her words

18. According to the author, men view the primary purpose of government to be
    A. educating the people
    B. solving the "mass of public problems"
    C. obtaining as much power as possible
    D. economics
    E. health

19. The argument shifts from a discussion of warfare to a discussion of politics in the first sentence of which of the following paragraphs?
    A. paragraph 4
    B. paragraph 5
    C. paragraph 6
    D. paragraph 7
    E. paragraph 9

20. The tone of the passage is best described as
    A. ambivalent
    B. reverent
    C. condescending
    D. accusatory
    E. indifferent

21. To present her argument, Gilman primarily uses which of the following rhetorical strategies?
    A. process
    B. definition
    C. cause and effect
    D. narration
    E. description

Questions 22–30 are based on a film by Ernest J. Gaines, author of *The Autobiography of Miss Jane Pittman* and *A Lesson Before Dying*, who is part of the fifth generation of his family to be born on the Riverlake plantation. This is his introduction to a short film titled *An Obsession* (2000), which is about a cemetery on the Riverlake plantation which he bought and is dedicated to preserving.

An obsession of mine concerns a half-acre of land in south-central Louisiana. This plot of land is surrounded by sugarcane fields on all sides, some of the rows coming within twenty feet of it. This plot of land is where my ancestors have been buried the past hundred years, where most of the people I knew as a child are now buried. This is Riverlake plantation, Point Coupee Parish, Oscar, Louisiana.

The first fifteen and a half years of my life were spent on this place. My ancestors for over a hundred years planted the sugarcane here, hoed the sugarcane, plowed it, cut it and, when it was time, hauled it to the mills. They, like too many others who worked this land, are buried here in unmarked graves because they could not afford the headstones.

A hundred years ago, the land was owned by one man who designated that the land would be a cemetery for the people on that plantation, but he did not give it to them, nor would he let them buy it. Today the land is owned by sixteen people who live all over the country and probably different parts of the world, some of whom I'm sure have never visited the plantation or know anything about the cemetery which lies there. Yet it is their land, and those who are buried there do not own even six feet of the ground.

Many rural cemeteries have been destroyed all over this country, and day and night I worry that the same fate may happen to this one. There is no law in the state of Louisiana that I am aware of that says it cannot be done. My wife and I and several friends from my childhood are trying to find a way to get control of the land. We have contacted lawyers to work with us and presently we are keeping the place clean of overgrowth, because that is one excuse landowners and developers use to plow under cemeteries. "We didn't know that one was there."

At a recent interview, I was asked where would I like to be buried and I answered that I'd like to be in the same place where my ancestors are. The interviewer asked me what would I like on my headstone and I said, "To lie with those who have no marks." These are the people for whom I wrote letters as a child, read their letters because many of them could not read nor could they write. Many of them had to go into the fields before they had a chance to go to school. Yet they're the ones responsible for my being here tonight. Not only did they encourage me to stay in school, but they, and only they, have been the source of all of my writings. I've said many times before that my novels, my short stories, are just continuations of the letters that I started writing for them some fifty years ago, and since I've tried to say something about their lives on paper— their joy, their sorrows, their love, their fears, their pride, their compassion—I think it is only my duty now to do as much as I can to see that they lie in peace forever.

22. The exigence for Gaines's passage is
    A. the need for funding to further the author's cause
    B. the possibility that the author may lose his plantation
    C. the growing possibility that the unmarked graves of slaves and other plantation workers may be lost to developers and farmers
    D. a protest movement to save unmarked graves of slaves
    E. the 400th anniversary of the first slave being brought into the Virginia colony

23. The function of the first paragraph is to
    A. establish the setting of the issue Gaines wishes to address
    B. begin developing the historical background of the location
    C. build a contrast between the accepted importance of the plantation to the lack of care paid to the cemetery
    D. emphasize that the cemetery has no name that might protect it
    E. develop the personal connection the author has with the location

24. Which item could most appropriately be added to end the series in paragraph 2 beginning with, *My ancestors for over a hundred years planted the sugarcane here . . .*
    A. and, when it was time, profited nothing from it
    B. and, when it was time, left the plantation to pursue new lives
    C. and, when it was time, were buried next to those fields
    D. and, when it was time, bought their freedom
    E. and, when it was time, reseeded the land for new crops

25. The thesis is located in which paragraph?
    A. 1
    B. 2
    C. 3
    D. 4
    E. 5

26. Which of the following is the major rhetorical strategy the author uses to support his thesis?
    A. appeal to emotions through historical anecdotes
    B. appeal to the audience's sense of guilt
    C. appeal to author's credibility through personal anecdotes
    D. appeal to reason through an overview of legal issues
    E. appeal to the audience's sense of historical precedence

27. Which of the following sentences could best be added to the end of paragraph 4?
    A. The destruction of these cemeteries across the nation is an example of systematic racism.
    B. It is urgent that we continue to speak up for the people buried in these cemeteries until we can find a lasting way to protect them.
    C. The lack of empathy on the part of these landowners needs to be punished in the civil court system.
    D. I speak to all of you today in the hopes that you will support our efforts to save these sites by contacting your local states representatives.
    E. It is necessary that permanent monuments are erected in these rural cemeteries to acknowledge the forgotten.

28. Which of the following best describes the author's purpose in including the following direct quotation in paragraph 5?

The interviewer asked me what would I like on my headstone and I said,
"To lie with those who have no marks."

   A. adds needed pacing
   B. presents an ironic counterbalance to the direct quotation in paragraph 4
   C. presents an illustration of the thesis
   D. appeals to the emotions of the audience
   E. emphasizes the author's reportorial approach to his subject

29. The rhetorical purpose of the set of dashes used in the last sentence is to
   A. supply an aside to the audience
   B. provide an overview of the author's literary works
   C. provide a continuation of the list begun at the start of this sentence
   D. emphasize what is stated in the sentence in the last paragraph beginning with *Not only did they encourage me . . .*
   E. enumerate what *their lives* consisted of

30. Carefully read the following two sentences:

I've said many times before that my novels, my short stories, are just continuations of the letters that I started writing for them some fifty years ago, and since I've tried to say something about their lives on paper—their joy, their sorrows, their love, their fears, their pride, their compassion—I think it is only my duty now to do as much as I can to see that they lie in peace forever. (Original sentence)

I've said many times before that my novels, my short stories, are just continuations of the letters that I started writing for them some fifty years ago, and since I've tried to say something about their lives on paper—their joy, their sorrows, their love, their fears, their pride, their compassion—It is my duty to see that they lie in peace forever. (A second version)

What does the original imply that the second version does not?
   A. The author will continue to write as much and as often as he can to benefit his ancestor's memories.
   B. The author will take his story to audiences across the Nation.
   C. The author is thinking about running for public office to secure the rights of his Louisiana ancestors.
   D. Instead of writing for and about his ancestors, the author will act on their behalf.
   E. The author is retiring from writing and will work solely to support the Riverlake Plantation cemetery.

Questions 31–41 are related to a 2007 essay written in response to a survey and commentary about what constitutes healthy eating.

To Eat or Not to Eat Healthy Foods

My friends and I are like the folks surveyed in a recent Reuters/Ipsos online poll. The majority favored limiting advertising of unhealthy food and soda. But, this majority also said a big NO to banning fast food restaurants. We want our drive-in burgers and tacos. How do we say "yes" to healthy foods and a healthy planet while still craving our Big Macs and fries? Several recommendations have already been made.   1

There are those who see our planet suffering from our love of beef. The carbon footprint left by our increasing "food production, processing, consumption, and waste disposal" (Hamerschlag) results in a huge amount of greenhouse gases released into our atmosphere and the pollution of our water. Our health is being adversely affected by our continued consumption of beef and processed meats. (Hamerschlag) For these groups, one possible solution would be to have everyone in the U.S. give up meat or cheese one day a week. Not counting the health benefits, they calculate the effects on emissions to be like "taking 7.6 million cars off the road." (Ewing)   2

Groups concerned about world hunger maintain that eating meat increases the number of hungry people. Why? Ezra Klein says that it takes 16 pounds of grain to produce one pound of meat—grain that hungry people can't eat because the grain is being sold and fed to livestock. The remaining grain is more expensive because there is less of it. What to do? For Klein and others: make meat more expensive. More expensive meat = less* meat consumption = more grain available = less hunger.   3

And, what about those who want us to eat a healthier diet? The research shows that "eating green is good for you." (Walsh)* As previously mentioned, red meat, processed food, etc., have a high carbon footprint, and they are also high in fat and calories. A "green diet of vegetables, fruits, whole grains, fish and lean meat like chicken" is also friendly to both our own health and the health of our planet. (Walsh) Mark Bittman and many other food experts would like to see high-fat, high-calorie processed foods taxed. He sees it as a way of saving billions of dollars in health care costs and saving "millions of lives." (Bittman)   4

It's hard to deny the findings of recent research. It's also hard to say "no" to burgers and fries or to that steak on the grill. Going "cold-turkey" and becoming a total vegan is not going to happen for me and not for most people in our country. Forcing it on us with high taxes and restrictive laws will only turn us into a nation of liars, sneaks, and criminals. Perhaps we can learn something from the way cigarettes have been treated in the past several decades: taxation, advertising, education, and ultimately self-interest. Right now, I'm listening to Jonathan Kaplan of the Natural Resource Defense Council who has said, "If you can't buy a Prius, you can certainly eat like one."   5

31. The writer wants to add the following sentence to the fourth paragraph to provide further information.

For instance, Thomas Walsh, the CEO of the Eat Healthy; Live Longer Institute, travels throughout the United States advocating for healthy eating.

Where would this sentence best be placed?
A. before the first sentence
B. after the second sentence
C. before the fourth sentence
D. after the fourth sentence
E. after the last sentence

32. The author uses which major rhetorical appeal to support and develop the thesis?
A. appeal of reason
B. appeal to emotions
C. appeal to authority
D. appeal to timeliness and opportunity
E. appeal to commonality

33. What is the rhetorical effect of using equal signs in the last sentence of paragraph 3?
A. continuation of the "mathematical" image
B. appeal to those who are convinced when confronted with cause and effect
C. a sense of irony
D. a sense of inevitability
E. a sense of balance

34. The author's purpose can best be stated as
A. advocating for a limit on the consumption of red meat
B. highlighting some of the difficulties related to food and the environment
C. criticizing those who recommend limiting meat production
D. reviewing the current state of research about food production and its effect on the environment
E. defending those who favor high taxes on both those who produce meat and those who consume it.

35. In context, which choice best combines the last two sentences in paragraph 4?
A. No change
B. To save billions of dollars and "millions of lives," Mark Bittman recommends taxing high-fat and high-calorie processed foods.
C. According to Mark Bittman and many other food experts, one way to save billions of dollars and "millions of lives" is to tax high-fat and high-calorie processed food.
D. Saving billions of dollars and saving "millions of lives," would be the major result of taxing high-fat and high-calorie processed food, argues Mark Bittman and many other food experts.
E. To encourage people to avoid high-fat, and high-calorie processed foods, Mark Bittman and other healthy food advocate taxing these foods, which will save billions of dollars in health care and save "millions of lives."

36. The logic of the fourth paragraph would be better served if the sentence beginning with *As previously mentioned, red meat . . .* were placed
A. at the beginning of the paragraph, before the sentence beginning with *And, . . .*
B. before the last sentence beginning with *He sees it . . .*
C. after the first sentence
D. before the next to last sentence beginning with *Mark Bittman . . .*
E. after the last sentence

37. The writer wants to more clearly introduce the thesis of the essay in the first paragraph. Which of the following versions of the first sentence beginning with *My friends and I . . .* would best serve that purpose?
    A. No change
    B. My friends and I recently saw a Reuters/Ipsos online poll.
    C. My friends and I are like most Americans when it comes to eating healthy.
    D. A recent Reuters/Ipsos poll indicates Americans are looking to government to solve the questions revolving around healthy eating.
    E. The results of a recent Reuters/Ipsos online poll about attitudes toward eating healthy should be of interest to us all.

38. In the last sentence of the first paragraph, the writer hopes to lead the reader into an examination of some of the recent research and recommendations of experts and organizations connected to healthy eating and to the environment. Which version of this last sentence best accomplishes this goal?
    A. No change
    B. This question and others related to healthy eating and the environment have been the subject of many research projects and recommendations.
    C. Here is what some of the experts in healthy eating recommend.
    D. It's difficult to come to any conclusion about healthy eating and the environment.
    E. Research seems to favor the government solving this problem.

39. The obvious exigence for this essay is
    A. an assigned writing prompt
    B. a concern for the environment
    C. fear of eating the wrong foods
    D. anger with climate change
    E. desire to change people's attitude toward healthy eating

40. Which of the following does the writer NOT assume about the audience?
    A. They have eaten fast food.
    B. They have had experience with paying taxes.
    C. They have a working knowledge of environmental science.
    D. They have an interest in protecting the environment.
    E. They have an interest in eating healthy.

41. The last sentence of the essay beginning with *Right now, I'm . . .* indicates to the reader that the writer most probably
    A. will find a compromise when dealing with food choices and their effects on the environment
    B. is confused about what to do about food choices and the environment
    C. will keep in mind the relationship between food choices and their effects on the environment when grocery shopping or eating out
    D. will advocate for corporations to become more active in protecting the environment
    E. will advocate for government taking a larger role in addressing this situation

Questions 42–45 are based on the following letter to the editor published in *Newsday* on August 23, 2019.

History Evolves as Scholars Learn More

When *The New York Times* published "The 1619 Project" on Aug. 18, 2019, there was a backlash from conservative critics about the integrity and accuracy of the project, which aims to reframe U.S. history with slavery as its foundation. [1]

Newsday columnist Cathy Young writes that "The 1619" project is "revisionist," a common pejorative used to discredit histories that highlight negative aspects of America's past ["A revisionist narrative of slavery," Opinion, Aug. 20, 2019]. In Young's view, "Increasingly, the prevailing view among progressives . . . is that the United States was founded on slavery and built on the backs of the enslaved." [2]

But all history is revisionist, as it is based on newly uncovered primary sources, scholarship, and contributions from groups—like enslaved Africans and African-Americans—excluded from previous accounts. The editors and authors of "The 1619 Project" would likely embrace the claim that theirs is a revisionist history that tells "the unvarnished truth," in the words of historian John Hope Franklin. [3]

While praising some parts of the "1619" study, Young maintains that the scholarship was questionable regarding the assertion that slavery was the cornerstone of the founding of this country and which still affects our American culture today. She writes that "we risk replacing one mythology with another that demonizes America and its achievements" and could make "ordinary Americans feel that patriotism is being made politically incorrect." This is a false dichotomy; history isn't a zero-sum endeavor, either patriotic or critical. It's both, because uncovering negative aspects from the past pushes us toward a brighter future. [4]

As a teacher of history, I must teach about the good, the bad and the ugly to help students think critically to understand the devastating impact of slavery and racism on our country. [5]

Dennis Urban,
History teacher

This is a letter to the editor, and by definition it is brief. If the author wished to further develop this into an essay of around 500–800 words, he might consider the following:

42. The location of the thesis of this letter is
A. all of paragraph one
B. the last sentence of paragraph 2
C. the first sentence of paragraph 3
D. he last sentence of paragraph 4
E. all of the last paragraph

43. The writer is considering placing the last sentence someplace else in the letter. Considering the rhetorical situation, including the exigence, what would be the best placement?
A. as is
B. at the very beginning
C. before paragraph 2
D. before paragraph 3
E. before paragraph 4

44. The writer wants an effective transition from the introductory paragraph to the main idea of the text. Which of the following would best achieve this goal?
  A. Leave as is.
  B. One critic is a contributing editor to *Reason* magazine.
  C. A recent edition of this newspaper published one of these conservative opinions.
  D. One of these conservative writers is *Newsday* columnist Cathy Young who writes that . . . [sentence continues as in the original].
  E. I read one of these opinions in a recent edition of this newspaper.

45. The writer wants to add the following sentence to the text to provide additional information.

It should be noted that "1619 Project" was published to correspond with the 400th anniversary of the arrival of the first African slaves in Jamestown, the first English settlement in North America.

Where would the sentence best be placed?
  A. the beginning of the first paragraph
  B. the end of the first paragraph
  C. the beginning of the second paragraph
  D. the end of the second paragraph
  E. the end of the last paragraph

ANSWER KEY

1. A	16. E	31. B
2. E	17. E	32. C
3. B	18. C	33. A
4. D	19. C	34. B
5. B	20. D	35. C
6. E	21. C	36. D
7. B	22. C	37. E
8. E	23. A	38. B
9. A	24. C	39. A
10. D	25. D	40. C
11. C	26. A	41. C
12. B	27. B	42. C
13. D	28. B	43. A
14. B	29. E	44. D
15. E	30. D	45. B

Explanations of Answers to the Multiple-Choice Questions

Explanations to the Samuel Johnson Essay

1. **A.** Although references to poetic style and to Dryden are contained in the passage, they are included to illuminate the character of Pope. Each of the details and examples in the essay is used to further the characterization of Pope.

2. **E.** No references to body versus soul are in the passage. We do find references to both the prose and the poetry of Pope and Dryden. We are told of Pope's monetary concerns, and we can infer the contrast between Pope's broken body and healthy mind.

3. **B.** This two-sentence paragraph provides an introduction to the topic (Pope), takes a position about Pope, and indicates the organization of the presentation.

4. **D.** A careful reading of this passage allows you to locate each of the devices, except satire.

5. **B.** Lines 20–21 clearly state that the two men were equally gifted.

6. **E.** Lines 9 and 10 tell the reader that Pope's humor was condescending. Lines 14–15 allude to his use of ridicule, and the reader may infer that these characteristics were carried over into Pope's writing.

7. **B.** The author sets up several comparisons between Dryden and Pope. Each of these comparisons has Pope the better of the two.

8. **E.** Carefully read lines 23 and 24 and you will see a direct correlation between those lines and choice E.

9. **A.** This is a fairly straightforward interpretation of a figurative line. The idea of "long on the wing" naturally leads the reader to think of endurance.

10. **D.** If you go to lines 25–29, you will see that Pope demanded perfection of himself and his writing. This characteristic is further extended with the clause in line 29.

11. **C.** Both words indicate a practiced, continuous, and extreme control of the work at hand. Even the "velvet of the lawn" indicates a tightness, a smoothness, and a richness of form and content.

12. **B.** If it were a contest, Pope would be declared the winner by Johnson. A close reading of both the structure and the content of the paragraph leads the reader to Pope. When discussing Dryden and Pope, Pope has the last work. This allows Pope to linger in the reader's mind. "Frequent" with Dryden and "perpetual" with Pope is another indication of Samuel Johnson's preference.

Explanations to the Gilman Essay

13. **D.** Although Gilman touches upon each of the choices in the passage, A, B, C, and E are details used to support her argument that a man-managed nation is an imperfect culture.

14. **B.** The question requires the student to be familiar with methods of logical reasoning and logical fallacies. Gilman presents the syllogism men use to deny women the right to vote:
Those who fight may vote.
Women do not fight.
Therefore, women may not vote.
"Those" is understood to be men. The first premise is incorrect, as is the second premise. This being the case, the conclusion is invalid.

15. **E.** Throughout this text, Gilman is making direct reference to the words and concepts she cites that are employed by society's male leadership.

16. **E.** Because the argument of the passage is to criticize the aggressive nature of politics in a male-managed society and to point out the results of combining politics and warfare, the question demands details that support the idea of aggression being detrimental to society. The only choice that does not reflect this idea is E.

17. **E.** Paragraph 4 is a listing of the ill-effects of the supremacy of power/might, and each of the other cited paragraphs illustrates this claim. All except for E, which is not an example of that idea.

18. **C.** Look carefully at the second paragraph to see the ranking Gilman sets up as the male-

centered priorities. The only one ranked over the others is fighting and the ability to kill.

19. C. Syntactically, the phrase, "Similarly in politics" is an indicator that a comparison is being drawn between what came before and what comes after. No other phrase does this.

20. D. Because this is an argumentative selection, the author is expected to take a position on an issue. Because of this, the choices of "ambivalent" and "indifferent" are immediately eliminated. Keeping in mind the diction of the piece, you can see that "reverent" and "condescending" are also inappropriate.

21. C. If you read the passage carefully, you cannot avoid the cause-and-effect sequencing throughout the excerpt. Look at paragraphs 2, 3, 4, 6, and the last. Remember that an author can use many different techniques in the same work, but only one will be predominant, and that strategy is what reinforces the author's purpose.

The Gaines Passage

22. C. Exigence identifies what compelled the author to compose the given text, in other words, the immediate cause for this writing/speaking/visual event. Even though each of the items is related to the general topic, only **C** cites the reason for this particular text at this particular time.

23. A. This first paragraph provides the audience with a context and background in which Gaines locates a part of his past, his heritage. Each of the other choices is referenced throughout the rest of the passage.

24. C. Given that the topic of this paragraph is the work and death life cycle of the plantation workers, introducing ideas related to profit, freedom, and renewed farming would not be logical. Only **C** makes a further comment on that life cycle.

25. D. The first sentence in paragraph 4 (**D**) presents the subject of the text, Gaines's position on the topic, and the organizational pattern of the passage. The other choices are separate claims made that are related to the development of the thesis.

26. A. Each of the choices plays a role in the development of the thesis, but the MAJOR rhetorical strategy is found in choice **A**. It cites the appeal to emotions AND briefly states how that is accomplished. Choice B only mentions a specific emotion without comment. Choice C only points to personal anecdotes. Choices D and E are also details without that sense of says/does.

27. B. The subject of paragraph 4 is the attempts at preserving the plantation. Choice **B** is the only sentence that includes Gaines and his wife, plus the cause they support. Each of the other choices addresses only one part of the equation or goes off in another direction.

28. B. Paragraph 4 ends with the direct quotation, "We didn't know that one [cemetery] was there." In other words, "Out of sight, out of mind." With his saying he wants his headstone to reference those whom no one can name, Gaines gives recognition to those who are unknown. **B** is the only choice that indicates this idea.

29. E. These dashes follow one of the prescribed uses of this punctuation mark. The dashes in this instance indicate emphasis on the scope of the lives of Gaines's ancestors. **E** is the only choice that cites this.

30. D. . . . *I think it is* <u>only</u> *my duty* <u>now</u> *to* <u>do as much as I can</u> *to see that they lie in peace forever.* Notice that in the second version the words *only* and *now* are omitted as well as the phrase *do as much as I can*. The audience can infer that Gaines sees his previous duty of writing for and about his ancestors as completed. It is time to actively work for the preservation of the cemetery. **D** addresses both of these components. He does not indicate that he is giving up writing all together.

Eating Healthy Passage

31. B. Since the claim of this paragraph is that there are many who want us to eat healthy foods and since sentences two and three attribute quoted information to Walsh, **B** is a sentence that would appropriately introduce Walsh to the audience. Choices C, D, and E are all related to Bittman. Placing a sentence before or after sentences four or five would not be logical and would confuse the reader.

32. **C.** The development of the appeal to authority (**C**) supports the thesis. Paragraphs 2, 3, 4, and 5 make specific reference to attributed experts related to the given data and examples in support of the thesis.

33. **A.** Using the mathematical theme established in paragraph 3, the author creates an image/analogy (**A**) of the algebraic equation to reinforce the claim that eating meat leads to hunger.

34. **B.** Although some would see the purpose of this essay as advocating for a limit on eating red meat (A), there are other goals developed. Choice D identifies the main purpose as reviewing the current state of research; however, citing one or two examples of the research is not all of it. The only choice that is inclusive of the other goal(s) is **B**.

35. **C.** Choices B, D, And E do combine the two sentences; however, each of these sentences presents problems with awkward construction or missing information. Choice **C** presents a clear and complete combination.

36. **D.** Because it references earlier details that compose the subject of the last two sentences, **D** would smoothly lead the reader into an understanding of what follows. Logic and clarity are not served by any of the other choices.

37. **E.** Choices A, B, and C incorrectly make it appear that the essay will center on the writer and his friends. D presents misinformation about what will be the thesis. Choice **E** clearly introduces the reader to the context and thesis of this essay.

38. **B.** Choice **B** uses *This* to refer to the rhetorical question that immediately precedes the sentence, and it connects it to the subject and organization pattern of the essay to follow. This is the thesis. The other choices do not offer the needed structure to appropriately connect to the rest of the essay.

39. **A.** Remember exigence simply means the "boot in the butt" that pushes the writer/author to act. Also, always remember to read introductory material. In this case, we are told

that the essay is a response to a given prompt. Given this information, it should be clear that the exigence is choice **A**.

40. **C.** There is nothing in the essay that depends on the audience knowing specifics about scientific/mathematical formulas, equations, and experiments (**C**). The other choices A, B, D, and E are the basis for the writer's appeal and organization of material.

41. **C.** The last sentence with its direct quotation does not lead the audience to infer that the writer is advocating for any government or corporate policies. (Choices D, E) Nor is there a hint of compromise or confusion. (Choices A, B) With the reference to both cars and food, the audience is encouraged to see the interconnection between what they buy and eat and their effect on the environment. (**C**)

Letter to the Editor

42. **C.** *But all history is revisionist, as it is based on newly uncovered primary sources, scholarship, and contributions from groups—like enslaved Africans and African-Americans—excluded from previous accounts.* This sentence presents the author's position with an indication of the type of reasoning that will support the assertion. Prior to this paragraph, the writer has provided context and needed background information that sets up his argument (A & B). The fourth paragraph continues the argument (D), and the last paragraph provides the reader with information about the author's credibility (E).

43. **A.** This is added information that highlights the writer's credibility/expertise. It does not develop the argument. If the writer were to have this sentence at the very beginning, the reader would be expecting the text to develop a claim about teaching about slavery to high school students (B). Placing this sentence anywhere else in the text (C, D & E) would break the logical flow.

44. **D.** Because of the required brevity of a letter to the editor, any added words/phrases must serve a specific purpose. In this case, the writer wants to refer to the first paragraph and lead the reader into a discussion of a

specific, conservative critic who has written about this "1619 Project." He does this clearly and succinctly by adding the introductory phrase. Choice B could be a little confusing because it identifies a writer for *Reason* and then re-identifies that writer as a *Newsday* columnist. The information in choice C is already provided in that first sentence of paragraph 2. This is just repetitious. Choice E is a given. Why state it? It's extra wording for no real purpose.

45. **B.** The first paragraph presents context and needed background information. Choice B provides important information to those who would not be familiar with the "1619 Project." Placing it at the end of the first paragraph allows this information to smoothly follow the timeline and exigence that was already established. This would not happen with its placement anywhere else in the text.

Introduction to Chapters 5, 6, and 7

The essay part of the AP Language and Composition exam emphasizes three major skills:

- Analysis
- Argument
- Synthesis

The additional 15 minutes is to allow time for careful reading and annotation of each of the prompts and all of the resources provided for the synthesis essay. <u>You are not required to spend this time only reading prompts and sources. But we recommend that you do so.</u>

You may begin once you feel you have an understanding of the demands of each prompt. Remember: READ THE PROMPT.

The heading of Section II looks something like this:

Section II

Number of questions—3

Percent of total grade—55

Each question counts one-third of the total section score.

You will have a total of 2–2¼ hours to write, which you may divide any way you choose. Because each essay carries the same weight, do NOT spend an inappropriate amount of time on any one question.

Chapters 5, 6, and 7 of this book introduce you to each of the three essay types.

BEFORE BEGINNING TO WORK WITH ANY OF THE ACTUAL ESSAY PROMPTS IN THIS BOOK, READ THE REVIEW OF THE PROCESSES AND TERMS IN THE COMPREHENSIVE REVIEW SECTION. ALSO, COMPLETE SOME OF THE ACTIVITIES RELATED TO EACH OF THE SPECIFIC ESSAY TYPES.

CHAPTER 5

Introduction to the Rhetorical Analysis Essay

IN THIS CHAPTER

Summary: Complete explanation of the analysis essay and its purpose as it is presented on the AP English Language exam.

Key Ideas

✪ Learn the types of analysis prompts you might encounter on the AP English Language exam.

✪ Learn about the rubrics and rating of the AP English Language essay.

✪ Learn the basics of reading and notating a given passage.

✪ Learn the basics of constructing your response to the prompt.

✪ Examine student models that respond to the diagnostic exam's analysis essay prompt.

✪ Learn how the rubrics were used to rate the student sample essays.

After your brief break, you will be given your free-response booklet that contains all three prompts: synthesis, analysis, and argument. You should spend the initial 15 minutes carefully reading each of the prompts. Then, read the sources provided for the synthesis prompt. The remaining 120 minutes are for you to compose your three essays.

On the cover of the booklet you will find the breakdown of the three essays and the time suggested for each.

Section II

Total Time—2¼ hours

Number of questions—3

Percent of total grade—55

Each question counts one-third of the total section score.

Note: You will have a total of 2¼ hours to write. This includes 15 minutes of recommended reading and annotation time. However, each essay carries the same weight, so do <u>NOT</u> spend an inappropriate amount of time on any one question.

The next step is to quickly turn the pages of the packet and skim the given selections. This should take you less than a minute.

Some Basics

Just What Is an AP English Language Analysis Essay?

Generally, the student is presented with a prose passage that can be drawn from various genres and time periods. Although the specific tasks asked of the student may vary from year to year, they will involve the analysis of language, including **rhetorical strategies** that the author uses to address the rhetorical situation. (If you are in doubt about a term used in the prompt, you can usually check its meaning in the glossary at the end of this book.)

> You may be extremely lucky and find a familiar piece by a familiar author. This certainly can enhance your comfort level. But, don't try to plug into the question everything you know about that author or selection if it does not exactly fit the prompt. Likewise, do not be rattled if you are unfamiliar with the work. <u>You will be familiar with the approaches necessary to analyze it</u>. Remember, this exam reaches thousands of students, many of whom will be in a similar situation and equally anxious. Be confident that you are thoroughly prepared to tackle these tasks and have fun doing so.

What Is the Purpose of the Analysis Essay?

"Doing close readings of editorial columns in newspapers and magazines is a real help to my students as they prepare to attack both multiple-choice questions and analysis essays."
—Chris S.,
  AP teacher

The College Board wants to determine your facility with reading, understanding, and analyzing challenging texts. They also want to assess how well you manipulate language to communicate your written analysis of a specific topic to a mature audience. **The level of your writing should be a direct reflection of your critical thinking.**

AP is looking for connections between analysis and the passage. For example, when you become aware of one of the author's rhetorical choices, identify it and connect it to the prompt. Don't just list items as you locate them.

Types of Rhetorical Analysis Essay Prompts

What Kinds of Questions Are Asked in the Rhetorical Analysis Essay?

Let's look at a few of the TYPES of questions that have been asked on the AP English Language and Composition exam in the past. These types may seem more familiar to you if you see them in the form of prompts.

- Analyze an author's view on a specific subject.
- Analyze rhetorical devices used by an author to achieve his or her purpose.
- Analyze rhetorical elements in a passage and their effects.
- Analyze the author's tone and how the author conveys this tone.
- Compare and/or contrast two passages with regard to style, purpose, or tone.
- Analyze the author's purpose and how he or she achieves it.
- Analyze some of the ways an author re-creates a real or imagined experience.
- Analyze how an author presents him- or herself in the passage.
- Discuss the intended and/or probable effect of a passage.

You should be prepared to write an essay based on any of these prompts. Practice. Practice. Practice. Anticipate questions. Keep a running list of the kinds of questions your teacher asks.

It's good to remember that the tasks demanded of you by the question remain constant. What changes is the source material on which you base your response to the question. Therefore, your familiarity with the terms and processes related to the types of questions is crucial.

Don't be thrown by the complexity of the passage. *You* choose the references you want to incorporate into your essay. So, even if you haven't understood everything, you *can* write an intelligent essay—AS LONG AS YOU ADDRESS THE PROMPT and refer to the parts of the passage you do understand.

Watch for overconfidence when you see what you believe to be an easy question with an easy passage. You are going to have to work harder to find the nuances in the text that will allow you to write a mature essay.

Rating the Rhetorical Analysis Essay

How Do the AP Readers Rate My Essay?

It's important to understand just what it is that goes into rating your essay. This is called a **rubric**, but don't let that word frighten you. A rubric is just a fancy, professional word that simply means the **rating standards that are set and used by the people who read the essays**. These standards are fairly consistent, no matter what the given prompt might be. The only primary change is in the citing of the specifics in a particular prompt.

As experienced readers of AP exams, we assure you that the exam readers are trained to reward both what students DO (analytic) and what students DO WELL (holistic) in addressing the question. They are NOT looking to punish you. They are aware of the time constraints and read your essay just as your own instructor would read the first draft of an essay you wrote on a 40-minute exam. These readers do look forward to reading an interesting, insightful, and well-constructed essay.

So, let's take a look at these rubrics.

6-Point Rubric for the Rhetorical Analysis Essay

THESIS = 1 Point

- **1 pt.** Addresses the prompt with a clearly defensible thesis.
- **0 pts.** Merely repeats the prompt, or statement is vague, avoids taking a position, or presents only an obvious fact.

DEVELOPMENT WITH EVIDENCE = 4 Points

- **4 pts.** With specific references to the text, the writer develops the thesis with conclusions and inferences that are the result of explaining the relationship between what the author says and what the rhetorical strategy does.
- **3 pts.** Development may be uneven, limited; there may be minor instances of description rather than analysis; there may be minor errors or weak links between thesis and support.
- **2 pts.** Development repeats, oversimplifies, or misinterprets cited references; may misinterpret or misunderstand the chosen rhetorical strategies; points made are not supported by the text.
- **1 pt.** Merely summarizes the text, or references to the text are not clear or relevant; merely restates points made in the text.
- **0 pts.** May lack a thesis; or presents irrelevant or too few references to the text in support of a clear thesis; or does not address the prompt; or writes about something totally unrelated to the prompt.

Note: Writing that lacks grammatical or syntactical control that interferes with a clear presentation of ideas cannot earn a 4.

SOPHISTICATION (Complexity and Style) = 1 Point

- **1 pt.** (sophistication of thought or development of complex argument) Writer develops the thesis with nuanced explanation of evidence; and/or recognizes and discusses a broader context; and/or recognizes and engages with opposition; and/or makes strong, convincing rhetorical choices in developing the thesis; and/or prose is especially convincing or appropriate.
- **0 pts.** Oversimplifies complexities of the text or the thesis; and/or diction and/or syntax do not enhance the presentation; and/or may overuse sweeping generalizations.

> REMEMBER, THIS ESSAY IS REALLY A FIRST DRAFT. THE READERS KNOW THIS AND APPROACH EACH ESSAY KEEPING THIS IN MIND.

Remember: PROMPT is another word for QUESTION.

"Throughout the year, I have students mimic the styles of various authors. We then present the pieces to the class, which tries to identify the author being imitated. Through this process, the students become more cognizant of what makes up style, tone, syntax, and diction."
—Denise C., AP teacher

The Unicorn 6

Many students are eager to know, "Just what is a **6**? And, just how can I get that magical **1** in sophistication?" Let's call this the search for the unicorn.

Here's what this unicorn looks like.

The very first thing to understand is that a **6** is NOT based on one thing. It depends on a combination of several factors. Writing a really terrific thesis statement does not guarantee a **6**. Writing a single, well-developed body paragraph is not going to earn a **6**. And, a spectacular conclusion alone does not equal a **6**. What does earn a sighting of that unicorn is having each of the sections of the essay working very well together. . . .

When the student essays are read, they are scored **1-4-1**. The reader does not look at the complete essay and say, "Yes, that is a **4**." or "Wow! That's a **6**." Instead each essay is scored according to the three areas: Thesis = **1**; Evidence and Commentary = **1, 2, 3, 4**; Sophistication = **1**.

It would be a good idea to become familiar with the rubric specifics for each of the categories.

For those who are concerned about what constitutes a good thesis, let's take a look at a specific thesis as it appears in a rhetorical analysis essay's introduction.

Author Liz Addison wrote an essay in 2007 called "Two Years Are Better Than Four." In this essay she uplifts community colleges as a response to Rick Perlstein's comment that "college as America used to understand it is coming to an end." **Addison undermines Perlstein's idea of the American college experience, provides a background of her own experience with higher education, and illustrates a hypothetical situation to show where her loyalties lie in order to persuade the reader that attending community college is a valid option for education.**

This is a good intro with a good thesis. There is nothing wrong with it. It does what it's supposed to do. It responds to the prompt and provides a claim that is defensible. It also gives a clear idea as to what the line of reasoning (organization of ideas) will be.

So, just what would turn this from good to great? How about placing this idea in a broader context? Within an interesting scenario? In the context of a striking quotation? Or a rhetorical question?

For example:

Which of these two scenarios is more likely? At the five-year high school reunion picnic, Rory wears his community college sweatshirt; OR Roxanne wears her Yale University sweatshirt. Your answer is the reason Liz Addison wrote "Two Years Are Better Than Four" in response to Rick Perlstein's comment that "college as America used to understand it is coming to an end." The thesis. . . .

In this introduction, the writer uses an interesting scenario. It captures the reader's attention and leads easily to the thesis. With this scenario and the thesis, the reader has a clear idea where the writer is going and how.

The body of the essay will support and illustrate that thesis with evidence that is relevant and commentary that offers insight into the implications, consequences, or questions raised by the evidence. It will use transitions as well as clear and mature diction and syntax to lead the reader easily through the claims and evidence being presented in support of the thesis.

The conclusion will not be just a type of summary with a reference to the thesis. It will present a final comment that connects the idea presented in the essay to a broader concept to which the reader can relate.

If the essay were to correspond to the preceding comments, the individual parts of the essay would earn 1-4-1, for a total of 6.

This information will hold true for all three of the free response essays.

A Consideration of Complexity

The rubrics applied to all three essays on the AP English Language exam refer to *complexity* when describing the sophistication point in the rating process:

- *Complex* understanding of the rhetorical situation
- Crafting a nuanced argument by consistently identifying and exploring *complexities* or tensions

A brief review and practice with *complexity* can be helpful.

Complexity = complicated, intricate, multiple layering

In addition to these synonyms, *complexity*, when dealing with literary, visual, musical texts, involves probing/searching beneath the initial layer and first impressions. It involves looking for the unspoken words, passion, motivation, hopes, fear, secrets, and so on. *Complexity* investigates the real WHY of the text.

Think of *complexity* as the opposite of *Cliff Notes*, *Spark Notes*, or *WikiSummaries*.

The process of analyzing the complexity of a text would progress from considering the obvious points of the text:

- Apply S O A P Stone first. The text SAYS.
- Peel back the first layer (SAYS) and consider DOES/HOW (the techniques, etc.).
  — Look for conflicts/tensions
  — Look for patterns
- Determine the results of SAYS/DOES—the WHY.
  — What is implied
  — What can be inferred
  — Any insights
- Discuss how and why the patterns, tensions, conflicts that you found are related to both the text and the prompt.

Assume that the following brief excerpt is located in the opening chapter of an auto-biography of a famous actor:

> *M&Ms has been my favorite candy since I was a kid, because I remember going to the movies with my Dad, and we always shared a box of M&Ms. They never lasted for the whole film, but Dad always let me have the last one or two. He would gently shake the box, and, as if awarding me a prize, slowly place the M&M box in the upturned palm of my hand.*

1. Can you apply SOAPStone and SAYS/DOES to this passage?
2. What can be inferred about the author? About the dad? About the relationship between them?

Note: When you answer the questions in number 2, you are involved with the complexity of the text. If you were to relate your comments to the world outside of this specific anecdote, you would also be involved with complexities.

Timing and Planning the Rhetorical Analysis Essay

Just How Should I Plan to Spend My Time Writing This Type of Essay?

Remember, timing is crucial. With that in mind, here's a workable strategy:

- 1–3 minutes reading and working the prompt.
- 5 minutes reading and making marginal notes regarding the passage.
  — Try to isolate two references that strike you. This may give you your opening and closing.
- 10 minutes preparing to write. (Choose one or two of these methods with which you're comfortable.)
  — Highlighting

— Marginal mapping
— Charts or key word/one word/line number outlining
* 20 minutes writing your essay, based on your preparation.
* 3 minutes proofreading.

Working the Prompt

> For the purposes of this text, highlighting refers to any annotative technique, including underlining, circling, marginal notes, or using colored markers. The AP exam does NOT permit the use of highlighters, but this technique is valuable in other circumstances.

How Should I Go About Reading the Prompt?

To really bring the answer home to you, we are going to deconstruct a prompt for you right now. (This is the same question that is in the Diagnostic/Master exam you first saw in the introduction to this book.)

You should plan to spend 1–3 minutes <u>carefully</u> reading the question. This gives you time to really digest what the question is asking you to do. ANNOTATE, ANNOTATE.

Here's the prompt:

The following paragraphs are from the opening of Truman Capote's *In Cold Blood*. After carefully reading the excerpt, compose a well-written essay that analyzes how Capote uses rhetorical strategies to convey his characterization of Holcomb and its citizens.

* Respond to the prompt with a defensible thesis that relates to the prompt.
* Select and use evidence to develop and support the line of reasoning.
* Explain the relationship between the evidence and the thesis.
* Demonstrate an understanding of the rhetorical situation.
* Use appropriate grammar and punctuation in communicating the argument.

> In the margin, note what time you should be finished with this essay. For example, the test starts at 1:00. You write 1:40 in the margin. Time to move on.

Here are three reasons why you do a 1–3-minute careful analysis of the prompt.

1. Once you know what is expected, you will read in a more directed manner.
2. Once you internalize the question, you will be sensitive to those details that will apply.
3. Once you know all the facets that must be addressed, you will be able to write a complete essay demonstrating adherence to the topic.

> TOPIC ADHERENCE, WHICH MEANS STICKING TO THE QUESTION, IS A KEY STRATEGY FOR ACHIEVING A HIGH SCORE.

DO THIS NOW.
Highlight, circle, or underline the essential terms and elements in the prompt.
(Time yourself) How long did it take you? _____
(Don't worry if it took you longer than 1–3 minutes with this first attempt. You will be practicing this technique throughout this review, and it will become almost second nature to you.)

Compare our highlighting of the prompt with yours.

The following paragraphs are from the **opening** of <u>**Truman Capote's** *In Cold Blood*</u>. After carefully reading the excerpt, compose a well-written essay that <u>analyzes how Capote uses rhetorical strategies to convey</u> his <u>characterization of Holcomb and its citizens.</u>

In this prompt, anything else you may have highlighted is extraneous.

Note: You are free to choose your own selection of techniques, strategies, and devices. Not only must you identify appropriate rhetorical strategies, etc., you must also indicate the effect of each strategy you choose to discuss. If you only identify strategies without discussing their effects, your essay will be incomplete.

Review terms related to elements of style and techniques and methods of analysis.

> Sometimes the incidental data given in the prompt, such as the title of the work, the author, the date of publication, the genre, etc., can prove helpful.

Reading and Notating the Passage

Finally, READ THE PASSAGE. Depending on your style and comfort level, choose one of these approaches to your **close reading**.

1. A. Read quickly to get the gist of the passage.
   B. Reread, using the highlighting and marginal notes approach discussed in this chapter.
2. A. Read slowly, using highlighting and marginal notes.
   B. Reread to confirm that you have caught the full impact of the passage.

Note: In both approaches, you MUST highlight and make marginal notes. There is no way to avoid this. Ignore what you don't immediately understand. It may become clear to you after reading the passage. Practice. Practice. Concentrate on those parts of the passage that apply to what you highlighted in the prompt.

There are many ways to read and analyze any given passage. You have to choose what to use and which specifics to include for support.

Don't be rattled if there is leftover material.

We've reproduced the passage for you below so that you can practice both the reading and the process of deconstructing the text. Use highlighting, arrows, circles, underlining, notes, numbers, whatever you need to make the connections clear to you.

DO THIS NOW.
Spend between 8 and 10 minutes "working the material."

DO NOT SKIP THIS STEP. It is time well spent and is a key to the high score essay.

Excerpt from the opening of *In Cold Blood*

The village of Holcomb stands on the high wheat plains of western Kansas, a lonesome area that other Kansans call "out there." Some seventy miles east of the Colorado border, the countryside, with its hard blue skies and desert-clear air, has an atmosphere that is rather more Far Western than Middle West. The local accent is barbed with a prairie twang, a ranch-hand nasalness, and the men, many of them, wear narrow frontier trousers, Stetsons, and high-heeled boots with pointed toes. The land is flat, and the views are awesomely extensive; horses, herds of cattle, a white cluster of grain elevators rising as gracefully as Greek temples are visible long before a traveler reaches them.

Holcomb, too, can be seen from great distances. Not that there is much to see—simply an aimless congregation of buildings divided in the center by the main-line tracks of the Santa Fe Railroad, a haphazard hamlet bounded on the south by a brown stretch of the Arkansas (pronounced "Ar-kan-sas") River, on the north by a highway, Route 50, and on the east and west by prairie lands and wheat fields. After rain, or when snowfalls thaw, the streets, unnamed, unshaded, unpaved, turn from the thickest dust into the direst mud. At one end of the town stands a stark old stucco structure, the roof of which supports an electric sign—Dance—but the dancing has ceased and the advertisement has been dark for several years. Nearby is another building with an irrelevant sign, this one in flaking gold on a dirty window—HOLCOMB BANK. The bank closed in 1933, and it is one of the town's two "apartment houses," the second being a ramshackle mansion known, because a good part of the local school's faculty lives there, as the Teacherage. But the majority of Holcomb's homes are one-story frame affairs, with front porches.

Down by the depot, the postmistress, a gaunt woman who wears a rawhide jacket and denims and cowboy boots, presides over a falling-apart post office. The depot, itself, with its peeling sulphur-colored paint, is equally melancholy; the Chief, the Super Chief, the El Capitan go by every day, but these celebrated expresses never pause there. No passenger trains do—only an occasional freight. Up on the highway, there are two filling stations, one of which doubles as a meagerly supplied grocery store, while the other does extra duty as a cafe—Hartman's Cafe, where Mrs. Hartman, the proprietress, dispenses sandwiches, coffee, soft drinks, and 3.2 beer. (Holcomb, like all the rest of Kansas, is "dry.")

And that, really, is all. Unless you include, as one must, the Holcomb School, a good-looking establishment, which reveals a circumstance that the appearance of the community otherwise camouflages: that the parents who send their children to this modern and ably staffed "consolidated" school—the grades go from kindergarten through senior high, and a fleet of buses transport the students, of which there are usually around three hundred and sixty, from as far as sixteen miles away—are, in general, a prosperous people. . . . The farm ranchers in Finney County, of which Holcomb is a part, have done well; money has been made not from farming alone but also from the exploitation of plentiful natural-gas resources, and its acquisition is reflected in the new school, the comfortable interiors of the farmhouses, the steep and swollen grain elevators.

Until one morning in mid-November of 1959, few Americans—in fact, few Kansans—had ever heard of Holcomb. Like the waters of the river, like the motorists on the highway, and like the yellow trains streaking down the Santa Fe tracks, drama in the shape of exceptional happenings, had never stopped there. The inhabitants of the village, numbering two hundred and seventy, were satisfied that this should be so, quite content to exist inside ordinary life . . .

Now, compare your reading notes with what we've done. Yours may vary from ours, but the results of your note taking should be similar in scope.

Notice that, in the sample, we have used a kind of shorthand for our notations. Rather than repeating the specific elements or points each time they are found in the text, we have numbered the major points.

    1 = Something old West and insignificant about Holcomb
    2 = The starkness of the town
    3 = People reflecting the setting
    4 = Contrast between first three paragraphs and the last two

This saves precious time. All you need do is list the categories and number each. Then, as you go through the text, number specifics that support these categories.

Excerpt from the opening of *In Cold Blood*

The village of Holcomb stands on the high wheat plains of western Kansas, a lonesome area that other Kansans call "out there." Some seventy miles east of the Colorado border, the countryside, with its hard blue skies and desert-clear air, has an atmosphere that is rather more Far Western than Middle West. The local accent is barbed with a prairie twang, a ranch-hand nasalness, and the men, many of them, wear narrow frontier trousers, Stetsons, and high-heeled boots with pointed toes. The land is flat, and the views are awesomely extensive; horses, herds of cattle, a white cluster of grain elevators rising as gracefully as Greek temples are visible long before a traveler reaches them.

Holcomb, too, can be seen from great distances. Not that there is much to see—simply an aimless congregation of buildings divided in the center by the main-line tracks of the Santa Fe Railroad, a haphazard hamlet bounded on the south by a brown stretch of the Arkansas (pronounced "Ar-kan-sas") River, on the north by a highway, Route 50, and on the east and west by prairie lands and wheat fields. After rain, or when snowfalls thaw, the streets, unnamed, unshaded, unpaved, turn from the thickest dust into the direst mud. At one end of the town stands a stark old stucco structure, the roof of which supports an electric sign— Dance—but the dancing has ceased and the advertisement has been dark for several years. Nearby is another building with an irrelevant sign, this one in flaking gold on a dirty window—HOLCOMB BANK. The bank closed in 1933, and it is one of the town's two "apartment houses," the second being a ramshackle mansion known, because a good part of the local school's faculty lives there, as the Teacherage. But the majority of Holcomb's homes are one-story frame affairs, with front porches.

Down by the depot, the postmistress, a gaunt woman who wears a rawhide jacket and denims and cowboy boots, presides over a falling-apart post office. The depot, itself, with its peeling sulphur-colored paint, is equally melancholy; the Chief, the Super Chief, the El Capitan go by every day, but these celebrated expresses never pause there. No passenger trains do—only an occasional freight. Up on the highway, there are two filling stations, one of which doubles as a meagerly supplied grocery store, while the other does extra duty as a cafe—Hartman's Cafe, where Mrs. Hartman, the proprietress, dispenses sandwiches, coffee, soft drinks, and 3.2 beer. (Holcomb, like all the rest of Kansas, is "dry.")

And that, really, is all. Unless you include, as one must, the Holcomb School, a good-looking establishment, which reveals a circumstance that the appearance of the community otherwise camouflages; that the parents who send their children to this modern and ably staffed "consolidated" school—the grades go from kindergarten through senior high, and a fleet of buses transport the students, of which there are usually around three hundred and sixty, from as far as sixteen miles away—are, in general, a prosperous people. . . . The farm ranchers in Finney County, of which Holcomb is a part, have done well; money has been made not from farming alone but also from the exploitation of plentiful natural-gas resources, and its acquisition is reflected in the new school, the comfortable interiors of the farmhouses, the steep and swollen grain elevators.

Until one morning in mid-November of 1959, few Americans—in fact, few Kansans—had ever heard of Holcomb. Like the waters of the river, like the motorists on the highway, and like the yellow trains streaking down the Sante Fe tracks, drama in the shape of exceptional happenings, had never stopped there. The inhabitants of the village, numbering two hundred and seventy, were satisfied that this should be so, quite content to exist inside ordinary life . . .

Developing the Opening Paragraph

After you have marked your passage, review the prompt. Now, choose the elements you are able to identify and analyze those that support Capote's view. To demonstrate, we have chosen structure, tone, and selection of detail.

Now, it's time to write. Your opening statement is the one that catches the eye of the reader and sets the expectation and tone of your essay. Spend time on your first paragraph to maximize your score. A suggested approach is to relate a direct reference from the passage to the topic. Make certain that the topic is very clear to the reader. This reinforces the idea that you fully understand what is expected of you and what you will communicate to the reader. As always, identify both the text and its author in this first paragraph.

Now, you try it. Write your own first paragraph for this prompt. Write quickly, referring to your notes. Let's check what you've written:

- Have you included author, title?
- Have you addressed "Capote's view of Holcomb"?
- Have you specifically mentioned the elements you will refer to in your essay?

Here are four sample opening paragraphs that address each of the above criteria:

A

In the opening of *In Cold Blood*, Truman Capote presents a picture of the town of Holcomb, Kansas. Through structure, selection of detail, and a detached tone, he makes it clear that he views Holcomb as dull and ordinary.

B

Holcomb, Kansas. Holcomb, Kansas. Even the sound of the place is boring and unin-teresting. Moreover, Truman Capote seems to agree with this in his opening to *In Cold Blood*. I, too, would be inclined to pass by this sleepy, bland, and undistinguished hamlet. This view is developed through the author's tone, structure, and selection of detail.

C

"Like the waters of the river, like the motorists on the highway, and like the yellow trains streaking down the Sante Fe tracks, drama in the shape of exceptional happenings, had never stopped here." This is the town of Holcomb, Kansas. Using a reportorial tone, specific structure, and selection of detail, Capote introduces the reader to this unremark-able town in the opening of *In Cold Blood*.

D

In Cold Blood is a very appropriate title, because Capote presents a cold and unemo-tional view of Holcomb, Kansas. His tone, structure, and selection of detail create a dis-tant and detached picture of this desolate farm community.

Each of these opening paragraphs is an acceptable beginning to this AP English Lan-guage and Composition exam essay. Look at what each of the paragraphs has in common:

- Each has identified the title and author.
- Each has stated which stylistic elements will be used.
- Each has stated the purpose of analyzing these elements.

However, observe what is different about the opening paragraphs.

- **Sample A** restates the question without elaborating. It is to the point and correct, but it does not really pique the reader's interest. (Use this type of opening if you feel unsure or uncomfortable with the prompt.)
- **Sample B** reflects a writer who really has a voice. He or she has already determined Capote's view and indicates that he or she understands how this view is created.
- **Sample C** immediately places the reader into the passage by referring specifically to it.
- **Sample D** reveals a mature, confident writer who is unafraid to make his or her own voice heard.

Note: There are many other types of opening paragraphs that could also do the job. Into which of the above samples could your opening paragraph be classified?

Writing the Body of the Essay

What Should I Include in the Body of This Analysis Essay?

1. Obviously, this is where you present *your* analysis and the points you wish to make which are related to the prompt.

2. Adhere to the prompt.

3. Use specific references and details from the passage.
- Don't always paraphrase the original. Refer directly to it.
- Place quotation marks around those words/phrases which you extract from the passage.

4. Use "connective tissue" in your essay to establish adherence to the question.
- Use the repetition of key ideas in the prompt and in your opening paragraph.

- Try using "echo words" (that is, synonyms: *town/village/hamlet; bland/ordinary/ undistinguished*).
- Use transitions between paragraphs (see Chapter 8).

5. Apply SAY/DOES/HOW when writing a rhetorical analysis essay for AP English Language.
- Develop evidence.
- Observe (SAYS) the author's use of rhetorical choices.
- Analyze (DOES/HOW) the intended effect of the choices and the way(s) in which this effect is achieved.

To understand the process, carefully read the sample paragraphs below. Each develops one of the elements asked for in the prompt. Notice the specific references, application of says/does/how (a couple examples are highlighted for you in paragraphs **B** and **C**), and the "connective tissue." Also notice that details which do not apply to the prompt are ignored.

A

This paragraph develops **tone.**

Throughout the passage, Capote maintains a tone which resembles a detached reporter who is an observer of a scene. Even though the impact of the passage is seeing Holcomb in a not-to-positive light, the author rarely uses judgmental terminology or statements. In describing the town, he uses words such as "float," "haphazard," "unnamed," "unshaded," "unpaved." Individuals are painted with an objective brush showing them in "denim," "stetsons," and "cowboy boots." Capote maintains his panning camera angle when he writes of the buildings and the surrounding farm land. This matter-of-fact approach is slightly altered when he begins to portray the townspeople as a whole when he uses words like "prosperous people," comfortable interiors," and "have done well." His objective tone, interestingly enough, does exactly what he says the folks of Holcomb do. He "camouflages" his attitude toward the reality of the place and time.

B

This paragraph develops **structure.**

Capote organizes his passage spatially. He brings his reader from "great distances" to the periphery of the village with its borders of "main line tracks" and roads and river and fields, to the heart of the town and its "unnamed, unshaded and unpaved streets." As the reader journeys through the stark village, he is led eventually from the outskirts to the town's seemingly one bright spot—the prosperous Holcomb school. Capote develops our interest in the school by contrasting it with the bleak and lonely aspects of the first three paragraphs. He shifts our view with the word "unless" and focuses on the positive aspects of the town. Holcomb "has done well" in spite of its forbidding description. The passage could end now, except that Capote chooses to develop his next paragraph with the words—"until one morning"—thus taking the reader on another journey, one of foreshadowing and implication. Something besides wheat is on the horizon.

C

This paragraph develops selection of **detail.**

In selecting his details, Capote presents a multilayered Holcomb, Kansas. The town is first presented as stark and ordinary. It is a "lonesome area" with "hard blue skies," "flat land" and "aimless buildings." The ordinary qualities of the village are reinforced by his references to the "unnamed" streets, "one-story framed houses" and the fact that "celebrated extremes never pass there." Details portray the citizens of Holcomb in the same light. Ranch hands speak with "barbed" and nasal twangs. They wear the stereotypical "cowboy" uniform and so does the "gaunt" postmistress in her "rawhide jacket." Once this description is established, the author contrasts it with an unexpected view of the town. He now deals with the appearance of Holcomb's "camouflages," the "modern" school, the "prosperous people," the "comfortable interiors" and the "swollen grain elevators." If Capote chooses to illuminate this contrast, does it indicate more to come?

> Study Group: Approach a subject in a joint manner. After you've deconstructed the prompt, have each person write a paragraph on a separate area of the question. Come together and discuss. You'll be amazed how much fun this is, because the work will carry you away. This is a chance to explore very exciting ideas.

We urge you to spend more time developing the body paragraphs rather than worrying about a concluding paragraph, especially one beginning with *"In conclusion,"* or *"In summary."* To be honest, in such a brief essay, the reader can remember what you have already stated. It is not necessary to repeat yourself in a summary final paragraph.

If you want to make a final statement, try to link your ideas to a particularly effective line or image from the passage. (It's a good thing.)

> Look at the last line of Sample **B** on structure.
>
> ***Something other than wheat is on the horizon.***
>
> Or, look at the last line of Sample **C** on selection of detail.
>
> ***If Capote chooses to illuminate this contrast, does it indicate more to come?***
>
> Each of these two final sentences would be just fine as a conclusion to the essay. A conclusion does not have to be a paragraph. It can be the writer's final remark/observation in a sentence or two.

DO THIS NOW.
    Write the body of your essay. Time yourself.
    When you write the body of your essay, take only 15–20 minutes.
    Find a way to time yourself, and try your best to finish within that time frame.
    Because this is practice, don't panic if you can't complete your essay within the given 20 minutes. You will become more and more comfortable with the tasks presented to you as you gain more experience with this type of question.
    Refer to the Comprehensive Review section in Step 4 of this book on developing the body of an AP Language and Composition essay.
    Note: Sharing your writing with members of your class or study group will allow you and all of the participants to gain more experience and more of a comfort zone with requirements and possibilities.

Sample Student Essays

Here are two actual student essays with comments on each.

Student Sample A

Truly successful authors have the ability to convey their view of a place without actually saying it, to portray a landscape in a certain light simply by describing it. In the provided excerpt taken from the opening paragraphs of <u>In Cold Blood</u>, Truman

1

Capote does just this. Through his use of stylistic elements such as selection of detail, imagery, and figurative language, Capote reveals his own solemn and mysterious view of Holcomb, Kansas, while setting the stage for an imminent change.

Beginning in the first line of the passage, Capote selects the most boring details of life in the small town in order to portray its solemnity. He draws attention to the physical isolation of Holcomb by referring to it as the place that "other Kansans call 'out there.'" In addition, he speaks of the parameters of the small town, pointing out that it is enclosed on all sides by rivers, prairies, and wheat fields. He describes the town as remote and unaffected, desolate and boring, continually mentioning the old, peeling paint and "irrelevant signs" that dot the landscape. Capote also gives the village a feeling of laziness in his writing, describing it as an "aimless congregation of buildings" and a "haphazard hamlet." He obviously feels that the town lacks liveliness, that it is bland and unchanging, simple and average. Almost looking down on the village and its inhabitants, the author characterizes the people in broad categories and focuses on their outward appearances and superficial similarities instead of delving more deeply into their abilities or livelihoods. This reveals that he views the people and their surroundings as one-dimensional and simplistic. The idea that he may summarize an entire town, generalize about its people and not be far from the truth, contributes greatly to Capote's solemn view of Holcomb. One gets the feelings from the author's selection of detail that he wishes there was something more interesting, deeper, to share with his audience, and is disappointed by the cursory nature in which he must approach the description of such a melancholy place.

In addition to including the most boring of details, Capote uses a great deal of imagery to describe the town and its residents. Focusing mostly on visual appeal, he describes the "sulphur-colored paint" and "flaking gold" to reveal the town's atrophying appearance and has-been status. Portraying the area as one that has seen better days, Capote writes about the "old stucco structure" that no longer holds dances, the crumbling post office, and the bank that now fails to serve its original purpose. Combining visual imagery with hints of desolation and obsoleteness, Capote attempts to reveal the gray and boring nature of the town through its appearance. He does not, however, rely only on visual details; in describing the local accent as "barbed with a prairie twang," he uses both auditory and visual appeal to make one imagine a ranch-hand's tone of voice and pattern of speech as he describes the monotonous events of his farming days. The "hard blue skies and desert-clear air" contribute to a feeling of emptiness, an emotional vacancy that seems omnipresent in the small town. Finally, even "the steep and swollen grain elevators" that represent the town's prosperity are seen in a solemn and mysterious light, as Capote makes certain to mention that the townspeople camouflage this abundance without explaining why they choose to do so.

Capote also uses a great deal of figurative language and contrasts to portray the small town as solemn and dead, yet somewhat mysterious. The area's intrigue lies more in its paradoxes than in its appearance, more in what Capote fails to explain than what he discusses. With the simile, "a white cluster of grain elevators rising as gracefully as

Greek temples," he almost points toward a happy, prosperous side of the town for the first and perhaps only time in this passage. Not long after this sentence, however, the author describes the streets as "unnamed, unshaded, unpaved," returning to his description of the village as desolate and empty, so destroyed that it is almost primitive.

This is not the only contrast of Capote's opening paragraphs; it seems the entire passage paints the town as quiet and simple only so that it may shock us with what is to come. The author uses personification at the end of the passage, stating that "drama . . . had never stopped there." The position of these words, just after he discusses the positive aspects of the school and its students' families, results in yet another contrast, another mysterious solemnity. Finally, in the last paragraph of this excerpt, when Capote writes "until one morning . . . few . . . had ever heard of Holcomb," the reader becomes aware that the solemn nature of this town is about to change. It becomes clear that the reader has been somewhat set up by Capote, made to view the town in the same way the author does, so that we may then realize the shock of the approaching aberration.

5

Through his use of stylistic elements, Capote builds the perfect scenery for the setting of a murder, the perfect simple town waiting for a complicated twist, a faded flower or ghost town that has surely seen better days. By the end of the passage, he has already warned the reader that everything he has stated about Holcomb is about to change, that the quiet and solitude, the blandness of the small town, may soon be replaced by very different descriptions.

6

Student Sample B

Holcomb, Kansas, a village containing two hundred and seventy inhabitants, has skipped over the drama of life, according to Truman Capote. The square town is described spatially with houses, rivers, fields of wheat, stations, a bank, and a school. In Truman Capote's In Cold Blood, an image of the town of Holcomb is presented through precise types of diction, syntax, imagery, and tone.

1

In order to convey a Western dialect used in Holcomb, Capote refers to the town as, "out there," and addresses the pronunciation of the Arkansas River with an informative, "Ar-kan-sas." Throughout the town there are quite a few signs which transmit the ghostliness present there. For example, "—Dance—but the dancing has ceased and the advertisement has been dark for several years," and "HOLCOMB BANK," which is later on discussed as being closed down, demonstrate the vacantness of the town. To create a better concept of the land itself, Capote uses alliterative devices and an allusion when he states, "horses, herds of cattle, a white cluster of grain elevators rising as gracefully as Greek temples are visible long before a traveler reaches them." This magnifies the field-like setting, and some of the town's old remnants of massive buildings. Altogether, the author's utilization of diction devices greatly personifies the town.

2

Although not a glaring feature of the excerpt, the sentence structure plays an important role in developing the author's viewpoint. He predominantly utilizes compound sentences, and complex with some prepositional phrases. The use of parallel

3

structures such as, "Like the waters of the river, like the motorists on the highway, and like the yellow trains streaking down the Sante Fe tracks . . ." greatly adds to the monotony of the town. "(Holcomb, like all the rest of Kansas, is 'dry')." is one of the numerous similes found throughout the passage that create a sense of vacancy within the town.

Capote's use of all of these literary devices envelope the reader into picturing what   4
Holcomb looks like, a worn out, rustic town filled with "grain elevators," or fields and fields of wheat. The reference to the grain and wheat exemplifies the daily activities that occur in the town. After all of the rural descriptions, a vision of the school is given, as it "camouflages" into the mix. Reading about all of the emptiness of the town, then envisioning a school that is the pride of the town provides insight into the type of people the inhabitants of Holcomb are. For example, they are described as, "in general, a prosperous people." Overall, a precise and objective image of the town, along with the townspeople is certainly focused on in the passage.

Encompassing all of the author's literary, stylistic approaches, one is able to "hear" a   5
voice or tone in the reading. A feeling of desolation, weariness, and loneliness should be derived from reading about this town, and a sense of rejuvenation is experienced toward the closing of the excerpt due to descriptions of the school. In exemplifying that the town has pride in one area, which is education, it leaves the reader with a sense of hope in the town and in its inhabitants. A strong voice toward Holcomb of its rugged, run down, and exhausted institutions is present.

Truman Capote's excerpt from <u>In Cold Blood</u>, which objectively describes   6
Holcomb, a town in Kansas, is profoundly written because of its abundance of allusions, alliteration, imagery, and particular syntax utilized. Capote's detailing enables one to envision what the town looks like because of spatial and in-depth descriptions.

Rating the Essays

Let's Take a Look at a Set of Rubrics for This Analysis Essay

Let's take a look at a set of rubrics for this rhetorical analysis essay. (If you want to see actual AP rubrics as used in a recent AP Language exam, log on to the College Board website: <www.collegeboard.org/ap>. As you probably know, essays are rated on a 6–1 scale, with 6 the highest and 1 the lowest. Since we are not there with you to personally rate your essay and to respond to your style and approach, we are going to list the criteria for high-, middle-, and low-range papers. These criteria are based on our experience with rubrics and reading AP Language essays.

A **HIGH** range essay can be a 6 or a 5. **MIDDLE** refers to essays in the 4 to 3 range. And the **LOW** scoring essays are rated 2 to 1.

Note: For our purposes, scoring comments will be followed by one of three letters to indicate one of the three areas used in the AP English Language rubric for the rhetorical analysis essay. Thesis = (A), Evidence/Commentary = (B), Sophistication = (C)

High-Range Essay (6, 5)

- Indicates complete understanding of the prompt via a defensible thesis (A)
- Integrates the analysis of Capote's view of Holcomb with his tone (B)
- Explores the implications of the contrasts within the excerpt (B)
- Identifies and analyzes rhetorical elements, such as imagery, diction, structure, selection of detail (B)
- Cites specific references to the passage (B)
- Illustrates and supports the points being made (B)
- Is clear, well-organized, and coherent (B and C)
- Offers a variety of insights or viewpoints about the complexity within the text (C)
- Reflects the ability to manipulate language at an advanced level (C)
- Contains, if any, only minor errors/flaws (C)

Mid-Range Essay (4, 3)

- Refers accurately to the prompt via a defensible thesis (A)
- Refers accurately to the stylistic elements used by Capote (B)
- Provides a less thorough analysis of the development of Capote's view of Holcomb than the higher-rated paper (B)
- Is less adept at linking techniques to the purpose of the passage (C)
- Demonstrates writing that is adequate to convey the writer's intent (C)
- May not be sensitive to the contrasts in the excerpts and their implications (C)

Low-Range Essay (2, 1)

- Does not respond adequately with a defensible thesis (A)
- Demonstrates insufficient and/or inaccurate understanding of the passage (B)
- Does not link rhetorical elements to Capote's view of Holcomb (B)
- Underdevelops and/or inaccurately analyzes the development of Capote's view of Holcomb (B)
- Fails to demonstrate an understanding of Capote's tone (B)
- Demonstrates weak control of the elements of diction, syntax, and organization (C)

Student Essay A

This is a **high-range** paper for the following reasons:

- It indicates complete understanding of the prompt and the passage via a strong, defensible thesis. (A)
- It uses mature diction [paragraph 1: "Capote reveals . . . imminent change"], [paragraph 2: "Capote also gives . . . simplistic"], [paragraph 3: "the hard blue skies . . . to do so"].
- It integrates references to support the thesis of the essay [paragraph 2: "Capote also gives . . . hamlet"], [paragraph 3: "Focusing . . . has-been status"], [paragraph 4: "with the simile . . . passage"]. (B)

- It grasps subtleties and implications [paragraph 1: "Capote reveals . . . change"], [paragraph 2: "One gets . . . place"], [paragraph 4: "The area's . . . discusses"], [paragraph 6: "By the end . . . descriptions"].   (B and C)
- It introduces specifics in a sophisticated manner [paragraph 3: "He does not . . . farming days"], [paragraph 5: "The author . . . solemnity"].   (B and C)
- It uses good "connective tissue" [paragraphs 2 and 3: "in addition"], [paragraph 4: "Capote also uses . . ."], [paragraph 5: "This is not the only contrast . . ."].
- It creates original and insightful comments [paragraph 2: "one gets . . . melancholy place"], [paragraph 3: "He does not . . . farming days"].   (B and C)
- It presents a conclusion that introduces unique observations and brings the reader directly to what may follow this passage.   (B and C)

This is a high-range essay that indicates a writer who "gets it"—who clearly understands the passage and the prompt and who can present ideas in a mature, controlled voice.

Student Essay B

This is a **mid-range** essay for the following reasons:

- It sets up an introduction that indicates the writer's understanding of the prompt with a defensible thesis.   (A)
- It cites appropriate specifics, but often does not adequately integrate these into the analysis [paragraph 2: "In order . . . present there"], [paragraph 3, sentence 2].   (B)
- It uses frequently awkward diction and syntax [first line of paragraph 2], [last sentence of paragraph 2], [all of paragraph 5].   (C)
- It demonstrates good topic adherence. (B and C)
- It reveals a facility with stylistic analysis [paragraph 2: "To create . . . reaches them"], [paragraph 3, sentence 3].   (B)
- It presents a conclusion that does not add anything to the impact of the essay. (B and C)

This mid-range paper indicates a writer who understands both the prompt and the process of analysis. However, the essay does not address the subtle, underlying purpose of the passage and ignores the foreshadowing and contrast. The writer's frequently awkward and disconnected diction and syntax prevent it from achieving the level of the high-range essays.

Now It's Your Turn

1. Try a little reverse psychology. Now that you are thoroughly familiar with this passage, construct two or three alternate AP level prompts. (Walk a little in the examiner's shoes.) This will help you gain insight into the very process of test-making.

2. Find other examples of descriptions of setting you can analyze in the same way as you did with the Capote excerpt. You might want to investigate works by John Steinbeck, Joan Didion, Peter Matthiessen, and, certainly, Sebastian Jung's *The Perfect Storm*.

Other Types of Rhetorical Analysis Essays

Are There Other Types of Rhetorical Analysis Questions on the Exam?

You bet. Another analysis prompt you can expect on the exam asks the student to <u>analyze the author's intended effect on the reader and how the author re-creates an experience. Still another type is comparison and contrast</u>. This prompt can be based on either a fiction or a nonfiction passage.

What Am I Expected to Do When Asked to Identify the Author's Intended Effect on the Reader?

No one can ever know what an author intended, unless you could personally approach the writer and ask, "Tell me, just exactly what did you intend the effect to be on your reader when you wrote this passage?" And, we all know that this is not a possibility for 999 out of 1,000 authors. This said, keep the following in mind.

The AP Comp test makers obviously believe that there is a clear, definite effect on the reader; otherwise, they would not be asking you to identify it. When writing about effect, think about your **personal** reaction to the text. While reading it, or as a result of reading it, how do you *feel* (happy, sad, angry, amused, perplexed, uplifted, motivated, informed, inspired, "connected"—you get the idea)?

What Should I Try to Include in My Essay When I'm Asked to Analyze How an Author Re-creates an Experience?

Think about this. Have you ever tried to re-create your own personal experience for your friends, your family, or your teacher? Ask yourself what you did to ensure that your listeners would really feel as if they were actually there. Were you trying to be humorous or serious? You chose what you would say to introduce this experience, didn't you? Did you set up the scene with descriptions of the setting, the people? Did you tell them why you were there? What kind of details did you choose to include? Why those, and not others? What kind of language did you use? (You were quite aware that your audience responds to certain kinds of language manipulation.) Did you center the tale on yourself, the action, a person, or group of people? Did you emphasize actions, reactions, dialogue? Did you tell the story in chronological order, or did you move back and forth in time? Did you interject personal comments? Did you tell the story so that the listeners felt a part of the experience or set apart from it? Did you emote or try to remain aloof?

Get the picture? This is the type of questioning that should be part of your process of analysis when asked how an author re-creates an experience.

What Do I Do About the Comparison and Contrast Essay?

The comparison and contrast essay is not difficult, but it demands that you have organizational control over your material. First, carefully read the prompt and understand what you are being asked to compare and contrast. With this in mind, carefully read and annotate each of the given texts, looking for major points to support and illustrate your thesis. Next, decide on the structure you want to use to present your points:

- Point by point
- Subject by subject
- A combination of both of the preceding

Note: The comparison/contrast essay is rarely being used on the exam. But, it is the type of prompt and analysis you should be comfortable and familiar with.

"Working the Prompt"

KEY IDEA

As you did with the previous essay, the very first thing you must do is to read and deconstruct the prompt carefully. What follows is a sample prompt that you could find in the essay section of the exam.

- Plan to spend 1–3 minutes carefully reading the question.
- After this initial reading, highlight the essential terms and elements of the prompt.

Carefully read the following excerpt from Louisa May Alcott's nonfiction narrative *Hospital Sketches* (1863). In a well-written essay, analyze how Alcott develops her argument concerning human compassion in a time of war.

- Respond to the prompt with a defensible thesis that relates to the prompt.
- Select and use evidence to develop and support the line of reasoning.
- Explain the relationship between the evidence and the thesis.
- Demonstrate an understanding of the rhetorical situation.
- Use appropriate grammar and punctuation in communicating the argument.

Time yourself. How long did it take you? _____
Compare your highlighting of the prompt with ours.

Carefully read the following excerpt from <u>**Louisa May Alcott's nonfiction narrative**</u> <u>*Hospital Sketches* (1863)</u>. In a well-written essay, <u>**analyze how Alcott develops her**</u> <u>**argument concerning human compassion in a time of war.**</u>

Notice that the prompt asks you to do TWO things. You must identify Alcott's argument AND analyze how the author constructs her argument. <u>If you address only one of these areas, your essay will be incomplete, no matter how well written it is.</u>

Review terms and strategies related to purpose, effect, organization.

Follow the process for reading the passage we illustrated for you in the first section of this chapter. Remember, you are going to do a close reading that requires you to highlight and make marginal notes (glosses) that refer you to the section of the prompt that this citation illustrates.

DO THIS NOW.
Spend between 8 and 10 minutes "working the material."
Do not skip this step. It is key to scoring well on the essay.

"Death of a Soldier"

As I went on my hospital rounds with Dr. P., I happened to ask which man in the room suffered most. He glanced at John. "Every breath he draws is like a stab; for the ball pierced the left lung and broke a rib. The poor lad must lie on his wounded back or suffocate." 1

"You don't mean he must die, doctor?" 2

"There's not the slightest hope for him." 3

I could have sat down on the spot and cried heartily, if I had not learned the wisdom of bottling up one's tears for leisure moments. The army needed men like John, earnest, brave, and faithful; fighting for liberty and justice with both heart and hand. 4

John sat with bent head, hands folded on his knee, and no outward sign of suffering, till, looking nearer, I saw great tears roll down and drop upon the floor. It was a new sight there; for, though I had seen many suffer, some swore, some groaned, most endured silently, but none wept. Yet it did not seem weak, only very touching, and straightway my fear vanished, my heart opened wide and took him in. Gathering the bent head in my arms, as freely as if he had been a little child, I said, "Let me help you bear it, John." 5

Never, on any human countenance, have I seen so swift and beautiful a look of gratitude, surprise and comfort. He whispered, "Thank you, m'am, this is right good! I didn't like to be a trouble; you seemed so busy . . ." 6

I bathed his face, brushed his bonny brown hair, set all things smooth about him. While doing this, he watched me with the satisfied expression I so liked to see. He spoke so hopefully when there was no hope. "This is my first battle; do they think it's going to be my last?" 7

It was the hardest question I had ever been called upon to answer; doubly hard with those clear eyes fixed upon mine. "I'm afraid they do, John." 8

He seemed a little startled at first, pondered over the fateful fact a moment, then shook his head. "I'm afraid, but it's difficult to believe all at once. I'm so strong it don't seem possible for such a little wound to kill me." And then he said, "I'm a little sorry I wasn't wounded in front; it looks cowardly to be hit in the back, but I obeyed orders." 9

John was dying. Even while he spoke, over his face I saw a gray veil falling that no human hand can lift. I sat down by him, wiped drops from his forehead, stirred the air about him with a slow wave of a fan, and waited to help him die. For hours he suffered dumbly, without a moment's murmuring: his limbs grew cold, his face damp, his lips white, and again and again he tore the covering off his breast, as if the lightest weight added to his agony. 10

One by one, the other men woke, and round the room appeared a circle of pale faces and watchful eyes, full of awe and pity; for, though a stranger, John was beloved by all. "Old boy, how are you?" faltered one. "Can I say or do anything for you anywheres?" whispered another. 11

"Take my things home, and tell them that I did my best." 12

He died then; though the heavy breaths still tore their way up for a little longer, they were but the waves of an ebbing tide that beat unfelt against the wreck. He never spoke again, but to the end held my hand close, so close that when he was asleep at last, I could not draw it away. Dan, another patient, helped me, warning me as he did so that it was unsafe for dead and living flesh to lie so long together. But though my hand was strangely cold and stiff, and four white marks remained across its back, even when warmth and color had returned elsewhere, I could not but be glad that, through its touch, the presence of human sympathy, perhaps, had lightened that hard hour. 13

When they had made him ready for the grave, I stood looking at him. The lovely expression which so often beautifies dead faces soon replaced marks of pain. The ward master handed me a letter, saying it had come the night before but was forgot. It was John's letter, come just an hour too late to gladden the eyes that had longed for it so eagerly.   14

After I had cut some brown locks for his mother, and taken off the ring to send her, I kissed this good son for her sake, and laid the letter in his hand. Then I left him, glad to have known so genuine a man, and carrying with me an enduring memory of a brave Virginia blacksmith, as he lay serenely waiting for the dawn of that long day which knows no night.   15

Now, compare your reading notes with ours. As we said earlier, your notes may vary from ours, but the results should be similar in scope.

"**Death** of a **Soldier**"

focus/subject?

simile
details

As I went on my **hospital** rounds with Dr. P., I happened to ask which man in the room **suffered most**. He glanced at John. "Every **breath** he draws **is like a stab**; for the ball **pierced** the left lung and **broke** a rib. The poor lad **must** lie on his **wounded back** or **suffocate**."   1

dialogue
Pity/inevitable death

"You don't mean he must die, doctor?"   2
"There's not the slightest hope for him."   3

too busy to cry

I **could have** sat down on the spot and **cried** heartily, if I had not learned the wisdom of **bottling up one's tears for leisure moments**.   4

(emotional appeal to Americans who can empathize with John)

The army needed men **like John, earnest, brave, and faithful; fighting for liberty and justice with both heart and hand**.

prayer?
He has time to cry; she not
//

John sat with **bent head**, **hands folded** on his knee, and no outward sign of suffering, till, looking nearer, **I saw great tears** roll down and drop upon the floor. It was a new sight there; for, though I had seen **many suffer, some swore, some groaned, most endured silently, but none wept**. Yet it did not seem weak, only **very touching**, and straightway my fear vanished, my heart opened wide and took him in.   5

simile
Dialogue—begin to identify with nurse

Gathering the **bent head** in my arms, as freely **as if he had been a little child**, I said, "**Let me help you bear it, John**."

Never, on any human countenance, have I seen so swift and beautiful a look of gratitude, surprise and comfort. He whispered,   6

dialogue = real John
//

"Thank you, m'am, this is right good! I didn't like to be a trouble; you seemed so busy . . ."

I bathed his face, brushed his bonny brown hair, set all things smooth about him. While doing this, he watched me with the satisfied expression I so liked to see. He spoke so hopefully when there was no hope. "This is my first battle; do they think it's going to be my last?"   7

dialogue

It was the hardest question I had ever been called upon to answer; doubly hard with those **clear eyes fixed upon mine**. "I'm afraid they do, John."   8

dialogue

(Dialogue—real insight into character)

He seemed a little startled at first, pondered over the fateful fact a moment, then shook his head. "I'm afraid, but it's difficult to believe all at once. I'm so strong it don't seem possible for such a little wound to kill me." And then he said, "I'm a little sorry I wasn't wounded in front; it looks cowardly to be hit in the back, but I obeyed orders." 9

short metaphor
imagery

[John was dying.] Even while he spoke, over his face I saw a gray veil falling that no human hand can lift. I sat down by him, **wiped drops** from his forehead, stirred the air about him with a **slow wave of a fan**, and waited to help him die. For hours he suffered dumbly, without a moment's murmuring: his **limbs grew cold**, **his face damp**, his **lips white**, and again and again he **tore the covering off his breast**, as if the lightest weight added to his agony. 10

imagery

how to think

One by one, the other men woke, and round the room appeared a **circle of pale faces and watchful eyes**, **full of awe and pity**; for, though a stranger, **John was beloved** by all. "Old boy, how are you?" faltered one. "Can I say or do anything for you anywheres?" whispered another. 11

dialogue

dialogue-character

"Take my things home, and tell them that I did my best." 12

obj. short

[He died then]; though the heavy breaths still tore their way up for a little longer, they were but the **waves of an ebbing tide that beat unfelt against the wreck**. He never spoke again, but to the end held my hand close, so close that when he was asleep at last, I could not draw it away. Dan, another patient, helped me, warning me as he did so that it was unsafe for dead and living flesh to lie so long together. But though my hand was strangely cold and stiff, and four white marks remained across its back, even when warmth and color had returned elsewhere, I could not but be glad that, through its touch, the presence of human sympathy, **perhaps, had lightened that hard hour**. 13

metaphor

lasting physical effect

(reinforces her purpose as a nurse)

When they had made him ready for the grave, I stood looking at him. The lovely expression which so often beautifies dead faces soon replaced marks of pain. The ward master handed me a letter, saying it had come the night before but was forgot. **It was John's letter, come just an hour too late to gladden the eyes that had longed for it so eagerly**. 14

(ironic detail—sentimental)

nurse's role
how to think
of John

After I had cut some brown locks for his mother, and taken off the ring to send her, I kissed this good son for her sake, and laid the letter in his hand. Then I left him, glad to have known **so genuine a man**, and carrying with me an enduring memory of a brave Virginia blacksmith, as he lay serenely **waiting for the dawn of that long day which knows no night**. 15

beautiful metaphor

The Opening Paragraph

Remember, your opening paragraph is going to set the subject and tone of your entire essay. Make certain that your reader knows precisely where you intend to take him or her. This clarity of purpose will give your reader confidence in what you have to present. Some of the questions you should ask yourself about your opening paragraph include.

- Have you cited the author and title?
- Have you identified the author's intended effect on the reader?
- Have you specifically mentioned which strategies, devices, or elements you will consider in your analysis of Alcott's re-creation of her experience?

Remember, this information can be provided to your reader in may different ways. You can be direct or inventive. Whatever you choose to do, be confident and clear.

Below are four sample opening paragraphs that address the prompt for the Louisa May Alcott analysis essay.

We recognized many areas we could develop in this analysis essay. Pacing is obvious in this brief narrative. Alcott tells of her experience in chronological order and uses a combination of short, direct sentences to balance longer, figurative ones. We could have just concentrated on dialogue, but we chose to include it with our discussion of selection of detail, diction, imagery, and tone.

Sample A

In Hospital Sketches, Louisa May Alcott presents a sentimental retelling of an episode she experienced as a Civil War nurse. As she tells of her encounter with a dying soldier, Alcott uses details, imagery, and diction to make her reader emotionally identify with her and her subject. These strategies and devices evoke a sentimental and sorrowful response in the reader.

Sample B

"John was dying." Such a direct statement for such a tragic and moving event. But, Louisa May Alcott does more than just objectively present a medical report of the death of a Civil War soldier in Hospital Sketches. Rather, through diction, selection of details, imagery, and tone, Alcott emotionally involves her reader in this sentimental re-creation of one young blacksmith's death.

Sample C

War is hell. But, occasionally an angel of mercy on a mission braves the horror to save a lost soul. Louisa May Alcott, a Civil War nurse, was such an angel—and perhaps her presence helped the troubled soul of a dying blacksmith reach the rewards of heaven he so deserved. Through imagery, diction, selection of detail, and tone, Alcott allows her readers to join her in this sentimental and awe-inspiring narrative from Hospital Sketches.

Sample D

My only previous connection with Louisa May Alcott was with Little Women. What a very different scene she presents in her story from Hospital Sketches. The reader is made to come face to face with the death of a wounded Civil War soldier as he is tended by a most caring nurse. This moving and sentimental narrative is developed through imagery, diction, selection of detail, and tone.

Although each of these opening paragraphs is different, each does the expected job of an introductory AP Comp analysis essay.

- Each cites the author and title.
- Each identifies the author's intended effect on the reader.
- Each states which strategies/devices will be discussed in the analysis of Alcott's narrative.

Let's take a look at what is different about each of these introductory paragraphs.

- **Sample A** restates the prompt directly. It is to the point without elaboration, but it enables the reader to immediately know the focus of the essay.
- **Sample B** uses a direct quotation from the text to grab the reader's attention. It is obvious that this is a writer who understands how language operates.
- **Sample C** imposes a personal viewpoint immediately and establishes a metaphor that will most likely be the unifying structure of the essay.
- **Sample D** makes reference to one of Alcott's other works as the scene is being set. The writer does not spend any additional time referring to the other work. It merely provides a kind of "stepping-stone" for both the writer and the reader.

Into which of the above samples could your opening paragraph be classified?

Writing the Body of the Essay

What Should I Include in the Body of This Analysis Essay?

Your strategy here should be the same as on the previous essay:

1. Present *your* analysis and your prompt-related points.
2. Adhere to the question.
3. Use specific references and details from the passage.
4. Use connective tissue—repetition, "echo words," and transitions—to establish coherence.

For more detail, refer back to the first discussion of this subject, earlier in this chapter.

To understand the process, carefully read the sample paragraphs below. Each develops one of the elements asked for in the prompt and cited in the introductory paragraph. Notice the specific references and the "connective tissue." Also notice that details that do not apply to the Alcott prompt are ignored.

This Paragraph Develops Diction

Throughout her account, Alcott's diction manipulates emotional responses in her readers. Words such as "earnest," "brave" and "faithful" establish John as a soldier worthy of sympathy, while "liberty and justice" rally the reader to his side with their patriotic connotations. Once the reader is involved, Alcott directs the tragic scene with words intended to bring forth more negative emotional responses: "suffering, tears, groans, and wept" emphasize John's pain. Yet, when the author says, "very touching," "fear vanished," and "my heart opened wide," the reader also wants to help John bear his pain. Alcott balances the negative side of death by using words that will make the reader more at ease during this uncomfortable passage. "Beautiful, gratitude and comfort" relax the reader and allow him to feel good about Alcott and her caregiving. Then, her direction changes as the young man is dying. He is now "cold, damp, white, and in agony." When the reader's heart is breaking, Alcott chooses words to lift the moment. The other men are "full of awe and pity," like the reader. In this way, the diction unites the reader, John, and Alcott. She makes certain that her concluding choices are comforting and positive. The "hard hour" has been "lightened." His expression is now "lovely and beautiful."

This Paragraph Develops Selection of Details

Louisa May Alcott chooses very special details to include in her development of scene and character. Dialogue is one of these details which provides tangible insights into the character of John. The immediacy and reality of John's inevitable death is brought straightforwardly home to the reader in paragraphs 2 and 3. "You don't mean he must die, doctor?" "There's not the slightest hope for him." John's politeness and unassuming personality are observed when we hear him respond to the nurse in paragraph 6. And, his youth and sense of honor are heartbreakingly presented in the dialogue in paragraph 7 and the end of paragraph 9. This sense of duty and honor is reinforced with his last words, ". . . tell them that I did my best." Selection of details also help the reader to understand and feel the horror of war and its casualties. The pain and coldness of death is almost brutally punctuated in paragraph 5, where Alcott chooses to emphasize others not crying while John does. Alcott chooses to tell us about the letter from John's mother that was not delivered until after his death to add more pathos and irony to an already tragic scene. And, to select the detail of her placing this letter into the dead soldier's hands prior to his burial heightens the reader's emotional involvement.

This Paragraph Develops Imagery

It might be easy to become dulled to pain in a war hospital filled with dying men. To prevent this and to personalize the experience, Alcott uses imagery to re-create the events of John's death. The reader can feel that "every breath he draws is like a stab." The image of suffocation tightens our throats as we read about his pain, but we, like Alcott, must learn to "bottle up our tears" as we envision through her simile the nurse as mother and soldier as child. The metaphor of "a gray veil falling that no human hand can lift" softens the death of the soldier while heightening the finality. The concluding metaphor reassures the reader of salvation as she, the writer, allows John into the "dawn of that long day which knows no night."

This Paragraph Develops Tone

As a result of her selection of details, diction, and imagery, Louisa May Alcott creates a scene with a predominant tone of sorrow. Re-creating the death scene of this young soldier, the author chooses those details that emphasize that pain and sorrow, both in herself and in her patient. She chooses to tell of the undelivered letter prior to the soldier's death, which further reinforces the reader's sense of sorrow and pity. Words like "suffering," "wept," "cold," "white," "in agony," help to convey and evoke sadness in the reader. And, the piteous situation is further developed when John's face is described as "lovely and beautiful" after his death. Imagery is also employed to create this tone of sorrow or sadness. Images of suffering, loss, and grief throughout, together with the final metaphor of "a gray veil falling that no human hand can lift," sadly portray the passing of this young Virginian blacksmith into eternity.

DO THIS NOW.

- Write the body of your essay. Time yourself.
- Allow 15–20 minutes to write your body paragraphs.

Here are two actual student essays with comments on each.

Student A

Louisa May Alcott experiences the worst part of war—suffering. Each day brings her 1
in contact with new bloodied men brought in on stretchers, and only a few walk out. She
has to live with their souls on her mind. One soldier, John, is described as a "brave" young
man who fought for "liberty and justice." But, he is suffering. Alcott writes with an
emotional tone about this soldier whom she helps "live" through his final moments. She
obviously retells this story so that her readers can begin to understand the anguish of war.

This chronologically organized story spans two hours, from life to the end of life. It 2
is said that no man should die alone, and Alcott helps this young man to die with the
comfort of one who cares for him. Alcott's diction includes adjectives to describe his
slow drift towards heaven with words like "his limbs grew cold, his face damp, his lips
white . . ." These characteristics added together with the metaphorically imposed "gray
veil" all lead up to his death. John's last words, "tell them that I did my best," symbolize
both his life and his death. From then on, he said nothing and waited to enter his next
life. Though he dies, Alcott hangs on as if trying to keep him from leaving. When
she finally lets him go, four white marks stay on her hand, symbolizing John's lasting
presence.

". . . Many suffer, some swore, some groaned, most endured silently, but none wept." 3
However, John was the exception. He let his emotions go, and his pain was answered
by a caring nurse. Alcott appeals to the reader's emotions with such words as "crying,"
"suffering," "pity," and "awe," that express the extremes of feeling present in the hospital
ward. A man in pain, about to die, should be pitied, especially when his life is about to
be cut short. All his childhood dreams are to go unfulfilled. It is a waste of a "genuine
man." Alcott uses this not only to tell of her experiences in war, but also to clarify for her
reader the devastation of war. Alcott's balanced sentences enhance her story. In paragraph
7, John says, "This is my first battle; do they think it's going to be my last?" Alcott
uses this question to illustrate the shock soldiers feel when faced with death. How can
anyone believe a doctor who tells him he is dying. This shock, on the part of the soldier
illustrates the human horror of war—people die!

Alcott also uses irony to emphasize the sadness of this boy's death. Just an hour after 4
he passes on, another doctor brings in a letter for John. It is just too late. If he had seen it,
maybe it would have put one last sparkle in his eyes before he shut them forever.

The ending of the passage summarizes the entire experience of so many of those who 5
fought in the Civil War. Here was a young man who was very human. He was an average
boy from Virginia who worked as a blacksmith. He had had a regular life and a regular
job until this terrible war. That was when this regular life ceased to exist: John's and pre–
Civil War America.

Having witnessed this young soldier waiting for the "dawn of that long day which 6
knows no night," people should cry and be awe struck at the consequences of war.

Student B

In this excerpt from <u>Hospital Sketches</u> by Louisa May Alcott, she constructs her story to deeply move the reader by re-creating her personal experience as a nurse. Alcott's rhetorical strategies, including diction, imagery and selection of details, help to emphasize the pain and the sorrow which filled the U.S. Army hospital.

1

A reason why Alcott's excerpt was very successful in helping the reader understand the atmosphere during the Civil War is through her choice of words. The repetition of "hope," reveals that although she and John hoped that he would survive, it was inevitable that he would die, for he had been deeply hurt. Alcott reveals her sympathy and care for this man named John by asking the doctor how long he has to live. She also helps us understand that during the war precious lives were taken away. "The army needed men like John, earnest, brave, and faithful." Alcott even reveals to her readers that having this companionship with John wasn't an easy job. She would have to answer heartbreaking questions, such as "Do they think it's going to be my last?" Telling a person that they won't live for long may be one of the hardest jobs Alcott may have had.

2

In addition to Alcott's diction, the details which she presents for her readers give the story an even more melancholy effect. She doesn't simply just state how many men were injured or how they were injured. Rather, she writes about her short encounter with the man named John. "John sat with bent head . . . and no outward sign of suffering, till . . . I saw great tears roll down and drop upon the floor." It's like this simple example shows the sadness and grief felt by this young man who was brave and fought for liberty. She reveals the soft side of a soldier. Alcott re-creates her experience by presenting the details of her relationship with John. "I sat down by him, wiped drops from his forehead, stirred the air . . . waited to help him die." She even displays the gradual physical change of the dying human body. "His limbs grew cold, his face damp, his lips white . . ." She also includes a small conversation between John and another injured man who, although a stranger, still had pity and sympathy for him. She also appeals to emotion by adding his mother in the story. She, as a friend, cuts his hair and kisses him for her instead at the grave.

3

Furthermore, the use of imagery also added to the re-creation of the Civil War scene. She describes John's pain as "every breath he draws is like a stab; for the ball pierced the left lung and broke a rib." With this quotation, it is evident that his pain was great. Alcott also shows the slow deterioration of John. "I saw a gray veil falling that no human hand can lift." This reveals that John's death is inevitable and there was nothing any human could do, but she could play the role of a friend. Alcott also displays the strength of John, how he wished to live, as "heavy breaths still tore their way up for a little longer."

4

Alcott describes her experience of the Civil War by telling a personal story. She reveals great love and generosity for John. Through this, it helps us understand the true power of human companionship.

5

Rubrics for Alcott Essay

As we said previously in this chapter, you can view actual AP English Language and Composition rubrics by logging on to the College Board website.

Note: For our purposes, scoring comments will be followed by one of three letters to indicate one of the three areas used in the AP English Language rubric for the rhetorical analysis essay. Thesis = (A), Evidence/Commentary = (B), Sophistication = (C)

High-Range Essay (6, 5)

- Indicates a complete understanding of the prompt via a defensible thesis (A)
- Clearly identifies and illustrates the author's intended effect on the reader (B)
- Presents various rhetorical strategies, devices, and elements used by the author to re-create her experience (B)
- Clear, well-organized, and coherent (B and C)
- Demonstrates a mature writing style (C)
- Thoroughly cites specific references from the text to illustrate and support points being made (B)
- Minor errors/flaws in diction/syntax, if any (C)

Mid-Range Essay (4, 3)

- The mid to high range essays identify rhetorical strategies PLUS the purpose/effect of the strategies (B)
- Refers accurately to the prompt via a defensible thesis (A)
- Refers accurately to the author's intended effect on the reader (A)
- Presents a less thorough analysis of how Alcott re-creates her experience than the higher rated essays (B)
- Is less adept at linking strategies and devices to the creation of effect or re-creation of the experience (B)
- Demonstrates writing that is adequate to convey Alcott's assertion (B)
- May not be sensitive to the more subtle strategies employed by Alcott (C)
- A few errors/flaws in diction/syntax may be present (C)

Low-Range Essay (2, 1)

- Does not respond adequately with a defensible thesis (A)
- Demonstrates insufficient and/or inadequate understanding of the passage and prompt (B)
- Does not clearly identify the author's intended effect on the reader or does not illustrate or supply support for the intended effect (B)
- Underdevelops and/or inaccurately analyzes Alcott's re-creation of her experience (B)
- Demonstrates weak control of the elements of diction, syntax, and organization (B and C)

Scoring for Student A Essay

This is a high-range essay for the following reasons:

- Indication of a mature writer [paragraph 2, sentence 3], [paragraph 3, sentences 2 and 3] (A)
- Clear understanding of the author's intended effect on the reader and applies it to a larger context [last paragraph] (B and C)
- Strong integration of textual support with rhetorical strategies [paragraph 4], [paragraph 5, sentence 1] (B)
- Strong topic adherence and connective tissue (B and C)
- Interesting and appropriate insights derived from the text [last paragraph] (C)

This high-range essay is well organized, with a strong, mature voice that has a clear point of view together with a well-developed analysis.

Scoring for Student B Essay

This is a mid-range essay for the following reasons:

- Identifies the intended effect on the reader [paragraph 1, sentence 1], [paragraph 3, sentence 1] (A and B)
- Adequately develops cited textual references (B)
- Shows understanding of rhetorical devices [paragraph 4] (B)
- Good transitions ("connective tissue") (B and C)
- Frequently uses awkward syntax [paragraph 2, last 3 sentences], [paragraph 3, last 2 sentences] (C)
- Interesting and appropriate insights derived from the text [last paragraph] (C)
- Minor technical errors, such as apostrophes and commas (C)

This mid-range essay is indicative of a writer who understands the text and the prompt. The student is able to choose the obvious rhetorical strategies and devices and relate them to Alcott's purpose with less fully developed analysis in comparison with the high-range papers.

Rapid Review

- Analysis is the study of rhetorical strategies.
- Your writing reflects your critical thinking.
- Review the types of analysis questions asked on previous exams.
- Always address the prompt.
- Review the rubrics to understand the rating system.
- Remember, the essay on the exam is a first draft.
- Follow a timing strategy for writing the exam essay.
- Carefully analyze the prompt.
- Practice topic adherence.
- Employ close reading and highlighting of the given passage.
- "Work" the material.
- Write your essay and check against models.
- Use echo words.
- Form a study group.
- Read sample essays and rubrics.
- Score your own essays.

A VIEW OF THE RHETORICAL SITUATION

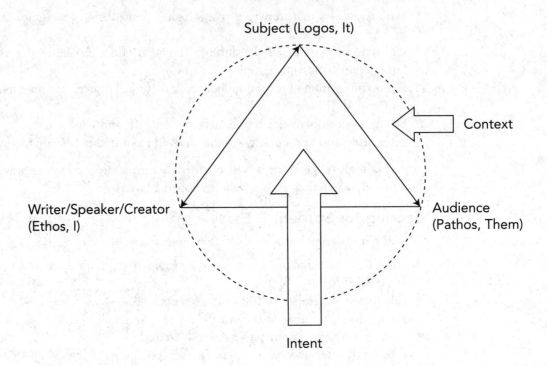

This diagram is an enhanced look at Aristotle's classical rhetorical triangle. All writers must be aware of three focus points:

1. **The subject.** What are you going to write about?
2. **The audience.** For whom are you writing?
3. **YOU, the writer.** How you going to engage this audience?

BUT, not only must the writer address these three focal points, she must be fully aware of **WHY (intent)** she is presenting this writing and the **SITUATION (context)** in which this writing is being presented.

CHAPTER 6

Introduction to the Argument Essay

IN THIS CHAPTER

Summary: Examination of the argument essay and its purpose as it is presented in the AP English Language exam.

Key Ideas

✪ Learn to take a position/stand on a situation given in the argument prompt.

✪ Familiarize yourself with strategies to support your position.

✪ Learn the basics of constructing the argument essay in response to the AP English Language prompt.

Some Basics

The second type of essay on the AP English Language exam is the argument essay. Many students believe it to be the easiest of the three essays to write. Unfortunately, too many students spend too little time in the actual planning of this essay and, as a result, present an underdeveloped, illogical, or off-topic piece. Although there is a great deal of latitude given for the response to the prompt, the argument essay demands careful reading and planning.

What Does the Argument Essay Require of Me?

Basically, you need to do three things

- Understand the nature of the position presented in the prompt
- Develop a position in response to the prompt
- Clearly and logically support your claim

What Does It Mean to Develop a Position?

Basically, this is a "So, what do YOU think?" prompt. You are asked to carefully read a passage or statement and to consider your own thoughts and where you stand on the issue. You are NOT being asked to confront the writer or speaker of the given text.

Timing and Planning the Essay

How Should I Approach the Writing of My Argument Essay?

Before beginning to actually write the essay, you need to do some quick planning. You could brainstorm a list of ideas, construct a chart, or create an outline. Whatever it is, you MUST find a way to allow yourself to think through the issue and your position.

Once I've Chosen My Position on the Given Issue, How Do I Go About Supporting It?

Remember that you've been taught how to write an argument throughout your school years, and you've even studied it in detail in your AP Comp course this year. Here is a brief overview of the kinds of support/evidence you could include to bolster your argument:

- facts/statistics
- details
- quotations
- dialogue
- needed definitions
- recognition of the opposition
- examples
- anecdotes
- contrast and comparison
- cause and effect
- appeal to authority

Just make certain to choose the strategy or strategies that are most familiar to you and with which you feel most comfortable. Don't try to "con" your reader or pad your essay with irrelevancies.

Does It Matter What Tone I Take in My Argument Essay?

The College Board and the AP Comp readers are open to a wide range of approaches. You can choose to be informal and personal, formal and objective, or even humorous and irreverent, and anything in between. Just be certain that your choice is appropriate for your purpose.

Will I Be Penalized for Taking an Unpopular, Unexpected, Irreverent, or Bizarre Position on the Given Issue?

As long as you are addressing the prompt and appropriately supporting your position, there is no danger of your losing points on your essay because you've decided to take a different approach. Your essay is graded for process and mastery and manipulation of language, not for how close you come to the viewpoint of your reader.

How Should I Plan to Spend My Time Writing the Argument Essay?

Learning to budget your time is a skill that can be most helpful in writing the successful essay. The following is a sample timeline for you to consider:

- 1–3 minutes reading and working the prompt
- 3 minutes deciding on a position
- 5–10 minutes planning the support of your position
- 20 minutes writing the essay
- 3 minutes proofreading

6-Point Rubric for the Argument Essay

THESIS = 1 Point

- **1 pt.**   Addresses the prompt with a thesis clearly, takes a position, and makes it clear HOW the thesis will be developed.
- **0 pts.**   Merely repeats the prompt, or statement is vague, avoids taking a position, or presents only an obvious fact.

DEVELOPMENT WITH EVIDENCE = 4 Points

- **4 pts.**   The writer presents support for the thesis clearly explaining the relationships between the evidence and the thesis.
- **3 pts.**   The development may be uneven, limited, incomplete; there may be minor errors or weak links between thesis and support.
- **2 pts.**   The development repeats, oversimplifies, or misinterprets cited evidence; points made are not supported by the text.
- **1 pt.**   The writer provides little or no commentary that links the evidence to the thesis.
- **0 pts.**   May lack a thesis; or presents irrelevant or too few references to the text in support of a clear thesis; or does not address the prompt; or writes about something totally unrelated to the prompt.

Note: Writing that lacks grammatical or syntactical control that interferes with a clear presentation of ideas cannot earn a 4.

SOPHISTICATION (Complexity and Style) = 1 Point

- **1 pt.**   (sophistication of thought or development of complex argument) Writer develops the thesis with nuanced explanation of evidence; and/or recognizes and discusses a broader context; and/or recognizes and engages with opposition; and/or makes strong, convincing rhetorical choices in developing the thesis; and/or prose is especially convincing or appropriate.
- **0 pts.**   Oversimplifies complexities of the text or the thesis; and/or diction and/or syntax does not enhance the presentation; and/or may overuse sweeping generalizations.

Working the Prompt

Before beginning to write, you MUST spend some time carefully reading and deconstructing the prompt. (We call this "working the prompt.") Your success depends upon your clearly understanding what is expected of you.

Below is the prompt of the third essay on the Diagnostic/Master exam.

In his famous "Vast Wasteland" address to the National Association of Broadcasters in May of 1961, Newton Minow, the Chairman of the Federal Communications Commission, spoke about the power of television to influence the taste, knowledge, and opinions of its viewers around the world. Carefully read the fol-

lowing, paying close attention to how timely it is today, especially in light of the Internet, smart phones, social media, and digital games, etc.

Minow ended his speech warning that "The power of instantaneous sight and sound is without precedent in mankind's history. This is an awesome power. It has limitless capabilities for good—and for evil. And it carries with it awesome responsibilities—responsibilities which you and [the government] cannot escape . . ."

Using your own knowledge and your own experiences or reading, write a carefully constructed essay in which you present and support your position on Minow's ideas about mass media and technology.

- Respond to the prompt with a defensible thesis that relates to the prompt.
- Select and use evidence to develop and support the line of reasoning.
- Explain the relationship between the evidence and the thesis.
- Demonstrate an understanding of the rhetorical situation.
- Use appropriate grammar and punctuation in communicating the argument.

DO THIS NOW.
Highlight the essential elements of the prompt.
    (Time yourself.) How long did it take you? _____
    Compare your highlighting of the prompt with ours.

In his famous **"Vast Wasteland"** address to the **National Association of Broadcasters** in May of **1961**, **Newton Minow**, the **Chairman of the Federal Communications Commission**, spoke about the **power of television to influence the taste, knowledge, and opinions of its viewers around the world**. Carefully read the following, paying close attention to how **timely** it is today, especially in light of the worldwide **Internet**.

Minow ended his speech **warning** that "**The power of instantaneous sight and sound is without precedent in mankind's history**. This is an **awesome power**. It has **limitless capabilities for good—and for evil**. And it carries with it **awesome responsibilities**—responsibilities which **you and [the government] cannot escape** . . ."

Using your **own knowledge** and your **own experiences** or **reading**, write a carefully constructed essay that **supports your position on Minow's ideas about mass media and technology**.

For this prompt, anything else you may have highlighted is extraneous.

Developing the Opening Paragraph

NOW, BEGIN TO PLAN YOUR ESSAY.
    Write your introductory paragraph. Make certain to

- refer specifically to the prompt; and
- clearly state your position on the given issue.

The following are three sample opening paragraphs.

A

I agree with Newton Minow's assertion to the National Association of Broadcasters that "The power of instantaneous sight and sound is . . . an awesome power . . . [with] capabilities for good—and for evil." However, I disagree with his placing the responsibility for this power squarely in the hands of the broadcasters and the government.

B

Imagine—you have limitless capabilities for good and evil—you, not Superman, can control the world with your super powers. And, what are your powers? Do you have x-ray vision, morphability, immortality? NO, you have the most awesome power ever devised—you can instantaneously influence the taste, knowledge, and opinions of mankind around the world. You are Supernet! and you have a super headache because you agree with Newton Minow, who warned the National Association of Broadcasters in 1961 that "You have an awesome responsibility."

C

Nowhere is the awesome power for good and evil of modern technology more clearly seen than in the Internet's pervasiveness and influence. Newton Minow was right on target in 1961 when he warned the National Association of Broadcasters that the power of TV has "limitless capabilities for good—and for evil."

Each of these opening paragraphs does the job required of an introduction to an argument essay on the AP English Language and Composition exam.

- Each cites the speaker and the occasion.
- Each clearly states the writer's position on the given issue.

Let's look at what is different about each of the paragraphs.

Sample A qualifies the assertion presented by Minow. The writer agrees with the potential of the power but disagrees about who should take responsibility.

Sample B agrees with Minow's position but treats the assertion in a lighthearted fashion. The reader can expect a humorous and possibly irreverent tone in the essay.

Sample C indicates a writer who has obviously decided to limit the area of the argument to that of the Internet and has chosen to agree with Minow.

Note: Given the subject matter, this prompt does not lend itself easily to a negative position. However, if a creative thinker and writer were to assert such a viewpoint, it would not be penalized.

Which of the above samples is similar to your opening paragraph? Are there any changes you would make in yours?

Developing the Body of the Essay

DO THIS NOW.

STRATEGY

— Plan the body of your argument essay.

A sample strategy for planning the Minow essay follows. After carefully reading and deconstructing the prompt, we decided to use Minow's own three-part warning to the NAB. We brainstormed for ideas that could be linked to each of the categories. (Remember, ideas about how to organize or approach your essay can sometimes be found in the excerpt itself.)

GOOD	EVIL	RESPONSIBILITY
— education	— promote hate	— laws
— warning of dangers	— distort reality	— censorship
— recognition of heroes	— help terrorists	— self-censorship
— involvement in humankind's achievements	— invasion of privacy	— prior restraint
	— threats to national security	— 1st Amendment
— instant communications with family and friends		— 4th Amendment
	— create mass hysteria	— financial gain
		— copyrights
— medical care	— exploit children	— parental control
— links to the world for the the disabled, elderly, isolated	— fraud	— v-chip
	— conspiracy	— personal checks and balances
	— subvert elections	
— entertainment	— brainwashing	

Once you've completed your initial planning, in our case brainstorming, you must choose those specific items you will be best able to use to support and develop your argument. We limited ours to the following.

GOOD	EVIL	RESPONSIBILITY
— instant communications	— promote hate	— personal checks and balances
— medical treatment	— exploit children	— laws
— entertainment	— create mass hysteria	

This type of chart will provide you as a writer with a structure for your presentation. You are now ready to write the body of your essay based on your carefully considered choices. Below are three sample body paragraphs which are based on the chart on page 100.

Body Paragraph on "Good"

One of the most rewarding applications of the Internet is its ability to provide instant communication between friends and family. A grandmother-to-be in New York is able to share in the moment by moment experience of her daughter's pregnancy and her granddaughter Daisy's birth in California through e-mail, scanned photos and quick videos. Likewise, the ability to instantly communicate with others may have saved the life of a doctor stranded at the South Pole. Her contact with medical resources and experts via the Internet enabled her to undergo surgery and treatment for breast cancer. Research and innovations in medical treatment are now available to those around the world via the "Net." Similarly, the ability for instant communication enables millions to enjoy concerts, sports events, theatrical presentations and other cultural activities without ever having to leave home. These wonderful benefits are all because of the fabulous and awesome technological creation—the Internet.

Body Paragraph on "Evil"

The other side of the mass communication coin has the face of evil on it. The Internet offers hate mongers unlimited access to anyone with a connection to the World Wide Web. Groups like the Neo-Nazis can spread their hate messages to susceptible minds via bright, entertaining and engaging websites. What looks like a simple, fun game can easily reinforce the group's hate-filled philosophy to unsuspecting browsers. With the potential for millions of "hits" each week, it does not take a rocket scientist to perceive the danger here. This danger is also present with the minds and bodies of curious and vulnerable young people. Because of its easy access and easy production, "kiddie porn" is both possible and available via the Internet and the films any number of porn sites offer for downloading with the mere click of a keyboard key. Through contacts made through e-mail and/or chat rooms on the Net, children can be easily fooled and led to contact those who would abuse their bodies and minds for a quick profit or cheap thrill. With instantaneous messaging, whether real or imagined, positive or negative, a single person or group can set into motion mass hysteria just by warning of an impending disaster, such as a flood, fire, bomb, poison, and so on. There are obviously many more possibilities floating out there in the ethernet. These are just three of the evil ones.

Body Paragraph on "Responsibility"

Just as there is the potential for both good and evil with regard to mass communication, so too is there the potential for both beneficial and destructive strategies related to responsibilities. The most powerful regulator of our responsibility as individuals is our finger and its power to press a button or double click on a key and to "just say no." With this slight pressure, we are able to exert monumental pressure on those who produce programs, websites, photos, documents, etc., which we find unacceptable. Who better to tell us what to watch, what to do, and what to think? All too often many people prefer to abdicate their personal responsibility and give that power to either the government or the communication industry. We must never forget that dictators target the control and censorship of mass media as the first step in the total control of the minds and hearts of the populace. The laws, which we as citizens of a democracy look to, must never impinge upon our First and Fourth Amendment rights. Each of us has the right of free speech, and each of us has the right to privacy. None of us has the right to harm others or to limit the rights of others; why, then, would we give that right to the communication industry or to the government?

> Regarding a concluding paragraph, our advice is to spend your time in planning and writing the body of your essay rather than worrying about a concluding paragraph. With a brief essay, you can be certain that your reader can remember what you've already said, so there is no need to summarize your major points or to repeat the prompt. If you feel you must have a concluding statement/remark, by all means do so. But, make certain it is a FINAL remark that is of interest and is appropriate to your purpose. You may want to use the last sentence of your last body paragraph as your concluding comment. For example, the final sentences in the first and third sample body paragraphs could be used as the conclusion to the essay.

DO THIS NOW.
Spend about 20 minutes writing the body of your essay. Make certain that your essay follows your plan.

Sample Student Essays

The following are two sample student essays.

Student A

When Newton Minow ended his speech in May, 1961, he warned that, "The power of instantaneous sight and sound is without precedent . . . [and] it has limitless capabilities for good—and for evil." I wholeheartedly agree with both Minow's position about modern technology, especially about how it relates to the Internet today and the responsibility facing its users.

Scene One—Pre-1980's. Big project. Long haul to the library, gazing despondently until your eyes resemble those of a zombie. Too many books, too little time, in short, just TOO much. Scene Two—mid-1990's. A two-foot walk to the computer, and Voila! All the information you'd ever need is at your fingertips. The Internet has truly revolutionized how people can obtain their information. Now, more than ever, it is easier and quicker to access all types of information from "Exactly what IS that fungus growing on my toe?" to "What are the names of every major river system in the continental United States?" The plethora of information enables people to almost cease the burdensome trip to the library and halt the overwhelming feelings of dread they find as they stare blankly at a stack of books. With the schedule of the typical American today, there's hardly enough time to breathe, nevermind attempting to fit that hour-long trip to the library in the time frame. With the birth of the Internet, people with access to a computer can locate information faster than ever. But, how are we to judge the acceptability of that information?

The awesome power of these new technological inventions, such as computers and the Internet, do not always produce, however, grade-A products. People have begun to utilize the Internet to recruit new cult members, to teach people how to build bombs, to teach hate. Basically, anything and everything evil can be posted on the "Net." Scene Three. Mr. Parker, a 75-year-old man from rural Indiana is in severe pain with abdominal cramps. Instead of attempting a two-hour drive to the nearest hospital, he makes it to his computer, logs on to the Internet in hopes of finding out what is wrong with him and in hopes of finding a quick remedy. Following the www's advice, he treats himself for stomach pain. Scene Four. Poor Mr. Parker dies hours later of acute appendicitis.

The Internet has the power to give birth to both good and evil. Today, as our society becomes more and more advanced, we rely more and more on anything that promises to make our busy lives less hectic. The easy way out, it seems, is always the right way in. Call it our American laziness, or call it our penchant to make learning easier, either way you slice it, the Internet has the potential for both positive and negative effects on society. Our responsibility is to find ways to exhibit our ability to distinguish between that which is beneficial and that which is destructive.

Student B

In his now famous address to the National Association of Broadcasters in May, 1961, FCC chairman Newton Minow spoke of the unprecedented power that those who control television's programming have over the American public, and how the mass media should be controlled and censored by the government, for it could wield awesome amounts of either good or evil. This assertion, that "television is a vast wasteland" rings true throughout the modern history of American society, especially in light of the global Internet. 1

There is no doubt that television has greatly altered the very psyche of Americans countless times since Minow's speech. From patriotic events like Neil Armstrong's first step on the moon and the "miracle on the ice" American victory over the Soviet Union in the 1980 Olympic hockey semi-finals, to historical events like Tiananmen Square, the assassination of JFK, and the fall of the Berlin Wall. Television has provided Americans with triumph—the Persian Gulf War—and tragedy—the Columbine massacre. Most importantly, however, it is entertainment for the masses, and is affordable to the point that 95% of Americans watch at least once a week, and this is where it goes awry. 2

Americans, due to the overwhelming economic prosperity and technological revolution of the last forty years, have become slovenly. We can get almost anywhere in the world within 24 hours via airplane and expect to be waited on while flying there. We drive to work everyday. We have every type of cuisine imaginable less than twenty minutes away, contrasting with several countries which don't have food, period. We have secure incomes, capital growth, and all of the material comforts of the day. We have the Internet, the new mass media which allows for anyone to learn about anything at anytime, anywhere. We are inactive, obese, materialistic, boring people, and television has adapted itself to fit our collective personas. Or possibly, we changed for television. 3

The nightly news is filled with images of death, suffering, pain, agony, misery, and other horrors that we gobble up because we as middle-class Americans have an infinitesimal chance of ever seeing it. The most popular TV shows are either irreverent comedies like "Seinfeld" and "Friends" with no actual cultural impact, or worse game shows like "Weakest Link" or "Survivor" that reward, in pride and prizes, ruthlessness, emotional warfare, and pointless competition that reinforces those attributes in the 30 million viewers they get every Monday and Wednesday night. The sensationalistic television programming caters to every evil desire we have, so it makes them grow inside us and want more, making us fervent to tune in next week for the next fantastic episode. God forbid they show a rerun. 4

Television has become a wasteland, and it's turning Western culture into one, too. One has to believe Newton Minow knew what he was talking about. In a classic quote from Catch-22, Joseph Heller writes that "There was a general consensus that the platitudes of Americanism were horsesh-t." I wholeheartedly agree. 5

Rating the Essays

You can view actual AP English Language and Composition rubrics by logging on to the College Board website.

Note: For our purposes, scoring comments will be followed by one of three letters to indicate one of the three areas used in the AP English Language rubric for the argument essay. Thesis = (A), Evidence/Commentary = (B), Sophistication = (C)

KEY IDEA

High-Range Essays (6, 5)
- Correctly identifies Minow's position regarding the power of television and other forms of mass communication via a defenisible thesis (A)
- Effectively presents a position about Minow's own ideas (A and B)
- Clear writer's voice (C)
- Defends his or her position by presenting carefully reasoned arguments making appropriate reference to specific examples from personal experience (B)
- Clear and effective organization (B and C)
- Effectively manipulates language (C)
- Few, if any, syntactical errors (C)

Mid-Range Essays (4, 3)
- Correctly identifies Minow's position and attitude about television and mass communications via a defensible thesis (A)
- Understands the demands of the prompt (A and B)
- Clearly states a position with regard to that of Minow (A and B)
- Presents a generally adequate argument that makes use of appropriate examples
- Ideas clearly stated (B)
- Less well-developed than the high-range essays (B)
- A few lapses in diction and/or syntax (C)

Low-Range Essays (2, 1)

- Inadequate thesis (A)
- Misunderstands, oversimplifies, or misrepresents Minow's position (B)
- Insufficient or inappropriate examples used to develop the writer's position (B)
- Lack of mature control of the elements of essay writing (C)

Student A
This is a high-range essay for the following reasons:

- A strong, mature voice willing to be creative as well as analytical (B and C)
- Clear statement/thesis about the writer's position on Minow's assertion (A)
- Overall structure clearly defined through "scenes" (B and C)
- Original illustrations and details to support writer's position (B)
- Tight focus (B)
- Mature vocabulary and sentence structure (C)
- Brief response to Minow's challenge about responsibility regarding the media (C)

This high-range essay, although brief, does the work of a mature, clear, and responsive writer. The assertion and support for it are well organized and developed in a very clear writer's voice.

Student B

This is a mid-range essay for the following reasons:

- Evidence that the writer understood the question and prompt via a defensible prompt (A)
- Indication of a writer's voice (B and C)
- Does not connect all parts of the essay, especially in paragraph 3, with the topic (B)
- Includes interesting and varied details and examples to support the thesis (B)
- Some obviously incorrect assumptions [paragraph 4, sentence 2] (B)
- A few problems with diction and syntax [fragment in paragraph 4, sentence 2]; ["slovenly" in paragraph 3, sentence 1], ["fervent" in paragraph 4, next to last sentence] (C)
- An interesting style and content (C)
- Does not really address the responsibility issue (B)

This mid-range essay indicates a writer who is a risk taker and intellectually curious. At times, the writer's enthusiasm seems to get in the way of a clear focus.

For this argument essay, almost all of the writers understood that Minow was commenting on the power of television and were able to comment on the timeliness of his assertions. In their essays, student writers attempted to distinguish between good and bad effects of modern technology, especially the Internet, and many illustrated their claims with fine examples of the power of this technology. They recognized the potential for inciting violence, for learning, for conformity, and for influencing political opinions and outcomes. The majority only touched upon power and influence, but the high-range essays recognized the subtlety of the responsibility of television and the Internet.

Most, if not all, student writers agreed with Minow, but few offered any real examination of the need for responsibility with regard to the advances in technology. Some were cautious about First Amendment rights, and a few saw the government as the chief "overseer."

Rapid Review

- Create an argument.
  - — understand the position or assertion
  - — agree, disagree, or qualify
  - — take a position, relate to an idea
  - — support your point of view
- Work the prompt.
  - — read and deconstruct the assignment
  - — highlight
- Plan the essay.
- Address the opposition.
- Allow for final remarks.
- Write the essay.
- Read the sample essays and rubrics.
- Score your own essay.

CHAPTER 7

Introduction to the Synthesis Essay

IN THIS CHAPTER

Summary: An introduction to the synthesis essay and its purpose as it is presented on the AP English Language exam.

Key Ideas

✪ Learn how the synthesis essay differs from the argument and analysis essays.

✪ Learn the process of dealing with many texts.

✪ Learn the strategies that can be used to incorporate specific texts into your essay.

✪ Learn the basics for constructing your response to the synthesis prompt.

Some Basics

What Is the Synthesis Essay on the Exam Like?

Basically, the student is presented with an introduction to and a description of an issue that has varying viewpoints associated with it. Accompanying this is a selection of sources that address the topic. These sources can be written texts that could include nonfiction, fiction, poetry, or even drama, as well as visual texts, such as photos, charts, artwork, cartoons, and so forth.

After carefully reading and annotating the sources, the student is required to respond to the given prompt with an essay that incorporates and synthesizes at least THREE of the sources in support of his position on the subject.

What Is the Purpose of the Synthesis Essay?

The College Board wants to determine how well the student can do the following:

- Read critically
- Understand texts
- Analyze texts
- Develop a position on a given topic
- Support a position on a given topic
- Support a position with appropriate evidence from outside sources
- Incorporate outside sources into the texts of the essay
- Cite sources used in the essay

The synthesis essay is a chance to demonstrate your ability to develop a "researched idea," using not only your personal viewpoint, but also the viewpoints of others. This essay is a reflection of your critical reading, thinking, and writing skills.

The Prompt

The first time you see a synthesis prompt, you may feel overwhelmed. After all, it's quite complex: three paragraphs long and several outside sources. Don't panic. Just begin at the beginning, and take it step by step.

The first step is to READ THE PROMPT!!!

- No, don't just skim it.
- Yes, read it word for word.
- Underline important words, phrases, instructions.
- Don't assume anything.

As an example of how to deal with a synthesis prompt, let's carefully read and annotate the eminent domain prompt from the diagnostic/master exam

A recent Supreme Court decision has provoked much debate about private property rights (eminent domain). In it the court ruled that the city of New London was within the bounds of the *Constitution* when it condemned private property for use in a redevelopment plan. This ruling is an example of the classic debate between individual rights vs. the greater good.

Carefully read the following sources, including any introductory information. Then, in an essay that synthesizes at least three of the sources for support, take a position on the claim that the governmental taking of property from one private owner to give to another to further economic development constitutes permissible "public use" under the Fifth Amendment.

Make certain to take a position and that your essay centers on your argument. Use the sources to support your reasoning; avoid simply summarizing the sources. You may refer to the sources by their letters (Source A, Source B, etc.) or by the identifiers given in the parentheses.

- Source A (*U.S. Constitution*)
- Source B (*60 Minutes*)
- Source C (*Kelo* decision)
- Source D (Koterba, editorial/political cartoon) (See the sources on pp. 31–35 in the Diagnostic Exam.)

- Source E (Broder)
- Source F (Britt, editorial/political cartoon)
- Source G (CNN and American Survey)

- Provide evidence from at least three of the provided sources to support the thesis. Indicate clearly the sources used through direct quotation, paraphrase, or summary. Sources may be cited as Source A, Source B, etc., or by using the description in parentheses.
- Explain the relationship between the evidence and the thesis.

- Demonstrate an understanding of the rhetorical situation.
- Use appropriate grammar and punctuation in communicating the argument.

1. Note the organization of the prompt.
   - The first paragraph gives important background information in order to establish context. This first paragraph will **always** provide background.
   - The second paragraph is the actual assignment – what are you required to do. The second paragraph is the true "meat" of the prompt. It **will change** with each new synthesis prompt you encounter.
   - The third paragraph provides instruction about how to construct your argument. This third paragraph will **always** provide organization information.
   - Each source is given a LETTER. The names of authors, etc. are given in parentheses.
2. Underline the important words and/or phrases. (We've already done that for you.) Note that ignoring any of the underlined words or phrases could seriously threaten your argument. That's what *important* means in this situation.
3. If you follow these two steps, you will have a working understanding of what is expected of you in this particular situation. If you have time, you might even want to write your assignment in ONE sentence. If you can do this, you really understand what your job is.

What Kinds of Synthesis Essays Can I Expect?

The synthesis essay has two primary approaches.

The first kind of synthesis essay is one you're probably familiar with. This is the essay in which you develop your thesis and support it with specific examples from appropriate sources. You could develop this type of synthesis essay using any of the rhetorical strategies, such as:

- Compare and contrast
- Cause and effect
- Analysis

The second kind of synthesis essay presents an argument. Here, you take a position on a particular topic and support this position with appropriate outside sources, while indicating the weaknesses of other viewpoints.

You should be ready to write either of these two types of synthesis essays. **Given the nature of the AP Language exam, however, it is more likely that you will be presented with a synthesis essay prompt that requires a response in the form of an argument.**

The important thing is to practice composing both types of synthesis essays. Practice. Practice. Being familiar and comfortable with the synthesis process is the crucial factor.

Don't be put off by the length and/or complexity of the introduction to the subject and the prompt. Remember, you are the one who will choose your position on the topic. And you are the one who chooses which sources to incorporate into your essay.

You can do this—AS LONG AS YOU ADDRESS THE PROMPT AND INCORPORATE AND CITE THE REQUIRED NUMBER OF SOURCES.

How Is the Synthesis Essay Rated?

As with the other essays on the AP Language exam, the synthesis essay is rated on a 6-point scale that is based on the AP Reader's evaluation of this first draft of an essay written in approximately 40 minutes. Here is a sample rubric for the synthesis essay.

6 Point Rubric for the Synthesis Essay

THESIS = 1 Point

- **1 pt.** Addresses the prompt with a thesis that makes it clear HOW the thesis will be developed.
- **0 pts.** Merely repeats the prompt, or statement is vague, avoids taking a position, or presents only an obvious fact.

DEVELOPMENT WITH EVIDENCE = 4 Points

- **4 pts.** With references to at least three of the given sources, the writer presents support for the thesis explaining the relationships between the evidence and the thesis.
- **3 pts.** With references to at least three of the given sources, the development may be uneven, limited; there may be minor errors or weak links between thesis and support.
- **2 pts.** With references to at least three of the given sources, the development repeats, oversimplifies, or misinterprets cited references; points made are not supported by the text.
- **1 pt.** With references to two or fewer of the given sources, the writer merely summarizes the referenced sources, or references to the text are not clear or relevant; provides little or no commentary that links the source to the thesis.
- **0 pts.** May lack a thesis; or presents irrelevant or too few references to the text in support of a clear thesis; or does not address the prompt; or writes about something totally unrelated to the prompt.

   Note: Writing that lacks grammatical or syntactical control that interferes with a clear presentation of ideas cannot earn a 4.

SOPHISTICATION (Complexity and Style) = 1 Point

- **1 pt.** (sophistication of thought or development of complex argument) Writer develops the thesis with nuanced explanation of evidence; and/or recognizes and discusses a broader context; and/or recognizes and engages with opposition; and/or makes strong, convincing rhetorical choices in developing the thesis; and/or prose is especially convincing or appropriate.
- **0 pts.** Oversimplifies complexities of the text or the thesis; and/or diction and/or syntax does not enhance the presentation; and/or may overuse sweeping generalizations.

Timing and Planning the Synthesis Essay

Before Writing

Before you begin to write your essay, you need to perform an important series of tasks.

   The first among these tasks is to wisely use the allotted, prewriting 15 minutes of reading time.

- Read ALL three of the prompts
- Deconstruct the synthesis prompt
- Read and annotate each of the given texts related to the synthesis prompt (see the sources on pp. 31–35 in the Diagnostic Exam)
- Decide how you will address the synthesis prompt

   The second of these tasks is to be aware of the timing of writing your essay. You've been told to open the test booklet and begin to write. Now what? Well, you've already read each of the three prompts and decided what position you're going to take on the synthesis essay. Here's what we recommend as a timeline for writing the synthesis essay:

- 5 to 6 minutes going back to the texts and deciding which you will use in your essay
- 8 to 10 minutes planning the support of your position
- 20 minutes writing the essay
- 3 to 4 minutes checking to make certain you've included at least the minimum number of sources and correctly cited each of them
- 3 minutes proofreading

Working the Prompt

As with the analysis and argument essays, you MUST spend time carefully reading and deconstructing the prompt. This entails your carefully reading and looking for key words, phrases, and other information that make your task clear. DO NOT FORGET TO READ ANY INTRODUCTORY MATERIAL PROVIDED. The introduction will set up the situation and give you any needed background information. Plan to spend about three minutes carefully reading both the introduction and the assignment, and highlighting the important terms and elements of the prompt.

The following is the prompt from the Diagnostic Master exam.

A recent Supreme Court decision has provoked much debate about private property rights. In this decision, the court ruled that the city of New London was within the bounds of the *U.S. Constitution* when it condemned private property for use in a redevelopment plan. This ruling is an example of the classic debate between individual rights versus the greater good.

Carefully read the following sources, including any introductory information. **Then, in an essay that synthesizes at least three of the sources for support, take a position that supports, opposes, or qualifies the claim that the government taking property from one private owner to give to another for the creation of further economic development constitutes a permissible "public use" under the Fifth Amendment.**

Make certain that you take a position and that the essay centers on your argument. Use the sources to support your reasoning; avoid simply summarizing the sources. You may refer to the sources by their letters (Source A, Source B, etc.) or by the identifiers in the parentheses below.

- Source A (*U.S. Constitution*)
- Source B (*60 Minutes*)
- Source C (*Kelo* decision)
- Source D (Koterba, editorial/political cartoon) (See the sources on pp. 31–35 in the Diagnostic Exam.)
- Source E (Broder)
- Source F (Britt, editorial/political cartoon)
- Source G (CNN and American Survey)

- Provide evidence from at least three of the provided sources to support the thesis. Indicate clearly the sources used through direct quotation, paraphrase, or summary. Sources may be cited as Source A, Source B, etc., or by using the description in parentheses.
- Explain the relationship between the evidence and the thesis.
- Demonstrate an understanding of the rhetorical situation.
- Use appropriate grammar and punctuation in communicating the argument.

DO THIS NOW.
Time yourself for this activity.
Highlight the essential elements of the prompt.
How long did it take you? _____

Compare your highlighting with ours.

<u>A recent Supreme Court decision has provoked much debate about private property rights.</u> In it, the court ruled that the city of New London was within the bounds of the *U.S. Constitution* when it condemned private property for use in a redevelopment plan. This ruling is an example of the <u>classic debate between individual rights versus the greater good.</u>

Carefully read the following sources, including any introductory information. **Then, in an essay that <u>synthesizes at least three of the sources</u> for support, <u>take a position that supports, opposes, or qualifies</u> the claim that the <u>government taking property from one private owner to give to another for the creation of further economic development constitutes a permissible "public use" under the Fifth Amendment.</u>**

Make certain that you take a position and that the essay centers on your argument. Use the sources to support your reasoning; avoid simply summarizing the sources. You may refer to the sources by their letters (Source A, Source B, etc.) or by the identifiers in the parentheses below.

- Source A (*U.S. Constitution*)
- Source B (*60 Minutes*)
- Source C (*Kelo* decision)
- Source D (Koterba, editorial/political cartoon) (See the sources on pp. 31–35 in the Diagnostic Exam.)
- Source E (Broder)
- Source F (Britt, editorial/political cartoon)
- Source G (CNN and American Survey)

Notice we have highlighted or underlined the essential parts of both the introduction and the prompt itself. All other words and phrases are nonessential.

> We now know a debate is centering around private property rights and public use for the greater good. We know the U.S. Supreme Court recently handed down a ruling supporting the principle of eminent domain, and we know we must take a position on this debate. And, lastly, we know we must choose at least three of the seven given sources.

Developing the Opening Paragraph

Now that you are aware of what is expected of you, you can begin to plan your essay.

> Before beginning the actual writing, we recommend you jot down a few notes about HOW you are going to present your material. There is no need to construct a formal outline. Simply create a brief listing of the major points you want to include and the order in which you will present them.

DO THIS NOW.
I have decided to use the following sources in my essay:
    Source ____ A ____ B ____ C ____ D ____ E ____ F ____ G
    When creating the opening paragraph, most student writers feel more in control if they:

— refer specifically to the prompt and/or introduction
— clearly state their position on the given topic

Now is the time to write your opening paragraph.

DO THIS NOW.

The position I'm going to take on this issue is _____ support _____ oppose _____ qualify.

The following are three sample introductory paragraphs.

A

Payday. As usual, the line at the bank drive-thru is a mile long, so Joe Citizen just sits and listens to the radio. This paycheck is especially important to him because it is the final payment on his castle—his home. Mr. Smith has a family waiting back at home for him. Even his dog will be happy to see Joe walk through the door. What Joe Citizen and his family don't know is this: waiting for Joe is a notice from his local government, a letter notifying him that his home and property are being taken, using the right of eminent domain. One has to ask, "Is this fair?" I think not.

B

Every time that my grandparents visit, I have to vacate my bedroom, so they can have a room of their own during their visit. It's always a painful few days because I'm locked out of the room that I've decorated, the room that holds all of my things; it's the room that's "mine." As my mother always says, "It's for the good of the family." But, no matter how much I feel deprived, I always know that I'll have it back in a few days. However, the results would be different if she applied the principle of "eminent domain." I would lose my room permanently, and it would be turned into a real guest room. I would not be a happy family member.

C

Today there is a wide-ranging debate about the individual's right to possess and protect his private property and the right of the government to seize a person's home and land needed for redevelopment that would benefit the entire community. Even though the principle of eminent domain is granted to the government in the *U.S. Constitution*'s Fifth Amendment, it should be used only in the most extreme circumstances.

Each of the previous opening paragraphs could be used to begin the synthesis essay demanded of the eminent domain prompt.

— Each introduces the subject and its context.
— Each clearly indicates the writer's position on the issue.

Let's examine these paragraphs.

Sample A clearly states a position in opposition to eminent domain. This writer tries to place his opinion in the context of a generic man and his family. This brief paragraph begins to indicate the writer's voice. By answering the rhetorical question, the writer emphatically declares a position.

Sample B uses personal experience to present an opposing opinion. By placing the general concept of eminent domain in the context of a very personal experience, the reader hears a real voice that defends private property rights with some exceptions.

Sample C presents an objective statement of the subject and its context. There is no indication of the personal in this introduction, and the reader can expect the objectivity to continue as the writer develops his qualifying essay.

Which of these introductory paragraphs is similar to yours? Are there any changes you would make in your opening? If so, what are they?

Developing the Body of the Essay

DO THIS NOW.

— Plan the body of your synthesis essay.

<u>Take a close look at the planning our writer did for this synthesis essay.</u>

Position on issue: qualifying position on eminent domain

Sources to use: (See the sources in the Diagnostic Master exam, pages 30–34.)

✔ Source A (*U.S. Constitution*)
Source B (*60 Minutes*)
✔ Source C (*Kelo* decision)
Source D (Koterba, editorial/political cartoon)
✔ Source E (Broder)
Source F (Britt, editorial/political cartoon)
✔ Source G (CNN and American Survey)

Points to make:

1. The *Kelo* decision + the Fifth Amendment = right of eminent domain. Empathize with private property owners.
2. *60 Minutes* interview to support negative idea of what happens when eminent domain takes private property.
3. Get into the idea of the greater good. Use *60 Minutes* interview with the mayor and the Broder points about the need for urban development to help blighted areas.
4. Use the *Washington Times* survey to support my position of leaning toward those who oppose this type of use of eminent domain.

With these points in mind, our writer is now ready to compose the body of the synthesis essay.

Body Paragraph Based on Point 1 (*Kelo* + Fifth Amendment)

Because of this experience, I can empathize with the home owners affected by the recent 5:4 Supreme Court decision *Kelo v. New London* that cited a section of the Fifth Amendment to the *U.S. Constitution* that states, "nor shall private property be taken for public use, without just compensation" (Source A). The Court ruled that New London, Connecticut, was within its constitutional rights to take private property and give it to another private individual in order to further the economic development of the city (Source C).

- Uses a transition to refer to the opening paragraph
- States empathy with those affected by the *Kelo* decision and summarizes both the case and the Fifth Amendment
- Appropriately cites the sources as directed in the prompt

Body Paragraph Based on Point 2 (*60 Minutes* interview + negative attitude)

Contrary to what the Court sees as "permissible public use" (Source C), I believe that a government taking a person's home or business away and allowing another private individual or company to take it over goes against the idea of our private property rights. A good example of this is the situation in Lakewood, Ohio, where the mayor wants to condemn a retired couple's home in order to make way for a privately owned, high-end condominium and shopping mall. As Jim Saleet said in his interview with *60 Minutes*, "The bottom line is this is morally wrong . . . This is our home . . . We're not blighted. . . . This is a close-knit, beautiful neighborhood" (Source B). The Saleets, who have paid off their mortgage, should be allowed to remain there as long as they want and pass it on to their children. Here, individual rights should prevail.

- Uses the transition device of repeating a phrase from the previous paragraph
- Maintains the personal with *I*
- Backs up personal position with the *60 Minutes* interview of the Saleets
- Appropriately cites the sources as directed in the prompt

Body Paragraph on Point 3 (Qualifying + Broder + *60 Minutes* and mayor)
However, I must also take into consideration the need for cities and states to improve troubled urban areas and clear blighted sections with new construction, tax revenues, and jobs (Source E). If governments are blocked from arranging for needed improvements and income, decline of cities and other areas could result. For example, the mayor of Lakewood, Ohio, Madeleine Cain, claims that the city cannot make it without more tax money coming in. As she sees it, Lakewood needs more money to provide required services. "This is about Lakewood's future. Lakewood cannot survive without a strengthened tax base," Mayor Cain told *60 Minutes* (Source B). Here, it sounds like the greater good should prevail.

- Introduces ambivalence with the transitional word "however"
- Uses both the Broder source and the mayor's words from the *60 Minutes* interview to illustrate and support the qualifying position
- Appropriately cites the sources as directed in the prompt

Body Paragraph Based on Point 3 (Qualifying + Broder)
Legal experts disagree about which of the two positions is the better one. Scott Bullock of the Institute for Justice sees the principle of eminent domain as an important one for government planning and building, but not for private development (Source E). On the other hand, John Echeverria, the executive director of the Georgetown Environmental Law and Policy Institute, sees a danger in legislators going to the extreme in the opposite direction and limiting essential powers of government. "The extremist position is a prescription for economic decline for many metropolitan areas around the country" (Source E).

- Transition created by referring to "the two positions"
- Uses the Broder source to give an overview of both sides of the issue
- Appropriately cites the sources as directed in the prompt and names authorities cited in the source material

> *Note:* This is just one example of the many ways this synthesis essay could be planned and developed. The important thing to remember is YOU MUST PLAN BEFORE YOU WRITE.

DO THIS NOW.
Spend about 20 minutes writing the body of your essay. Make certain that your essay follows your plan and that you cite your sources.

Writing the Conclusion

Now that you've written the intro and body paragraphs, you can't just drop your pen or leave your laptop and walk away. You need to end your essay with a final remark. This concluding idea is the last pertinent thought you want your reader to remember concerning the significance of the issue.

> ATTENTION. ATTENTION. Avoid final paragraphs that are merely summaries. This is not a lengthy, complicated presentation. Your reader can remember what you've said in the previous paragraphs.

DO THIS NOW.
Spend about five minutes quickly writing the concluding paragraph. Keep in mind what you said in your introduction and what you developed as your major points in the body of your essay.

<u>Now, take a look at our three sample conclusions.</u>

In the case of this synthesis essay, you'll recall that our writer wanted to make four major points. The body paragraphs developed three of those ideas. What to do with the fourth: "Use the *Washington Times* survey to support my position of leaning toward those who oppose this type of eminent domain."

Our writer realizes this could be an important source to solidify the qualifying position, and it brings both sides of the argument together.

The decision is made. Use Source G to develop the concluding paragraph. The following are three sample conclusions that make use of the survey.

A

It seems that there is no right position in all circumstances. According to a *Washington Times* survey, 60% of the American public is against local governments having the power to seize private homes and businesses (Source G). However, there may be times when the greater good has to win the toss.

B

Finally, 60% of the responders to a *Washington Times*/CNN survey opposed the right of eminent domain to local governments. Even though this may seem to be the most compelling position on this issue, there are going to be special circumstances when the greater good trumps private ownership.

C

Ultimately, I have to agree with the large majority of people who responded to recent polls conducted by both the *Washington Times* and CNN. When asked if local governments should be able to take over private homes and businesses, over 60% said "no" (Source G). But, I will have to be open to the possibility that public use and the greater good may, in some cases, be the only viable solution to a complicated problem.

Which of these concluding paragraphs is similar to yours? Are there any changes you would make in your ending? If so, what are they?

Sample Synthesis Essay from the Master Exam

The following is the complete essay that our writer developed for the eminent domain synthesis prompt, which is found in the Master exam.

Every time that my grandparents visit, I have to vacate my bedroom so that they can have a room of their own during their visit. It's always a painful few days because I'm locked out of the room that I've decorated, the room that holds all of my things; it's the room that's "mine." As my mother always says, "It's for the good of the family." But, no matter how much I feel deprived, I always know that I'll have it back in a few days. However, the results would be different if she applied the principle of "eminent domain." I would lose my room permanently, and it would be turned into a real guest room. I would not be a happy family member.

Because of this experience, I can empathize with the home owners affected by the recent 5:4 Supreme Court decision *Kelo v. New London* that cited a section of the Fifth Amendment to the *U.S. Constitution* that states, "nor shall private property be taken for public use, without just compensation" (Source A). The Court ruled that New London, Connecticut, was within its constitutional rights to take private property and give it to another private individual in order to further the economic development of the city (Source C).

Contrary to what the Court sees as "permissible public use" (Source C), I believe that a government taking a person's home or business away and allowing another private individual or company to take it over goes against the idea of our private property rights. A good example of this is the situation in Lakewood, Ohio, where the mayor wants to condemn a retired couple's home in order to make way for a privately owned, high-end condominium and shopping mall. As Jim Saleet said in his interview with *60 Minutes*, "The bottom line is this is morally wrong . . . This is our home . . . We're not blighted. . . . This is a close-knit, beautiful neighborhood" (Source B). The Saleets, who have paid off their mortgage, should be allowed to remain there as long as they want and pass it on to their children. Here, individual rights should prevail.

However, I must also take into consideration the need for cities and states to improve troubled urban areas and clear blighted sections with new construction, tax revenues, and jobs (Source E). If governments are blocked from arranging for needed improvements and income, decline of cities and other areas could result. For example, the mayor of Lakewood, Ohio, Madeleine Cain, claims that the city cannot make it without more tax money coming in. As she sees it, Lakewood needs more money to provide required services. "This is about Lakewood's future. Lakewood cannot survive without a strengthened tax base," Mayor Cain told *60 Minutes* (Source B). Here, it sounds like the greater good should prevail.

Legal experts disagree about which of the two positions is the better one. Scott Bullock of the Institute for Justice sees the principle of eminent domain as an important one for government planning and building, but not for private development (Source E). On the other hand, John Echeverria, the executive director of the Georgetown Environmental Law and Policy Institute, sees a danger in legislators going to the extreme in the opposite direction and limiting essential powers of government. "The extremist position is a prescription for economic decline for many metropolitan areas around the country" (Source E).

Ultimately, I have to agree with the large majority of people who responded to recent polls conducted by both the *Washington Times* and CNN. When asked if local governments should be able to take over private homes and businesses, over 60% said "no" (Source G). But, I will have to be open to the possibility that public use and the greater good may, in some cases, be the only viable solution to a complicated problem.

Sample Student Essays

Student A

Eminent domain. Two little words that strike fear in the hearts of homeowners all over the country. But what exactly is it anyway? Eminent domain is the power of the government to take privately owned property away for "public use" as long as the original owners are given "fair" compensation for it. (Source A) However, the more the government exercises this power given to it by the Fifth Amendment, the more the public feels the need to curtail it.

1

I agree with those opposing this governmental sledge hammer. My parents own their own house and have spent much of their lives paying off the mortgage, and now it is finally ours. I would never want to give it away—just compensation or not. The same appears to be true for Jim and Joanne Saleet who live in Lakewood, Ohio, who in a *60 Minutes* interview described their feelings about their mayor, Madeleine Cain, deciding to invoke this right of eminent domain. The mayor's reason for seizing this house that the Saleets "plan to spend the rest of their days [in] and pass on to their grandchildren" is not to build a needed highway or a hospital. NO, it is to build a high-end shopping mall (Source B). This is hardly justifiable—the neighborhood being seized is just your basic middle class suburbia—much like the house you most likely live in. Much like the house 80% of America lives in.

2

Since the Saleets, their neighbors in Scenic Park don't want to leave, the mayor has labeled Scenic Park, ironically enough, as "blighted." This has created a negative picture of the area in the public's mind. Jim Saleet told *60 Minutes*, "You don't know how humiliating this is to have people tell you, 'You live in a blighted area,' and how degrading this is. . . . This is an area that we absolutely love." (Source B) The intent of the new classier condos and mall is to raise Lakewood's property tax revenues, but so far, by calling the area "blighted," all they have done is to lower the reputation of Scenic Park. As Mr. Saleet said, "This is morally wrong, what they're doing here. This is our home." (Source B)

3

Some might say, "Well, this is just one small town example with just one guy's opinion." This is hardly so. In a CNN commissioned survey of 177,987 voters, 66% of those who responded said that local government should never be able to seize homes and businesses. Only 33% said it should be permitted for public use, and only a measly 1% voted to allow eminent domain for private economic development. (Source G)

4

Cities have claimed that invoking the right of eminent domain is being done to further "the greater good." And, yet, as the CNN survey shows, the masses who are supposedly benefiting from it either are not feeling this greater good or just plain don't appreciate

5

it. In either case, something tells me that if most people are not happy about a situation something ought to be done about it. (We are still living in a democracy aren't we?)

Some have tried to stop it. But, the Supreme Court ruled on February 22, 2005, in the case of *Kelo v. City of New London* that "the governmental taking of property from one private owner to give to another in furtherance of economic development constitutes a permissible 'public use' under the Fifth Amendment." (Source C) This decision not only went against what the vast majority of the public feels, but it also was made with a very narrow margin of 5:4. This is because the Fifth Amendment doesn't state any specifics regarding what public use is, only that the owner of the property seized must be duly compensated. 6

The Supreme Court's narrow margin of votes demonstrates how heavily disputed this topic is. The public feels that their individual rights are being infringed upon—and I'm on their side. 7

Student B

The debate over government's authority over private property and the seizing of it has been heard ever since the creation of the Constitution. For over two hundred years, both federal and local governments alike have been taking private property for public use (with compensation): a power known as eminent domain. While government officials have used this right to help build public services such as roads and railroad tracks, they have also used this power under the label of "economic development" to benefit private corporations that build these projects. 1

Government should be allowed to take private property only for the creation of public goods and services. This right is stated in the Fifth Amendment of the Constitution, which deals with the issue of private property rights (Source A). However, the term "public use" is ambiguous and is open for much interpretation. Eminent domain should be used to build services like roads and schools. As the nation grows, and new economic centers develop, there is a need for the creation of new roads. The land for these roads needs to be taken from somewhere, and often times the only option is to take land from private owners. A similar situation arises when towns need to build new schools because of growing population pressures. Scott G. Bullock of the Institute for Justice concurs when he says, "It [eminent domain] has an important but limited role in government planning and the building of roads, parks, and public buildings" (Source E). 2

Although the Supreme Court in *Kelo v. New London* ruled that eminent domain can be used to seize private property to sell to private buyers for economic development that would benefit a needy area (Source C), the results of this power can cause unnecessary displacement and pain for the individuals whose homes are part of this "buy out." The Saleets of Lakewood, Ohio, present one example of this situation. This couple has been living in their home for 38 years and feels that the government is morally wrong in trying to evict them from their house in order to create high priced condos and shopping malls. The area in question is not a run down locale; therefore, it doesn't need renovation. The 3 mayor of Lakewood claims the city needs money, and that the "area can be used for a higher and better use" (Source B).

However, it can also be argued that there is always room for improvement when it comes to the use of land, especially because of the ever changing needs and desires of people and governments. The United States was built on the principle of capitalism and private enterprise. It is not run with a planned economy as communist nations are. Therefore, the economy should be allowed to take its own course without government interference. The invisible hand of the free market guiding the economy has led and will continue to lead to better outcomes for the entire society.

4

Additionally, because the government is run by the people and for the benefit of the people, the public's opinion should be taken into consideration. In a recent CNN poll, only 1% indicated that it affirms the right of eminent domain for private economic development. While the poll doesn't display everyone's opinion, it is a good indicator of the attitudes of American citizens (Source G).

5

Clearly, eminent domain shouldn't be invoked for economic development by private developers. It should be limited to the construction of public services. However, this debate over property rights, and in a sense, individual rights versus the greater good, will continue for years to come as the conditions and outlooks of the American people change.

6

Rating the Essays

You can view actual AP English Language and Composition rubrics by logging on to the College Board website.

The rubrics for the synthesis essay are almost identical to the rubrics for the argument essay EXCEPT for the requirement of support coming from at least three sources.

Note: For our purposes, scoring comments will be followed by one of three letters to indicate one of the three areas used in the AP English Language rubric for the synthesis essay. Thesis = (A), Evidence/Commentary = (B), Sophistication = (C)

Student A
This is a high-range essay for the following reasons:

- Opening forcefully catches the reader's attention and immediately identifies the subject via a defensible thesis (A)
- Brings the reader into the conversation with the rhetorical question (B)
- Presents a brief overview of both sides of the debate (B)
- Integrates sources smoothly into the text of the essay (B)
- Uses proper citations (B)
- Utilizes transitions (B and C)
- Exhibits control of language, for example: parallel structure, punctuation, parenthetical statements, and diction (C)
- Recognizes the opposite position—"Some might say . . ." (B)
- Employs irony to comment on textual material (B and C)

- Incorporates not only sources, but also provides pertinent comments to develop the argument (B and C)
- Presents a succinct and straightforward final point (B and C)
- Presents a true voice (C)

Student B

This is a mid-range essay for the following reasons:

- Clearly takes a position on the issue via a defensible thesis (A)
- Uses appropriate evidence (B)
- Clearly incorporates sources into the text (B)
- Cites the opposition (paragraph 4) (B)
- Presents a personal opinion (paragraph 4) (B and C)
- Develops a clear organizational pattern (B and C)
- Uses good transitions (B and C)
- Develops a final paragraph that makes a clear statement (B)
- Uses a matter-of-fact voice (C)

Rapid Review

- Read ALL information in the prompt.
- Carefully read and annotate the prompt and the given texts.
- Choose your position on the issue.
- Choose suitable texts from among those given to support your position (choose at least three).
- Plan your essay.
- Write your essay in the allotted time.
- Check your essay to make certain you have cited your sources.
- Proofread.

STEP 4

Review the Knowledge You Need to Score High

CHAPTER 8

Comprehensive Review—
Rhetorical Analysis

IN THIS CHAPTER

Summary: Examine structure, purpose, and style as evidenced in the modes of discourse.

Key Ideas

✪ Learn the language of analysis and how to use it.
✪ Acquaint yourself with rhetorical strategies.
✪ Learn how selection of detail, subject matter, diction, and syntax contribute to style.
✪ Learn how topic adherence and connective tissue unify your essay.
✪ Understand the difference between active and passive voice.

Some Basics

What Is ANALYSIS?

For the AP English Language exam student, the definition of *analysis* is quite specific. It means that *you* are going to take apart a particular passage and divide it into its basic components for the purpose of examining how the writer develops his or her subject.

Are There Different Types of Analysis?

For the AP English Language exam, the *different types of analysis* include the analysis of structure, purpose, and style.

What Is *DISCOURSE*?

Discourse simply means "conversation." For the writer, this "conversation" takes place between the text and the reader. To communicate with the reader, the writer uses a particular method or combination of methods to make his or her idea(s) clear to the reader.

What Is *RHETORIC*?

Don't let professional jargon throw you. Rhetoric is basically an umbrella term for *all* of the strategies, modes, and devices a writer can employ to allow the reader to easily accept and understand his or her point of view.

What Is a *MODE OF DISCOURSE*?

Here's another piece of the lingo puzzle that you need not fear. Prose can be divided into FOUR primary categories. They are:

1. EXPOSITION: illustrates a point
2. NARRATION: tells a story
3. DESCRIPTION: creates a sensory image
4. ARGUMENTATION: takes a position on an issue and defends it

These are generally referred to as the *modes of discourse*. You should be able to distinguish among them, but do not become bogged down in worrying about these classes. They will be obvious to you. Being familiar with the professional terminology of this course is a way of beginning to develop a common vocabulary needed to discuss writing.

What Are *RHETORICAL CHOICES*?

Note: As used in AP Lang, the term *rhetorical choices* includes example, contrast and comparison, definition, cause and effect, process, analysis/division, classification, and literary devices, such as metaphor and parallelism. The writer may also employ descriptive and narrative strategies. These are the basic approaches a writer uses to tell a story, explain a point, describe a situation, or argue a position. (Modes of discourse, for those in the know.)

What Is the Analysis of *RHETORICAL STRUCTURE*?

Regardless of the length of a passage, the writer will employ one or more strategies to develop the purpose of the piece. Your job is to:

- Carefully read the passage
- Recognize and identify strategies used in the passage
- Determine how these strategies are utilized in the development of the author's purpose

The following diagram may be of help visualizing how to organize an analysis of the rhetorical structure OR, in other words, the line of reasoning.

THE LINE OF REASONING—THE CLAIM'S LINE OF DEFENSE

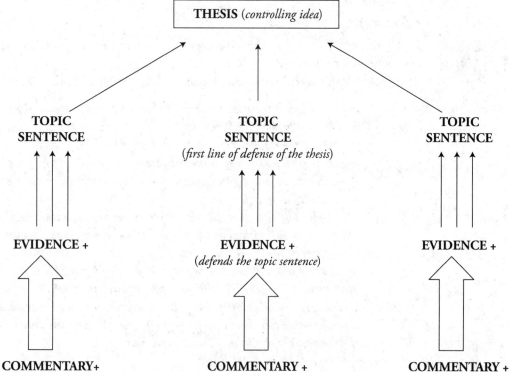

THESIS *(controlling idea)*

TOPIC SENTENCE

TOPIC SENTENCE
(first line of defense of the thesis)

TOPIC SENTENCE

EVIDENCE +

EVIDENCE +
(defends the topic sentence)

EVIDENCE +

COMMENTARY+

COMMENTARY +

COMMENTARY +

(student's opinion that ties the evidence to the topic sentence . . .
illustrates the "truth" of the topic sentence)

Based on an idea of Angie Kratzer

> After this, it is up to you to use your own rhetorical strategies/choices to present the points you want to illustrate in your analysis. Remember, your primary purpose is to analyze the passage. In so doing, you will probably employ one or more of the rhetorical strategies/choices, such as example, cause and effect, or contrast and comparison.

There Is So Much to Know, How Can I Prepare Myself for the Exam?

First, don't panic. You're in an AP English Language course, and you will have a year to become prepared. The work of this course centers on developing those analytical skills required by the AP English Language exam. In this chapter, we are going to provide you with a brief overview of the different rhetorical strategies. For each rhetorical strategy, we will do the following:

- define the term;
- cite examples;
- provide practice with analysis; and
- offer suggestions for writing your own AP essays using that strategy.

Rhetorical Strategies/Choices

Example

Definition: <u>Example</u> is a specific event, person, or detail of an idea cited and/or developed to support or illustrate a thesis or topic.

   Here is an excerpt from Jane Jacobs's "A Good Neighborhood" that uses examples.

> *Perhaps I can best explain this subtle but all-important balance between people's desire for essential privacy and their wish to have differing degrees of contact with people in terms of the stores where people leave keys for their friends. In our family, we tell friends to pick up the key at the delicatessen across the street. Joe Cornacchia, who keeps the delicatessen, usually has a dozen or so keys at a time for handing out like this. He has a special drawer for them.*
>
> *Around on the other side of our block, people leave their keys at a Spanish grocery. On the other side of Joe's block, people leave them at a candy store. Down a block they leave them at the coffee shop, and a few hundred feet around the corner from that, in a barber shop. Around one corner from two fashionable blocks of town houses and apartments in the Upper East Side, people leave their keys in a butcher shop and a bookshop; around another corner they leave them in a cleaner's and a drug store. In unfashionable East Harlem, keys are left with at least one florist, in bakeries, in luncheonettes, in Spanish and Italian groceries.*

Practice with Analysis

1. Underline the thesis statement.

2. The topic/subject of the passage is _____.

3. The purpose of the passage is to _____.

4. Does the passage contain an extended example? _____

5. The passage contains how many examples? _____

6. Briefly list the examples. _____

7. The organization is ___ chronological ___ spatial ___ least to most important ___ most to least important.

Remarks About the Passage

This informative passage uses a lengthy list of examples to indicate informally the relationship between people and businesses in a neighborhood. There is no single extended example, but rather a series of more than eight examples.

> It's a good idea to actually mark up the passage as you answer the analysis questions. It will give you practice and help this process to become second nature to you.

Contrast/Comparison

Definition: <u>Contrast/comparison</u> is a method of presenting similarities and differences between or among at least two persons, places, things, ideas, etc. The contrast/comparison essay may be organized in several ways including:

- Subject by subject—Subject A is discussed in its entirety and is followed by a full discussion of Subject B.
- Point by point—A major point related to Subject A is examined and is immediately followed with a corresponding point in Subject B.
- Combination—In a longer essay, the writer may employ both of the preceding strategies.

Here is an example of a passage that uses contrast/comparison from W. H. Auden's "Work, Labor, and Play."

> *Between labor and play stands work. A man is a worker if he is personally interested in the job which society pays him to do; and that which society views as necessary labor, is from his own point of view voluntary play. Whether a job is to be classified as labor or work depends, not on the job itself, but on the tastes of the individual who undertakes it. The difference does not, for example, coincide with the difference between a manual and a mental job; a gardener or a cobbler may be a worker; a bank clerk, a laborer. Which a man is can be seen from his attitude toward leisure. To a worker, leisure means simply the hours he needs to relax and rest in order to work efficiently. He is therefore more likely to take too little leisure than too much; workers die of coronaries and forget their wives' birthdays. To the laborer, on the other hand, leisure means freedom from compulsion, so that it is natural for him to imagine that the fewer hours he has to spend laboring, the more hours he is free to play, the better.*

Practice with Analysis

1. The topic/subject of the passage is _____.
2. Underline the thesis statement.
3. The purpose of the passage is to _____.
4. The items being compared/contrasted are _____.
5. One example of a comparison in the passage is _____.
6. One example of contrast in the passage is _____.
7. The pattern of development is ____ opposing ____ alternating.
8. The organization is ____ subject to subject ____ point by point ____ combination.

Remarks About the Passage

As with most of your AP contrast/comparison selections, the emphasis is on distinction and contrast. In this passage, the author uses a pattern of alternating points that develops the contrast between work, labor, and leisure.

Cause and Effect

KEY IDEA

Definition: Cause and effect establishes a relationship: B is the result of A. The cause-and-effect essay can emphasize the cause or the effect, or can treat both equally. It can detail a single cause with many effects, or several causes with a single effect, or any combination. The organization can present the cause or the effect first. All of this depends upon the intent of the writer. Depending on his or her purpose, the writer can choose to present the most important idea in the beginning, middle, or end. The author can also choose from myriad strategies to develop the cause and effect, such as:

- facts
- statistics
- authorities
- anecdotes
- cases
- real or imagined scenarios

It should be noted that, in some cases, the successful writer of a cause-and-effect essay anticipates and addresses reader objections and/or questions.

Here is an example of a passage using cause and effect from Thomas Hobbes's "Of the Natural Condition of Mankind" (1651).

> *From this equality of ability arises equality of hope in the attaining of our ends. And therefore if any two men desire the same thing, which nevertheless they cannot both enjoy, they become enemies; and in the way to their end (which is principally their own conservation, and sometimes their delectation only), endeavor to destroy or subdue one another. And from hence it comes to pass that where an invader has no more fear than another man's single power, if one plant, sow, build, or possess a convenient seat, others may probably be expected to come prepared with forces united to dispossess and deprive him, not only of the fruit of his labor, but also of his life, or liberty. And the invader again is in like danger of another.*

Practice with Analysis

1. Underline the thesis statement.

2. The topic/subject of the passage is _____.

3. The purpose of the passage is to _____.

4. List the causes. _____

5. List the effects. _____

6. The emphasis is on ____ cause ____ effect ____ causes ____ effects.

7. The passage makes use of ____ statistics ____ facts ____ authorities ____ anecdotes ____ cases ____ real/imaginary scenarios.

Remarks About the Passage

The entire focus of this paragraph is on the singular result of one person's envy for the possessions of another. If both cannot possess it, envy ensues, which leads to dispossession and/or violence.

Classification

Definition: Classification separates items into major categories and details the characteristics of each group and why each member of that group is placed within the category. It is possible to divide the categories into subgroups. The principle of classification should be made clear to the reader. (This is the umbrella term under which everything fits.)

Here is a passage that makes use of classification from Jane Howard's "All Happy Clans Are Alike."

> *. . . If blood and roots don't do the job, then we must look to water and branches, and sort ourselves into new constellations, new families.*

These new families, to borrow the terminology of an African tribe (the Bangwa of the Cameroons), may consist either of friends of the road, ascribed by chance, or friends of the heart, achieved by choice. Ascribed friends are those we happen to go to school with, work with, or live near. They know where we went last weekend and whether we still have a cold. Just being around gives them a provisional importance in our lives, and us in theirs. Maybe they will still matter to us when we or they move away; quite likely they won't. Six months or two years will probably erase each from the other's thoughts, unless by some chance they and we have become friends of the heart. . . . [Those] will steer each other through enough seasons and weathers so that sooner or later it crosses our minds that one of us . . . must one day mourn the other.

Practice with Analysis

1. The topic/subject of the passage is _____.

2. Underline the thesis statement.

3. The purpose of the passage is to _____.

4. Identify the principle of division/classification. _____

5. List the main subgroups. _____

6. Cite the major characteristic(s) of each subgroup. _____

Remarks About the Passage

This passage briefly details two classes of friends, one by chance and the other by choice. The thesis given at the beginning of the excerpt is stated in general terms that lead the reader to the specific classifications.

Process

Definition: Process is simply "how to" do something or how something is done. Process can have one of two purposes. It can either give instructions or inform the reader about how something is done. It is important to understand that a clear process presentation must be in chronological order. In other words, the writer leads the reader step by step, from beginning to end, through the process. A clear process essay will define necessary terms and will cite any precautions if needed.

Here is a passage that makes use of process from L. Rust Hills's "How to Care for and About Ashtrays."

To clean ashtrays the right way, proceed as follows. Take a metal or plastic or wooden (but never a basket) wastebasket in your left hand, and a paper towel in your right. Approach the ashtray that is to be cleaned. Put the wastebasket down on the floor, and with your released left hand pick up the ashtray and dump its contents of cigarette ends, spent matches, and loose ashes (nothing else should be in an ashtray!) into the wastebasket. Then, still holding the ashtray over the basket, rub gently with the paper towel at any of the few stains or spots that may remain. Then put the ashtray carefully back into its place, pick up the wastebasket again, and approach the next ashtray to be cleaned. It should never be necessary to wash an ashtray, if it is kept clean and dry. Throughout its whole lifetime in a well-ordered household, an ashtray need never travel more than three feet from where it belongs, and never be out of place at all for more than thirty seconds.

Practice with Analysis

1. Underline the thesis.

2. What is the topic/subject? _____

3. The general purpose is to ____ give specific directions ____ be informative.

4. List the major steps given in the selection. _____

5. Is the essay in chronological order? ____ yes ____ no

6. List any words that are defined. _____

7. Were there any other words that should have been defined? _____

   _____

8. List any precautions given. _____

9. The process presented is ____ clear ____ unclear ____ complete ____ incomplete.

Remarks About the Passage

The formal tone of such a menial process makes this small paragraph a bit humorous. Its clearly developed ashtray cleaning process is quite complete and needs no added definitions nor precautions.

Definition

Definition: Definition identifies the class to which a specific term belongs and those characteristics which make it different from all the other items in that class. There are several types of definitions: physical, historical, emotional, psychological, and relationship(s) to others.

An essay of definition can be developed using any of the rhetorical strategies, and the writer should decide whether to be serious or humorous.

Here is a passage that uses definition.

BUGDUST

The dinner was fine, the play funny; let's hope my drive home will easily top off a relaxing and rewarding evening. What a surprise! Brightly perched on my car's windshield is a yellow ticket which not so brightly announces that I am being fined $50.00 for an expired parking meter. Grabbing the thing and choking it, I exclaim, "Bugdust!"

Now, let's be honest. This ticket is neither an insect, nor is it dirt. So, am I blind, ignorant or just plain crazy? I hope none of the above. The expletive, "Bugdust," is my personal substitute for the ever-popular, overused and vulgar, four letter curses. My background forces me to avoid these common, rude and inappropriate four letter words. And, heaven only knows that over the years I've had many occasions where I would have loved to use them. For much of my young life, when I found myself in a situation which cried out for some sort of exclamation, I usually reverted to RATS! or CRUMB! Really harsh curses, huh? However, years ago I came upon a substitute by sheer accident.

I was helping out in the kitchen at my sorority house. While chopping onions, I accidentally slipped and cut my thumb quite badly. I really needed a way to express my surprise, pain, and fear. Nothing inside my head would allow me to scream the usual expletives words. (By the way, I sincerely believe that a good deal of money spent on psychotherapy could have been saved had I been able to "just say IT.") In that nanosecond, I wanted, I demanded that my mind come up with something—anything—that I could use. My mind obviously obeyed and began working at a frantic pace. "I hate insects; I hate housework." My mind works in strange ways; it's really warped. (Hmm, that's a word I should also define.) Put two abominable conditions together. Voila! Murf's rule = one new expression = BUGDUST. What a mind!

The people around me during the birth of this little word-gem said, "What the *@#?! does that mean?" I had to stop for a second. They were right. What did it mean? It was not the incinerated remains of a roach colony. It was not the unkempt environs of a roach motel. It was a way for me to say that I was monumentally angry. It was also a way for me to say I was hurting. It was original and ME.

Years have passed. And, so today . . .

It's 15°; it's snowing and icy; I'm cold. Let's shop. I join the rest of the universe at the supermarket. Heaven only knows one needs rice crispy treats in the house when it snows. What I don't need is the keys locked in my car. BUGDUST!

I'm doing 7 mph behind a 1965 Volkswagen Beetle being driven by its original owner. I miss the green light. I'm late for my dental appointment. BUGDUST!

And, into cyberspace . . . My computer just crashed. BUGDUST!

Practice with Analysis

1. Underline the thesis.

2. The topic/subject is _____.

3. The purpose is to _____.

4. The attitude of the writer is ____ serious ____ humorous.

5. To what class does the word being defined belong? _____

6. List the major rhetorical strategies used. _____

7. The definition is ____ historical ____ physical ____ emotional ____ psychological ____ relationship(s) to others.

8. Do you, as a reader, have an understanding of the definition presented? _____

9. Briefly state your understanding of the term. _____

Remarks About the Passage

The topic of the essay is the definition of the expletive *bugdust*. The thesis is the fifth sentence of the second paragraph. The primary purpose is to humorously narrate the invention of the word "bugdust." The rhetorical strategies used throughout the essay are example [paragraph 1] and anecdote [paragraphs 3 and 4]. The definition of *bugdust* is primarily emotional [last two sentences in paragraph 3 and the last two sentences in paragraph 4].

Now it's your turn. Write a paragraph that defines a favorite word that is special or unique to you or your friends or family. Choose an attitude and go for it. When finished, ask yourself the same analytical questions you asked for the sample essay.

Narration

Definition: Narration is nothing more than storytelling. There is a beginning, a middle, and an end. Moreover, there's a point to it—a reason for recounting the story that becomes clear to the reader. There should be a focus to the story as well. For example, your point might be that lying gets you into trouble. To illustrate this, you might focus on an anecdote about the repercussions of a specific lie you told your parents. Narration requires a specific point of view, such as:

- 1st person
- 3rd person omniscient
- 3rd person objective
- Stream of consciousness

A narrative generally revolves around a primary tension and employs character, plot, and setting. The point the author is trying to make corresponds to the literary term *theme*. The development of a narrative may be extended and fully developed or brief to support or illustrate the subject of an essay.

The following excerpt from "Death of a Soldier" by Louisa May Alcott is an example of a narrative.

> *John was dying. Even while he spoke, over his face I saw a gray veil falling that no human hand can lift. I sat down by him, wiped drops from his forehead, stirred the air about him with a slow wave of a fan, and waited to help him die. For hours he suffered dumbly, without a moment's murmuring: his limbs grew cold, his face damp, his lips white, and again and again he tore the covering off his breast, as if the lightest weight added to his agony.*
>
> *One by one, the other men woke, and round the hospital ward appeared a circle of pale faces and watchful eyes, full of awe and pity; for, though a stranger, John was beloved by all. "Old boy, how are you?" faltered one. "Can I say or do anything for you anywheres?" whispered another.*
>
> *"Take my things home, and tell them that I did my best."*

Practice with Analysis

1. The topic/subject is _____.

2. The purpose is to _____.

3. The focus is _____.

4. The point of view is ____ first person ____ third person objective ____ third person omniscient ____ stream of consciousness.

5. The setting is _____.

6. The main character(s) is/are _____.

7. The gist of the plot is _____.

8. List the sequence of the major events (beginning, middle, end)

   _____

   _____

Remarks About the Passage

This brief excerpt is enough of a story to allow you to identify the basic narrative elements. Employing the first person point of view, Alcott provides a beginning, middle, and ending to this episode that occurs in a hospital ward. Focusing on the boy's death, the author illustrates the quality of John's character.

Description

> KEY IDEA

Definition: <u>Description</u> is writing that appeals to the senses. It can be objective, which is scientific or clinical, or it can be impressionistic, which tries to involve the reader's emotions or feelings. Description can also be direct or indirect, and the organization can be as follows:

- Chronological
- Spatial
- Emphasizing the most important detail
- Emphasizing the most noticeable detail

To create his or her description, the writer can employ any or all of the following literary devices:

- Analogy
- Concrete, specific words
- Appeal to the senses
- Personification
- Hyperbole
- Contrast and comparison
- Onomatopoeia
- Other figurative language

The following excerpt from Charles Dickens's *Bleak House* uses description.

> *Fog everywhere. Fog up the river, where it flows among green aits and meadows; fog down the river, where it rolls defiled among tiers of shipping and waterside pollutions of a great (and dirty) city. Fog on the Essex marshes, fog on the heights, fog creeping into the cabooses of [coal barges]. Fog lying out on the yards, and hovering in the rigging of great ships; fog drooping on the gunwales of barges and small boats. Fog in the eyes and throats of ancient Greenwich pensioners, wheezing by the firesides of their wards; fog in the stem and bowl of the afternoon pipe of the wrathful skipper, down in his close cabin; fog cruelly pinching the toes and fingers of his shivering little 'prentice boy on deck. Chance people on the bridges peeping over the parapets into a nether sky of fog, with fog all round them, as if they were up in a balloon, and hanging in the misty clouds.*

Practice with Analysis

1. Underline the thesis.

2. The topic/subject of the passage is _____.

3. The description is ____ objective ____ impressionistic.

4. The passage contains examples of

   - ____ analogy, ex. _____
   - ____ concrete words, ex. _____
   - ____ imagery, ex. _____
   - ____ contrast/comparison, ex. _____
   - ____ personification, ex. _____
   - ____ onomatopoeia, ex. _____
   - ____ other figurative language, ex. _____

5. The intended effect is to _____.

Remarks About the Passage

In its appeal to the senses, this loaded passage about fog contains about every descriptive device possible to re-create the almost palpable scene for the reader.

About Style

> *Note:* Although the style is a designated component of AP English Literature, it is impossible to analyze an author's presentation and purpose without discussing the many elements associated with what we call style.

What Is Style?

Ask yourself a question—What is the difference between two comedians who are familiar to you? They may both be funny, but in different ways. What makes one comedian's humor different from the other's is his distinctive style.

Consider the following:

- Subject matter
- Language (diction)
- Pacing
- Selection of detail
- Presentation—body language
- Attitude toward the material
- Attitude toward the audience

This is what we call style. You do this all the time. You know Jennifer Lopez has a different style than does Adele.

If we were to give you two literary passages, you could probably tell which was written by Hemingway and which was written by Dickens. How would you know? Simple; you would use the same principles you considered with the two comedians:

- Subject matter
- Selection of detail
- Point of view
- Diction
- Figurative language/imagery
- Attitude
- Tone
- Pacing/syntax
- Organization

See how easy it is? The AP English Language and Composition exam expects you to be able to recognize and to explain how these elements function in a given passage.

How Do I Talk About Style?

You need to understand and to refer to some basic writing terms and devices. These include subject matter, selection of detail, organization, point of view, diction, syntax, language, attitude, and tone.

What follows is a brief review of each of these *elements of style*. In this review, we define each device, cite examples, and provide practice for you. (In addition, we have incorporated suggested readings and writing for you.)

Subject Matter and Selection of Detail

Since these two are dependent on each other, let's look at them together. Unlike the poor, beleaguered AP Comp student who is assigned a topic, each author makes a conscious decision about what he or she will write. (In most instances, so do you.) It is not hit or miss. The author wants to make a point about his or her subject and makes numerous conscious decisions about which details to include and which to exclude. Here's an example. Two students are asked to write about hamburgers. One is a vegetarian, and one is a hamburger fanatic. You've already mentally categorized the details each would choose to include in making his or her points about hamburgers. Got it? Selection of detail is part of style.

Note: Many authors become associated with a particular type of subject matter: for example, Mario Puzo with organized crime (*The Godfather*), Steven King with horror and suspense (*The Shining*), Upton Sinclair with muckraking (*The Jungle*). This, then, becomes part of their recognized style.

Think about a couple of your favorite writers, rock groups, singers, comedians, and so on and list their primary subjects and selection of details.

Organization

The way in which a writer presents his or her ideas to the reader is termed *organization*. You do this every day. For example, look at your locker. How are your books, jacket, gym clothes, lunch, and other things arranged in it? If someone else were to open it, what conclusion would that person draw about you? This is your personal organization. The same can apply to a writer and his or her work. Let's review a few favorite patterns of organization.

Writers can organize their thoughts in many different ways, including:

- Chronological
- Spatial
- Specific to general
- General to specific
- Least to most important
- Most to least important
- Flashback or fast-forward
- Contrast/comparison
- Cause/effect

As with your locker, an outside viewer—known here as the reader—responds to the writer's organizational patterns. Keep these approaches in mind when analyzing style. (You might want to make marginal notes on some of your readings as practice.)

Point of View

Point of view is the method the author utilizes to tell the story. It is the vantage point from which the narrative is told. You've had practice with this in both reading and writing. For AP Language purposes, here are a few examples:

- *First person:* The narrator is the story's protagonist. (I went to the store.)
  Here is an example from Charles Dickens's *The Personal History of David Copperfield.*

> *Whether I shall turn out to be the hero of my own life, or whether that station will be held by anybody else, these pages must show. To begin my life with the beginning of my life, I record that I was born (as I have been informed and believe) on a Friday, at twelve o'clock at night. It was remarked that the clock began to strike, and I began to cry, simultaneously.*

- *Third person objective:* The narrator is an onlooker reporting the story. (She went to the store.)

   Here is an example from Sinclair Lewis's *Elmer Gantry*.

   > *Elmer Gantry was drunk. He was eloquently drunk, lovingly and pugnaciously drunk. He leaned against the bar of the Old Home Sample Room, the most gilded and urbane saloon in Cato, Missouri, and requested the bartender to join him in "The Good Old Summer time," the waltz of the day.*

- *Third person omniscient:* The narrator reports the story and provides information that the character(s) is unaware of. (She went to the store unaware that in three minutes she would meet her unknown mother selling apples on the corner.)

   Here is an example from Evan S. Connell's *Mrs. Bridge*.

   > *Her first name was India—she was never able to get used to it. It seemed to her that her parents must have been thinking of someone else when they named her. Or were they hoping for another sort of daughter? As a child she was often on the point of inquiring, but time passed, and she never did.*

- *Stream of consciousness:* This is a narrative technique that places the reader in the mind and thought process of the narrator, no matter how random and spontaneous that may be (e.g., James Joyce's *Ulysses*).

   Here is an example from William Faulkner's *As I Lay Dying*.

   > *I dont know what I am. I dont know if I am or not. Jewel knows who he is, because he does not know that he does not know whether he is or not. He cannot empty himself because he is not what he is and he is what he is not. Beyond the unlamped wall I can hear the rain shaping the wagon that is ours . . . And then I must be, or I could not empty myself for sleep in a strange room. And so if I am not emptied yet, I am is.*

- *Interior monologue:* This technique reflects the inner thoughts of the character.

Diction

Diction, also termed *word choice*, refers to the conscious selection of words to further the author's purpose. Once again, place yourself in the writer's position. How would you describe your date last weekend to your parents? Your peers? Yourself? We're guessing you used different words (and selection of details) for each audience. And, may we say, "good choice."

That personal note out of the way, a writer searches for the most appropriate, evocative, or precise word or phrase to convey his or her intent. The author is sensitive to denotation, connotation, and symbolic aspects of language choices.

<u>Diction is placing the right word in the right place.</u> It is a deliberate technique to further the author's purpose or intent. Diction builds throughout a piece so that ideas, tone, or attitude are continually reinforced. You should be able to identify and link examples of specific diction to the ideas, purpose, tone, or intent of the passage.

For Example

Here is the bare-bones outline of a paragraph.

> *Jonathan I. was a thin guy. He seemed to be smart when he spoke. He didn't smile, and he looked like he was really feeling down.*

Here's how Oliver Sachs actually wrote his paragraph in *The Case of the Colorblind Painter* about one of his patients.

> *When we first saw him, on April 13, 1986, Jonathan I. was a tall, gaunt man, showing obvious recent weight loss. He spoke intelligently and well, both analytically and vividly, but in a soft and rather lifeless voice. He rarely smiled; he was manifestly depressed. We got a sense of inner pain, fear, and tension, held in with difficulty beneath his civilized discourse.*

Highlight those changes in words/phrases that transform the tone and effect of the passage.

In this brief paragraph that describes Oliver Sachs's first meeting with his subject, we can easily see the effect of diction. Jonathan is not just thin. He is a series: *tall* and *gaunt* and, most importantly, showing *obvious* signs of *recent weight loss*. This begins to set the reader up for the possibility that Mr. I. is not well. Using *soft* and *rather lifeless* to describe his voice further strengthens the impression of a man who is ill. Sachs calmly lists what he sees and draws conclusions from these details which allow him to state that Jonathan is *manifestly depressed*.

See how the diction enriches the paragraph. Here, the reader begins to get a feeling for Sachs's patient.

> Would you compose a sentence such as: *The author uses words. The author uses word choice.* Of course not. You'd make certain to describe what type of words the author uses. You'd choose the adjective or adverb that best describes that choice of words. You could also indicate what you think the author intended with this word choice.
>
> Here are a few descriptors that could be placed before *diction*: formal, informal, sarcastic, aggressive, academic, supportive, argumentative, forceful.
>
> To avoid *The author uses diction*, you might try one of the following:
>
> The author's diction creates a tone. (SAYS/DOES)
>
> The author's ___ language helps him/her to ___ because ___. (WHAT/WHY)
>
> Words/phrases such as "___" and "___" help to create a sense of ___. (WHAT/WHY)
>
> Words/phrases such as "___" and "___" help the author to ___. (SAYS/DOES)

Figurative Language and Imagery

Imagery is the written creation of sensory experience achieved through the use of figurative language. Figurative language includes the following:

- Analogy
- Sensory description
- Poetic devices, which include:
  — metaphor
  — simile

— hyperbole
— onomatopoeia
— personification
— oxymoron
— metonymy
— synecdoche
— alliteration
— assonance
— consonance

As an example, here is a passage excerpted from Thoreau's *Walden*, Chapter 4, "Sounds."

> *I watch the passage of the morning cars with the same feeling that I do the rising of the sun, which is hardly more regular. Their train of clouds stretching far behind and rising higher and higher, going to heaven while the cars are going to Boston, conceals the sun for a minute and casts my distant field into the shade, a celestial train beside which the petty train of cars which hugs the earth is but the barb of the spear. The stabler of the iron horse was up early this winter morning by the light of the stars amid the mountains, to fodder and harness his steed. Fire, too, was awakened thus early to put the vital heat in him and get him off. If the enterprise were as innocent as it is early! If the snow lies deep, they strap on his snowshoes, and, with the giant plow, plow a furrow from the mountains to the seaboard, in which the cars, like a following drill-barrow, sprinkle all the restless men and floating merchandise in the country for seed. All day the fire-steed flies over the country, stopping only that his master may rest, and I am awakened by his tramp and defiant snort at midnight, when in some remote glen in the woods he fronts the elements incased in ice and snow; and he will reach his stall only with the morning star, to start once more on his travels without rest or slumber. Or perchance, at evening, I hear him in his stable blowing off the superfluous energy of the day, that he may calm his nerves and cool his liver and brain for a few hours of iron slumber. If the enterprise were as heroic and commanding as it is protracted and unwearied!*

Can you recognize the different examples of figurative language used in this paragraph? List several now.

Syntax

Risking your closing the book, we are going to use the dreaded "G" word—*grammar*. Grammar refers to the function of words and their uses and relationship in a sentence. Syntax is the grammatical structure of sentences. Without syntax, there is no clear communication. It is the responsibility of the author to manipulate language so that his or her purpose and intent are clear to the reader.

Note: When we refer to syntax in the context of rhetorical analysis, we are not speaking of grammatical correctness, but rather of the deliberate sentence structure the author chooses to make his or her desired point.

We assume that you are already familiar with the basics of sentence structure and are able to recognize and clearly construct:

- phrases;
- clauses;
- basic sentence types: declarative, interrogative, imperative, exclamatory;
- simple sentences;
- compound sentences;

- complex sentences;
- compound–complex sentences;
- periodic sentence;
- cumulative sentence; and
- rhetorical question.

We also assume that you have a good working knowledge of:

- punctuation,
- spelling, and
- paragraphing.

If you are in doubt about any of these items, you could refer to grammar/syntax sites on the internet for explanations, examples, and practice activities. We also recommend *The Elements of Style* by Strunk and White. And, don't forget, your teacher is your major resource who can provide you with information and practice. Be honest with yourself. If you need help, get it early in the term.

Carefully read the following passage for *more practice with syntax.*

> *It struck eight. Bella waited. Nobody came.*
>
> *She sat down on a gilt chair at the head of the stairs, looked steadily before her with her blank, blue eyes. In the hall, in the cloakroom, in the supper-room, the hired footmen looked at one another with knowing winks. "What does the old girl expect? No one'll have finished dinner before ten."*
>
> — (*Mr. Loveday's Little Outing*; "Bella Gave a Party," Evelyn Waugh, 1936)

Did you notice the following syntactical elements and their effects in this selection?

- Short declarative sentences
  - — Repetitiveness is like the ticking of a clock
  - — Immediately introduces tension
- Simple declarative sentence beginning with subject/verbs
  - — Parallel structure with phrases beginning with *in*
  - — Pacing: clock ticking away time, uncaring
- Periodic sentence draws attention to the setting rather than the footmen
- Ends with a rhetorical question: reader drawn into the tension

You can see from just a brief analysis of the sentence structure of this passage that syntax plays an important role in the creation of character, setting, and tension.

We recommend that you choose brief passages from works which you study in your AP Comp class and practice this process on them throughout the year.

Here is a sentence structure activity you can use to review creating sentences using coordination and subordination.

Consider the following set of sentences.

I write.
I have a writing problem.
The problem is wordiness.
This tendency leads me somewhere.
It leads me to my writing awkward sentences.

These sentences confuse my readers.
I must edit my writing.
I must be very careful.

Rewrite this set of simple sentences THREE different ways, with each new sentence containing ALL of the information given. Each new sentence is to emphasize a different simple sentence (main clause) given in the original set. Bracket the clause you are emphasizing in each new sentence.

> You might wish to work on this type of activity throughout the year with your class or with an AP Comp study group that you have formed.

Tone and Attitude

We are guessing that these terms have confused you, as indeed, they have confused our own students in the past. Both terms refer to the author's perception and presentation of the material and the audience.

Tone, which often reinforces the mood of a piece, is easy to understand. Think of Edgar Allen Poe and the prevailing mood and tone of a short story such as "The Telltale Heart." There is no doubt that the single effect of this story is macabre horror, which clearly establishes the tone.

An author's attitude is not just the creation of a mood. It represents the stance or relationship the author has toward his or her subject. This type of analysis may require that you "read between the lines," which is the close reading of diction and syntax.

There are some basics for you to consider when determining tone and attitude.

The author can indicate several attitudes toward the reader:

- Talking down to the reader as an advisor
- Talking down to the reader as a satirist
- Talking eye-to-eye with the reader as an equal
- Talking up to the reader as a supplicant or subordinate

The attitude may also be formal or informal.

- Formal tends to use diction and syntax that are academic, serious, and authoritative.
- Informal is more conversational and engages the reader on an equal basis.

In "The Telltale Heart," it is fairly obvious that the diction and syntax help to create a macabre tone. At the same time, Poe's highly academic and mature diction and syntax create a formal attitude as he relates his tale to his reader as an equal.

Jonathan Swift in "A Modest Proposal" presents a satiric attitude as he speaks down to (instructs) his audience. Likewise, Charles Lamb in "A Dissertation on Roast Pig" engages his reader with an informal attitude in his satire.

If you want to see a subservient or subordinate attitude, see Chief Seattle's speech in our Practice Exam 1, essay question 2. Here, you will see how he employs diction and syntax to create a mocking humility that would serve his greater purpose.

The following is a list of adjectives often used to describe tone and attitude in a literary work. Feel free to add your own appropriate words.

bitter	objective	idyllic
sardonic	naïve	compassionate
sarcastic	joyous	reverent
ironic	spiritual	lugubrious

mocking	wistful	elegiac
scornful	nostalgic	gothic
satiric	humorous	macabre
vituperative	mock-serious	reflective
scathing	pedantic	maudlin
confidential	didactic	sentimental
factual	inspiring	patriotic
informal	remorseful	jingoistic
facetious	disdainful	detached
critical	laudatory	angry
resigned	mystified	sad
astonished		

> Be aware that tone and attitude are frequently described using a *pair* of words in the multiple-choice section of the AP English Language and Composition exam. For example: *bitter and disdainful*. Both adjectives must apply for the choice to be correct.

What follows is a set of activities that can provide practice in recognizing and analyzing tone and attitude. We suggest you try them as you progress through your AP Comp course. Consider the following passages:

Passage A

I am looking at a sunset. I am on the rim of the Grand Canyon. I have been on vacation for the past two weeks which I have been planning for over a year. I have always wanted to visit this geographic location. There are many people also looking at the same sight that I see. This is the first time I have witnessed this place and this event. There are many varied colors while this sunset is taking place. The sun disappears behind the Canyon walls, and darkness comes quickly after that.

Passage B

It was Monday morning. The sun was out, and I walked into the meeting. I was expecting to find some new people there. They were. I was introduced to them. The room was warm. Coffee was served. The meeting began, and the subject was our budget for the next year. There was discussion. I did not agree with many of the people there. A vote was taken after a period of time. The new budget was passed.

Passage C

I am looking at the new Wondercar. I am trying to decide whether or not to purchase or lease this car. It offers ABS, four-wheel drive, a V-8 engine, and the following extras: CD player, AC, power windows, door locks, etc., tinted glass, heated leather seats, a cellular phone, and luggage and ski racks. I would like the color forest green. The purchase price is $48,500. The monthly leasing payment after a $6,000 down payment would be $589.00 for three years.

Using your knowledge of tone, rewrite each of the above passages so that a specific tone is evident to your reader. Identify that tone/attitude. Once you have written the new passage, highlight those changes in diction and syntax which help you to create the tone and attitude you wanted.

Here is another activity that will allow you to practice your skills in analyzing tone and attitude:

Locate reviews of films, music, plays, cars, sports events, or teams—anything you can find that has been reviewed or criticized. These reviews can come from newspapers and/ or periodicals you locate in an actual publication, or they can be from a *real* newspaper or periodical with articles posted on the Web. We suggest that you cut them out or print them out from the Internet.

Under each review:

- Cite the source and the date of the review
- State the *tone* the reviewer has
- Underline those words and/or phrases (*diction*) used in the review that support and/or develop this *tone*

As an extra practice, you might try this. Follow the directions above. Only this time, you will be collecting the reviews for only *one* film, sports event, and so forth. Let's see. You could try the *New York Times, USA Today,* the *Wall Street Journal, Time, Newsweek, People,* or *Entertainment Weekly.* Of course, you may know of others. Terrific; feel free to use them.

Again, try this with your class or study group. The more the merrier.

The following may serve as a final look at our review of style. We have been taking a rather concentrated look at some of the components of what the experts call "literary" style. As you know, two of the major components of style are: (1) the types of sentences an author chooses to use (*syntax*); and (2) word choice (*diction*). Below is a sample paragraph that provides some further practice with these two areas. *This is the first, bare-bones draft.*

> *Last night was chilly. I went into New York City. I went to see a reading of a play. It was a new play. It was a staged reading. It was read at the Roundabout Theater. The Roundabout Theater is on Broadway. It is on the corner of 45th Street. The play was written by Ruth Wolf. She writes about historical people. This play is about Mary Shelley. She was the wife of Percy Bysshe Shelley. Percy B. Shelley was a poet. He is a very famous Romantic poet. Mary Shelley wrote books. She wrote <u>Frankenstein</u>. Many people know this novel. Many people really like the story. There were more than 200 people there. The play was long. It had two acts. It takes place in France and Italy. It also takes place in heaven and hell. There are three main characters. One character is Mary Shelley. One character is Percy B. Shelley. One character plays the archangel and the devil. There is a lot of talking. There is little action. I liked the talking. I wished there was more action. It is called a comedy. Many of the scenes were not comical. The play could not make up its mind. I do not think it will be produced.*

1. Now, using your knowledge of syntax and diction, rewrite this paragraph using coordination, subordination, phrases, and so forth.
2. Once you have written a revised paragraph, work with someone and REWRITE it in a **new and different** way.

Here's an example of one way to revise the passage.

> *Last night, I went into chilly New York City to see a staged reading of a new play at the Roundabout Theater on the corner of 45th and Broadway. Ruth Wolf, who is known for her productions about historical figures, has written a play about Mary Shelley, the wife of the Romantic poet Percy Bysshe Shelley. Many people know Mary Shelley as the author of the popular novel <u>Frankenstein</u>. The play takes place in France, Italy, heaven, and hell with main characters Mary herself, Percy B. Shelley, and an archangel who doubles as the devil. The drama contains much dialogue*

and very little action, which I sorely missed. Billed as a comedy, this play seemed to be unable to make up its mind between being a comedy or a serious tragedy. Because of this problem, I don't believe this play has a real chance of being produced.

The "Connective Tissue" Issue

Throughout this book, we use the term *connective tissue*. For us, this "tissue issue" has four components. The most obvious refers to transitions between paragraphs or sections of a piece. The other three are not as readily recognizable as is transition, but you need to know that they play a major role in the coherence of a written work. The mature reader and writer will learn to recognize and employ these elements:

- Transition—indicates a logical connection between ideas
- Subject consistency—the subjects of the main clauses in a sequence of sentences are consistent (inconsistency is often the result of passive voice)
  Example: no: The <u>photography</u> was by Ansel Adams. <u>I</u> have always been a fan of this great photographer. The <u>temptation</u> to buy the photo due to the price was quite strong.
  yes: <u>I</u> have always been a fan of the great photographer Ansel Adams. Because of the price of one of his photographs, <u>I</u> was tempted to buy it.

- Tense consistency—the use of the same tense throughout the selection
  Example: no: When I have driven to work, I always used the same route.
  yes: I always use the same route when I drive to work.

- Voice consistency—use of the active voice and avoidance of the passive voice when possible
  Example: no: The bear was seen when Tim opened the door.
  yes: Tim opened the door and saw the bear.

Note: Another method of creating cohesion and topic adherence is the use of "echo words" or synonymous words or phrases throughout the selection.

Those authors you recognize as good writers are skilled at building connective tissue. You should be able to recognize it and to employ it in your own work.

<u>The following is a guide to transitional words and phrases.</u>

Most often used and most "natural" transitions in sentences or brief sequences of sentences:

- and
- but
- or
- nor
- for
- yet

Some other commonly used transitions between paragraphs or sections of longer works:

- Numerical: first, second, third, primarily, secondly, and so forth
- Sequential: then, finally, next
- Additional: furthermore, moreover, again, also, similarly
- Illustrative: for example, for instance, to illustrate
- Contrast, comparison, alternative: on the other hand, nevertheless, conversely, instead, however, still
- Cause and effect: therefore, consequently, as a result, accordingly
- Affirmation: of course, obviously, indeed

Here is an activity that will provide practice with transitions. Using one of your essays, highlight all of the transitions and complete the following:

The following are the *transition words/phrases* that I have used to connect each paragraph to the one before it.

1: _____

2: _____

3: _____

4: _____

5: _____

6: _____

7: _____

8: _____

9: _____

10: _____

If you find that you are missing a needed transition between paragraphs, indicate that on the appropriate line that corresponds to that paragraph. Then, write the needed transitional word or phrase.

Note: This practice activity should be one which you do as often as possible. You may wish to do this type of editing with your class or study group. No matter how you do it, just DO IT.

Voice: Pen, Paper, Action!

Writing is a living process. Good writing moves the reader clearly from point to point. Voice and pacing play a major role in this process. Subjects are responsible for their actions. In the context of rhetorical analysis, the *first type of voice* is that "picture" of yourself as a writer that you consciously try to create for your reader. Just how do you want your reader to "see" and "hear" you: as confident, mature, knowledgeable, witty, reverent, friendly, caring, audacious . . . ? What? This first type of voice is the result of all of the elements that make up **style**.

And, one of those components is the *second type of voice*. This type of voice refers to *active* or *passive voice*, which simply is the relationship between the subject and its verb. Almost every instructor or writer who teaches says one thing—"Use ACTIVE voice."

Just What Is ACTIVE VOICE?

To answer this question, look at the following sentences:

> **The ball was thrown by Jessica.**

1. What is the subject? _____

2. What is the verb tense? _____

3. Is the verb simple or compound? _____

4. What is the prepositional phrase? _____

5. How many words are in the sentence? _____

Jessica threw the ball.

1. What is the subject? _____

2. What is the verb tense? _____

3. Is the verb simple or compound? _____

4. Is there a prepositional phrase? _____

5. How many words are in the sentence? _____

Which of the two sentences has the subject of the sentence doing the action? ____
Which one has the subject being acted upon? ____

> When the writing lets the reader know that the subject is *doing the acting*, you have ACTIVE VOICE. When the subject is acted upon or is the goal of the action, and, therefore, NOT responsible, you have PASSIVE VOICE.

With this information, now identify which of the two sentences above is active and which one is passive. Without doubt, we know you chose the second as active and the first as passive. Good for you.

Here's another example:

The treaty was signed last night.

Who signed the treaty? Whom do we blame if the treaty fails? We don't know, do we? Passive voice avoids responsibility. It is a primary tool of those who want to obfuscate or of those who lack confidence and decisiveness. Why not give the true picture and write:

Last night, the president of the United States and the president of Mexico signed a mutual defense treaty.

Here's a practice activity for you.

> *The huge red building was entered at the sound of the bell. Instructions were yelled at us by a mean-looking old lady. A crowd of six-year-olds was followed down a long hallway, up some steps, and down another corridor by me clutching my lunchbox. Mrs. Nearing's room was looked for. Our destination was reached when we were loudly greeted by a tall, black-haired woman. A tag was pressed to my chest after my name was asked and a tag was printed by her. Several big six-year-olds could be seen inside the room by me. The door was closed with a loud bang. The glass near the top of the door was kept from shattering by a network of wires. The wires were observed to be prison-like. So, back in school was I.*

You should have noticed that every sentence is written in the passive voice. Awkward and tedious, isn't it? Now, it's your turn. Rewrite this passage by simply changing all of the passive constructions into active voice.

Compare Your Revision with Ours

At the sound of the bell, I entered the huge, red building with hundreds of other kids. Just inside the entrance, a mean-looking old lady yelled instructions at us. I clutched my lunchbox and followed a crowd of other six-year-olds down a long hallway, up some steps, and down another corridor as we looked for Mrs. Nearing's room. I knew we had reached our destination when a tall, black-haired woman loudly greeted us. She asked me my name, then she printed it on a sticky tag and pressed it to my chest. Once inside the room, I could see several other kids my age, some of them BIG. Finally, Mrs. Nearing closed the door with a loud bang. A network of wires kept the glass near the top of the door from shattering. These wires looked like the bars of a prison to me. I was back in school.

Have you noticed that many sentences written in passive voice contain a prepositional phrase beginning with *by*? That *by*-phrase immediately following the verb (usually compound) can be a clue that you have passive voice at work in the sentence. GET RID OF IT, if you can.

Note: There are times when you deliberately want to use passive voice, but it should be a very conscious choice on your part. Here are four questions to ask yourself.

- Do you want to avoid stating who/what is responsible for an action?
- Is there a specific goal or effect that you wish to emphasize?
- Do you want to create a "special effect"?
- Do you want to sound "academic" and avoid using the dreaded "first person" responsibility?
- If you can answer a loud "yes" to any or all of these questions, then you may decide to employ passive voice.

Let's hear your voice—loud and clear! Take responsibility for what you think, say, and write. This is your voice. It is the real you. Give it life. Don't suffocate it.

Pacing

Pacing is the "movement" of a literary piece from one point to another. The primary component of pacing is syntax: sentence length, sentence type, and punctuation. There are several ways to add variety and pacing to your writing:

- using a mixture of sentence types, known as sentence variety;
- using the rhetorical question;
- using the imperative sentence;
- using the exclamatory sentence; and
- varying the beginnings of sentences.

For example, if you were to compose a brief paragraph about writing an AP English Language and Composition essay, you could write:

I like to write essays for AP Comp class. I like to think through an idea, and I like to try out different approaches to discussing an idea. My AP teacher gives us lots of time to prepare our essays. He gives us a topic. Then, he has us do an outline and then a first draft. We have our first draft read by a member of our peer group. I do my revision after this. I also read my essay aloud to someone. Then, I'm ready to hand it in to my instructor for grading.

Note that all the sentences begin with subject and verb. All the sentences, except for the second one, are simple. The second is no more than a compound sentence made up of two very simple main clauses. Do you feel the tediousness and immaturity of this paragraph? There is *nothing* grammatically wrong with any of the sentences. However, would you be happy with this paragraph if you had written it? Something is missing, and that something has to do with *pacing*.

Rewrite this paragraph so that there is a variety of sentences and sentence beginnings. How does your revision compare with ours?

> *Because I like to think through ideas and try different approaches to presenting an idea, I really enjoy my AP Comp class. Another reason for my enjoying writing essays is my AP teacher's approach to composition. For him and, therefore, for us, writing is not a quick, hit-or-miss assignment. After we choose a topic, Mr. Damon allows plenty of time for preparation, which includes outlining, writing the first draft, and reading by our peer groups. It is only after completing these steps that I revise and write the final draft I will submit for grading. It's a good plan.*

Says/Does

Analysis isn't just simply identifying the parts. It is also describing HOW each of the parts contributes to the whole. Rhetorical analysis is always interested in the rhetorical situation: context, audience, purpose.

When addressing a rhetorical analysis prompt, only listing the rhetorical elements doesn't do the complete job. You need a combination of two elements: SAYS (a summary of the <u>content</u>, what the author actually says) + DOES (an observation of the rhetorical techniques and their intended effect or purpose, in other words, <u>form and function</u>).

Here is a short list of what you could say a text does:

- Describes
- Narrates
- Lists
- Explains
- Emphasizes
- Compares
- Illustrates
- Evaluates
- Cites
- Supports
- Introduces
- Synthesizes

For example:

This writer discusses the beginning of an article about smartphones in the classroom.

> Dr. Lyons maintains that smartphones are an important tool that can be a boon to both instructor and student in the classroom. But she questions whether the benefits outweigh the costs. **(SAYS)** Using two charts and several direct quotations from students and education experts, Lyons introduces her thesis to the audience and starts them thinking about the subject. **(DOES)**

Try It Yourself

The following is an excerpt from *Bleak House* by Charles Dickens:

> *Fog everywhere. Fog up the river, where it flows among green aits and meadows; fog down the river, where it rolls defiled among tiers of shipping and waterside pollutions of a great (and dirty) city. Fog on the Essex marshes, fog on the heights, fog creeping into the cabooses of [coal barges]. Fog lying out on the yards, and hovering in the rigging of great ships; fog drooping on the gunwales of barges and small boats. Fog in the eyes and throats of ancient Greenwich pensioners, wheezing by the firesides of their wards; fog in the stem and bowl of the afternoon pipe of the wrathful skipper, down in his close cabin; fog cruelly pinching the toes and fingers of his shivering little 'prentice boy on deck. Chance people on the bridges peeping over the parapets into a nether sky of fog, with fog all round them, as if they were up in a balloon, and hanging in the misty clouds.*

SAYS: In this excerpt from *Bleak House*,

_____

_____

_____

_____

_____

DOES: To _____ the presence of fog everywhere on everything, Dickens uses (rhetorical techniques + effects of techniques)

_____

_____

_____

_____

_____

> *"For me, having an audience who gives me feedback is really important and helps me to see what needs to be revised."*
> —Jessica K.,
>   AP student

Note: You may also feel comfortable thinking about SAYS/DOES in terms of WHAT/WHY. *What* does the author *do*, and *why* does she *do it*? Remember that just identifying a rhetorical strategy/choice is not enough. You *must* discuss what effect the author intended for the given audience.

A Few Words About Coherence

Coherence is accepting your responsibility as a writer to "deliver the goods." Your reader has expectations you are obliged to meet.

- Basically, the reader looks for some kind of announcement as to what is to follow (the thesis, assertion, claim).
- Near the end of the introduction, the reader expects to find some hints about the major points that you will discuss in your piece of writing.
- The body of the presentation will develop the discussion of each major point.
- The reader will expect to be led logically from one major point to another via "connective tissue."

- The reader expects some sort of final comment or remark, not a summary. Among the many possibilities, this final "point" could be:
  — an interpretation of the significance of the points of your discussion;
  — a prediction;
  — an anecdote;
  — a question; or
  — a quote.

Make certain that your ending/conclusion is related to your discussion. Don't introduce new or irrelevant ideas or comments. Also, make sure that the final comment is consistent in tone and attitude with the rest of the paper.

Just as the reader has particular expectations of you as a writer, YOU have expectations when you read the writing of others and when you complete a rhetorical analysis of another's written work. Ask the very same questions that are asked of you.

An Essay Editing and Revision Template

We are going to provide you with a template for editing and revision that we recommend you use throughout the year for your own essays. The more you use this template for your own writing, the more comfortable you will be when it comes to analyzing the writing of others. It will become almost second nature to you.

Before you begin to write the revised draft of your essay, respond to each of the following *carefully*. If possible, ask for input from your peers. Read aloud to each other. *Listen* to what you have written.

The title of my essay is _____.

I will organize my essay using (a rhetorical strategy) _____.

The thesis of my essay is in the _____ paragraph.

My intended tone/attitude is _____.
I have used the following rhetorical devices/elements to create this tone:

_____ in paragraph _____ _____ in paragraph _____

_____ in paragraph _____ _____ in paragraph _____

_____ in paragraph _____ _____ in paragraph _____

_____ in paragraph _____ _____ in paragraph _____

_____ in paragraph _____ _____ in paragraph _____

_____ in paragraph _____ _____ in paragraph _____

_____ in paragraph _____ _____ in paragraph _____

_____ in paragraph _____ _____ in paragraph _____

_____ in paragraph _____ _____ in paragraph _____

The following are the *transition words/phrases* I have used to connect each paragraph to the one before it.

1: _____

2: _____

3: _____

4: _____

5: _____

6: _____

7: _____

8: _____

9: _____

10: _____

I use the _____ tense as the predominant tense in my essay.

I have checked the verbs in each of my paragraphs. They are *all* in the predominant tense *except*:

    1: _____ (tense) _____ Reason for using this tense is _____. (You must do this with each paragraph and with each verb.)

I have _____ sentences in my essay. _____ of them begin with the subject. _____ of them begin with a participle phrase. _____ of them begin with a relative clause. _____ of them begin with an adverbial clause. _____ of them begin with a prepositional phrase. _____ of them begin with an infinitive. _____ of them begin with a gerund.

I have _____ simple sentences in my essay; _____ compound sentences; _____ complex sentences; _____ compound-complex sentences.

I think I need to add more sentence variety to my presentation. _____ yes _____ no

I have made certain that there is a variety of sentence structures in my essay. _____ yes _____ no

My conclusion _____ *is* _____ *is not* a summary of what I have already said in my essay. If it is not a summary, identify the type of ending you have created. _____

I have discussed this inventory of my first draft with _____. These are the suggested areas for improving my essay:

The *major* things I have to work on when I revise my essay are:

Rapid Review

- Analysis is the deconstruction of a passage into its components in order to examine how a writer develops a subject.
- The AP English Language exam requires the analysis of structure, purpose, style.
- Discourse is conversation between the text and the reader.
- Rhetoric is a term for all of the strategies, modes, and devices a writer employs.
- There are four major modes of discourse:
  — exposition
  — narration

- — description
- — argumentation
- Rhetorical strategies are used to develop the modes of discourse:
  - — example
  - — comparison and contrast
  - — definition
  - — cause and effect
  - — process
  - — analysis
  - — classification
- Practice each of the rhetorical strategies.
- Style is the unique writing pattern of a writer.
- Style comprises:
  - — subject matter
  - — selection of detail
  - — organization
  - — point of view
  - — diction
  - — syntax
  - — language
  - — attitude
  - — tone
- Practice with stylistic devices.
- Review words that describe tone.
- Review "connective tissue":
  - — transition
  - — subject consistency
  - — tense consistency
  - — voice consistency
- Practice using active and passive voice.
- Practice recognizing pacing in professional writing and in your own essays by sentence variety:
  - — construction
  - — openings
  - — types
- Utilize rubrics to gauge your essays.

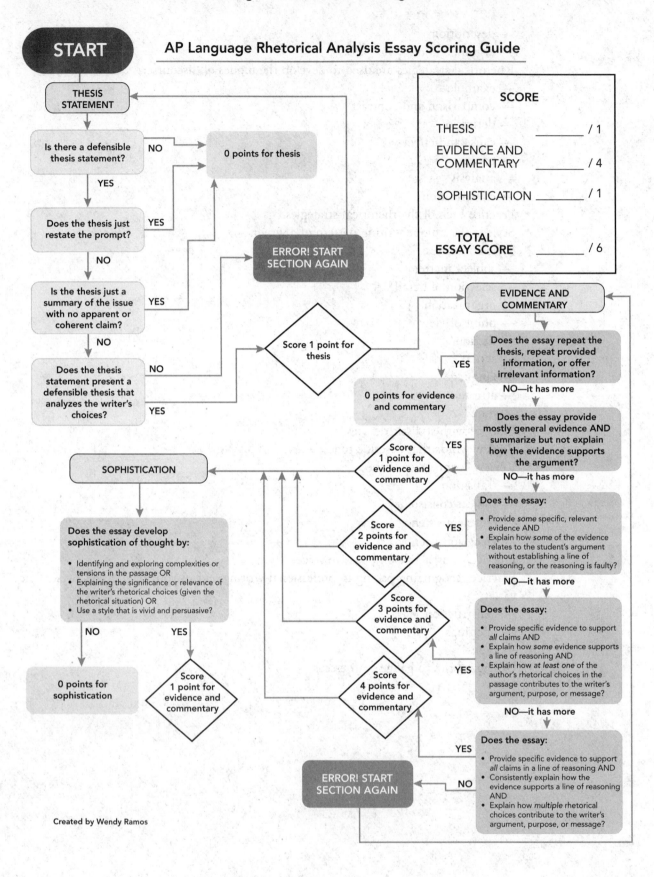

START

AP Language Rhetorical Analysis Essay Scoring Guide

THESIS STATEMENT

Is there a defensible thesis statement? — **NO** → 0 points for thesis

↓ **YES**

Does the thesis just restate the prompt? — **YES** → 0 points for thesis

↓ **NO**

Is the thesis just a summary of the issue with no apparent or coherent claim? — **YES** → 0 points for thesis

↓ **NO**

Does the thesis statement present a defensible thesis that analyzes the writer's choices? — **NO** → **ERROR! START SECTION AGAIN**

↓ **YES**

Score 1 point for thesis

SCORE

THESIS _____ / 1

EVIDENCE AND COMMENTARY _____ / 4

SOPHISTICATION _____ / 1

TOTAL ESSAY SCORE _____ / 6

EVIDENCE AND COMMENTARY

Does the essay repeat the thesis, repeat provided information, or offer irrelevant information?

YES → 0 points for evidence and commentary

NO—it has more

↓

Does the essay provide mostly general evidence AND summarize but not explain how the evidence supports the argument?

YES → Score 1 point for evidence and commentary

NO—it has more

↓

Does the essay:
- Provide *some* specific, relevant evidence AND
- Explain how *some* of the evidence relates to the student's argument without establishing a line of reasoning, or the reasoning is faulty?

YES → Score 2 points for evidence and commentary

NO—it has more

↓

Does the essay:
- Provide specific evidence to support *all* claims AND
- Explain how *some* evidence supports a line of reasoning AND
- Explain how *at least one* of the author's rhetorical choices in the passage contributes to the writer's argument, purpose, or message?

YES → Score 3 points for evidence and commentary

NO—it has more

↓

Does the essay:
- Provide specific evidence to support *all* claims in a line of reasoning AND
- Consistently explain how the evidence supports a line of reasoning AND
- Explain how *multiple* rhetorical choices contribute to the writer's argument, purpose, or message?

YES → Score 4 points for evidence and commentary

NO → **ERROR! START SECTION AGAIN**

SOPHISTICATION

Does the essay develop sophistication of thought by:
- Identifying and exploring complexities or tensions in the passage OR
- Explaining the significance or relevance of the writer's rhetorical choices (given the rhetorical situation) OR
- Use a style that is vivid and persuasive?

NO → 0 points for sophistication

YES → Score 1 point for evidence and commentary

Created by Wendy Ramos

CHAPTER > 9

Comprehensive Review—Argument

IN THIS CHAPTER

Summary: Experience why everything is an argument. Examine the process for presenting a position that others will understand and accept.

Key Ideas

✪ Learn the format for the basic argument essay.
✪ Learn the difference between deduction and induction.
✪ Become familiar with logical fallacies.
✪ Practice reading and evaluating an argument.

Some Basics

What Is ARGUMENT?

In its broadest sense, all writing is argument. It is the presentation and defense or support of a specific thesis, assertion, or claim. This thesis can be a strongly held belief, a critical view of an issue, a presentation of an insight, a search for the truth, or even a description of that mountain view that moved you to tears that you hope others will share. To convince the reader to accept the position, the writer provides support using objective facts or logical evidence, and sometimes, even emotional appeals.

You can find argument almost anywhere: from ads in your favorite magazine or on television to academic journals, from *"Peanuts"* to editorial cartoons, from letters to the editor of *Sports Illustrated* to editorials in the *New York Times*, and from a plea to your parents to a president's speech to the nation. Possibly the only writing that is not an argument is a piece that offers no support for a claim.

What Is the Difference Between Argument and Persuasion?

The intended results of each of these strategies is where the difference lies. ALL persuasion is a type of argument. The goal of an argument is to have you accept the writer's thesis. However, with persuasion, after you've accepted the position of the writer, the goal is to have you get moving and *do something*. For example:

ARGUMENT: Walking is necessary for good health.

PERSUASION: I want you to walk every day for good health.

What Does the AP Expect Me to Be Able to Do with an Argument Essay?

Most frequently, the AP exam will present you with a prompt that could be:

- A brief excerpt
- A quotation
- A statement
- An anecdote

You will then be directed to take a position regarding:

- Author's position
- Statement's main idea
- Narrative's main point
- A collection of statements or quotations

Other types of argument prompts will ask you to:

- Write an essay indicating which idea among a given set is more valid
- Explore the validity of an assertion

No matter which type of argumentation prompt is given, the AP expects you to be able to:

- Take a position on the issue or situation
- Support your position using your own experience, reading, and/or observations

How Do You Argue a Point or Position?

Basically, support for your position on an issue should be rational and logical, not emotional. It should be objective rather than biased (one-sided). This support can be developed using any of the rhetorical strategies and devices we've reviewed for you in Chapter 8.

The classical formula for an argument is:

1. Present the issue/situation/problem.
2. State your (writer's) assertion/claim/thesis.
3. Support your claim.
4. Acknowledge and respond to real or possible opposing views.
5. Make your final comment or summary of the evidence.

The order of the presentation can be varied, and any of the rhetorical strategies can be employed. You must make certain that your support/evidence is appropriate and effective.

The Argument

Your argument can be:

- **Ethical**—an appeal to the reader's good sense, goodwill, and desire to "do the right thing"
- **Emotional**—an appeal to the reader's fear, patriotism, and so forth
- **Logical**—an appeal to inductive and deductive reasoning
  - *Induction*: forming a *generalization* from a set of specific examples. (Example: Margo has 17 stuffed teddy bears, 3 stuffed cows, 11 monkeys, 4 camels, and 6 stuffed elephants. Margo loves to collect stuffed animals.)
  - *Deduction*: reaching a probable *conclusion* based on given premises. A *premise* is a proposition that is proven or taken for granted. (Example: All high school seniors at this high school must write a research paper. Sean is a senior at this high school. Therefore, Sean must write a research paper.)

Be aware that conclusions can be drawn from implicit premises. These can include:

- Universal truths
- Possibilities that the reader will readily accept
- Familiar sayings
- Facts that everyone, including the reader, knows

The three major types of arguments are:

- **Aristotelian**—a win or lose attempt to get audience to accept a position; think of lawyers at a trial
- **Rogerian**—attempt to find common ground in reaching an agreement; think of negotiations
- **Toulmin**—a formatted form of argument with six parts: claim, grounds, warrant, quantifier, rebuttal backing. Think of debates.

Deduction uses the syllogism. A **syllogism** is the format of a formal argument that consists of a

Major premise:	*All A are C.*	*"All lions are cats."*
Minor premise:	*B is A.*	*"Leonard is a lion."*
Conclusion:	*Therefore, B is C.*	*"Leonard is a cat."*

You could also say, "Because Leonard is a lion, he is a cat." In this instance, you have suppressed one of the premises. However, you are confident that most people would agree that all lions are cats. Therefore, you would feel confident in leaving out that premise. But, you must be very careful, because you could end up with what we call a **logical fallacy**.

Logical fallacies are mistakes in reasoning and fall into several categories.

- *Non sequitur argument:* This Latin phrase means "does not follow." This is an argument with a conclusion that does not follow from the premise. (Example: Diane graduated from Vassar. She'll make a great lawyer.)
- *Begging the question:* Here is a mistake in which the writer assumes in his or her assertion/ premise/thesis something that really remains to be proved. (Example: Taking geometry is a waste of time. High school students should not be required to take this course.)

- *Circular reasoning:* This mistake in logic restates the premise rather than giving a reason for holding that premise. (Example: I like to eat out because I enjoy different foods and restaurants.)
- *Straw-man argument:* Here is a technique we've all seen and heard used by politicians seeking election. The speaker/writer attributes false or exaggerated characteristics or behaviors to the opponent and attacks him on those falsehoods or exaggerations. (Example: You say you support allowing people under eighteen to drive alone. I'll never be able to understand why weak-willed drivers like you are willing to risk your life and the lives of all other drivers with these crazy teenagers on the road.)
- *Ad hominem argument:* This literally means to "argue against the man." This technique attacks the person rather than dealing with the issue under discussion. (Example: We all know Sam has several speeding tickets on his record. How can we trust him to vote for us on the issue of a trade agreement with Europe?)
- *Hasty generalization:* A person who makes a hasty generalization draws a conclusion about an entire group based on evidence that is too scant or insufficient. (Example: The veterinarian discovered a viral infection in five beagles. All beagles must be infected with it.)
- *Overgeneralization:* This is what we call stereotyping in most cases. Here, the writer/speaker draws a conclusion about a large number of people, ideas, things, etc. based on very limited evidence. (Example: All members of group A are not to be trusted.) Words such as *all*, *never*, *always*, and *every* are usually indicative of overgeneralization. It's best to use and to look for qualifiers (*some*, *seem*, *often*, *perhaps*, *frequently*, etc.) that indicate that the writer has an awareness of the complexities of the topic or group under discussion.
- *Post hoc argument:* This fallacy cites an unrelated event that occurred earlier as the cause of a current situation. (Example: I saw a black cat run across the street in front of my car five minutes before I was hit by a foul ball at the ball park. Therefore, the black cat is the cause of my bruised arm.)
- *Either/or argument:* With this fallacy, the writer asserts that there are only two possibilities, when, in reality, there are more. (Example: Tomorrow is April 15; therefore, I must mail in my tax return, or I will be arrested.)

There are several other categories of logical fallacies, but these are the most frequently encountered.

During the year, carefully read editorials or ads in the print media. Check to see if you can locate any logical fallacies. It might be beneficial to do this with your class or study group.

The following activities provide you with some practice with induction, deduction, and analogy.

Induction: If induction is the process that moves from a given series of specifics to a generalization, these are the possible problems:

- The generalization covers many unobserved persons, objects, etc.
- If the conclusion begins with ALL, any exception would invalidate the generalization.
- Cited facts are incorrect.
- Assumed connections are incorrect.
- Assumption is a conclusion NOT supported by the evidence.

Practice:

A. Write a conclusion for the following:
  1. Television network USBC's drama series won this year's Emmy for Best Dramatic Series.
  2. USBC won the Emmy for Best Comedy Series.
  3. USBC won the Emmy for Best Talk Show.

  4. *Therefore,* _____.

  Are there any possible weaknesses in your conclusion?

B. Carefully read the following and briefly explain the possible error in the conclusion.
  1. The 43rd U.S. president is a Yale graduate.
  2. The 42nd U.S. president was a Yale Law School graduate.
  3. The 41st U.S. president was a Yale graduate.
  4. The last seven presidents were college graduates.
  5. *Therefore,* the president of the U.S. must have a college degree.

Deduction: If deduction is the process of moving from a general rule to a specific example (A = B; C = B; Therefore, C = A.), these are the possible problems:

- Not *all* of the given A falls into the given B category. There are exceptions.
- The given category B is incorrect.
- The second statement is *not* true or is incorrect. Therefore, the conclusion is invalid.
- The truth of the third statement is in question.

Practice:

A. Carefully read the following. Assume that statements 1 and 2 are true. Briefly state the possible error of the conclusion.
  1. Some Japanese cars are made in the United States.
  2. Toyota is a Japanese car.
  3. *Therefore,* all Toyotas are made in the United States.

B. Carefully read the following. Assume that statements 1 and 2 are true. Briefly state the possible error of the conclusion.
  1. No eagles are flamingos.
  2. All flamingos are birds.
  3. Therefore, no eagles are birds.

Analogy: If analogy is an argument based on similarities, these are the possible problems.

- Accepting the totality of the analogy by never questioning that there are differences between/among the items being compared that could invalidate the argument or conclusion.
- Exaggerating the similarities.

Practice:

A. Briefly identify the analogy in the following:

Both the doctor and the teacher must have special knowledge. People select their own doctors; therefore, people should be allowed to pick their own teachers.

B. Briefly explain the mistake in the following:

Both 2-year-olds and 10-year-olds have two legs, two eyes, two ears, and two arms. Ten-year-olds can read and write. Therefore, 2-year-olds should be able to read and write.

Reading the Argument

In the multiple-choice section of the AP English Language exam, you are asked to read several selections, many of which are argumentative. Remember two very important points. No matter how brief or how lengthy the text is:

1. There is a rhetorical context with a
   - writer
   - occasion or situation
   - audience

Any good argument will effectively utilize and address each of these elements.

2. Don't make the mistake of evaluating an argument based simply on who wrote it. Don't confuse the messenger with the message.

   With this in mind, your task is to read the given text critically and to:

   - Determine who the speaker is, what the situation is, and who the audience is.
   - Identify the position of the speaker.
   - Check off the points made in support of the assertion.

   You can easily accomplish these three tasks by highlighting, underlining, checking, making marginal notes, or even outlining (if you have time). Once you have completed your initial reading, you need to ask yourself several questions. In the case of the actual AP English Language and Composition exam, your test makers will ask you the questions based on these points.

1. Are there any judgments in the presentation?
   — Evidence is needed to support judgments.

2. Recognize that fact is <u>not</u> the same as interpretation.
   — Fact: You know it with certainty and can verify it.
   — Interpretation: An explanation of the meaning and/or importance of a specific item.

   You must be able to distinguish between the two.

3. Distinguish between literal and ironic statements. Recognizing the difference between these two terms can save you from misreading the text.
   — Ironic: Saying the opposite from what you really mean, as in satire.
   — Clues to be aware of: diction, subject, selection of detail.
   — Literal: What you read is what is the reality.

4. Do not evaluate an argument based on its form. Look at the content. It's easy to be misled by "fabulous" writing.

Below is a checklist that functions as a rubric for the evaluation of any rhetorical argument.

— A clearly developed thesis is evident.
— Facts are distinguished from opinions.
— Opinions are supported and qualified.
— The speaker develops a logical argument and avoids fallacies in reasoning.
— Support for facts is tested, reliable, and authoritative.
— The speaker does not confuse appeals to logic and emotion.
— Opposing views are represented in a fair and undistorted way.
— The argument reflects a sense of audience.
— The argument reflects an identifiable voice and point of view.
— The piece reflects the image of a speaker with identifiable qualities (honesty, sincerity, authority, intelligence, etc.).

As practice, read the following editorial, which appeared in a recent teachers' newsletter.

Misters King and Prince could not have picked a more ironic day to have their anti-teacher tirade printed in Today's News *than on Tuesday, January 13. Here were Matt King, executive director of the conservative magazine* The Right Position, *and Ray Prince, the chief economist for the conservative Small Business Conference, showing their poisonous fangs in their hissy-fit against the state's teachers' union and the state's education department.*

Here were two cobras from the antiteacher snake pit posturing about the need to end tenure and to create charter schools. These, said the two vipers, are among the steps "needed to revitalize education in our area and across the state." Later in their column, they continued with "declining student performance in recent years" is indicative of poor teaching quality.

May I direct King and Prince to pages A5 and A28 of this very same Today's News *edition. In this article were the names of 74 (4 of them from New High School) Intel competition semifinalists out of a total of 144 in our state. With about 50% of the state's semifinalists, this and our neighboring county had MORE winning contestants and MORE participants than any other region in the country. This is MORE than half the national total of 300 . . . [and] "more than six times as many as the second-ranked state, which had 21 semifinalists and the third-ranked state, which had 19."*

Hmmm . . . now, let me think. Which speaks more loudly about teacher quality and student motivation: the negative nagging of King and Prince or the positive professionalism and performance represented by the Intel story? I daresay—no contest. And, this type of professional proficiency and dedication is part and parcel of the standards and goals of ALL our state teachers.

They would have to count the extraordinary number of national, state, and local awards our professionals and their pupils have earned. They would have to count the number of scholarships, volunteer hours, and AP courses our students have amassed. They would have to listen to a litany of academic awards, associations, and degrees with which our teachers are connected. They would have to read the hundreds of thank-you letters former students have written to their teachers.

They would have to acknowledge that their scaly agenda needs to be shed.

Rather than casting a "shadow over education" in this state, our teachers shine a bright light on the snake pits created by ignorance and negativity.

Let's Use the Argument Checklist on This Editorial

1. The <u>thesis</u> is that Mr. King and Mr. Prince are incorrect about their position to end tenure and create charter schools. These two are wrong when they say "our area needs to revitalize education."
2. <u>Facts are distinguished from opinion</u>. Facts include the number of Intel scholarships in paragraph 3; the comparison of the writer's area with other school districts in paragraph 3, and the number of awards, etc. associated with the writer's school. Opinion is obvious in the analogy established between Mr. King and Mr. Prince and snakes.
3. Some <u>opinions are supported and others are not</u>. In some cases, numbers are cited, and in other cases, generalizations are used.
4. The editorial <u>avoids fallacies in most instances</u>. However, the emotional appeal and arguing from analogy is present.
5. The <u>editorial is developed using induction</u>. A possible fallacy here revolves around whether or not what is true about one school district may be true about all other school areas or for all teachers and students.
6. The <u>facts used come from current newspapers</u>. The writer cites statistics and gives the source. The comparison between New High School and other schools and school districts is based on statistics and facts.
7. The author <u>uses both logic and emotion</u>. The facts and statistics are given in separate paragraphs. Emotional and analogical aspects of the argument are in opinionated sections of the editorial.
8. The <u>opposing views</u> of King and Prince are presented to illustrate the position of the columnists factually.
9. The <u>audience</u> is obviously teachers and those involved in education.
10. The <u>point of view</u> of the writer is clearly negative toward King and Prince and positive toward the condition of education in the writer's school district and state.
11. The editorial reflects a writer who is sincere, angry, confident, and willing to find support for the assertion.

Note: Each of these statements about the given editorial could also be turned into a multiple-choice question. Keep in mind that the writers of the AP English Language and Composition exam are aware of all of the preceding information and will base their questions on the assumption that you are also familiar with it and can recognize the elements of argument when you read them.

Writing the Argument

While the multiple-choice section of the exam will present you with specific questions about specific texts, the argument essay in the second section of the test requires that you compose *your own argument* based on a given excerpt, quotation, statement, or anecdote.

You will have to plan and write your argument knowing that the AP reader will be evaluating your presentation based on the major points we have just reviewed.

How Should I Go About Writing My Argument?

We invite you to compose an argument essay based on the following prompt. We will take you through the prewriting process.

> *In a recent* USA Today *op-ed piece, titled "Poor Suffer from Lack of Internet Access," Julianne Malveaux stated, "While the Internet has hardly caused the gap between the [lower and higher rungs on the economic ladder], it is one of the many things that have made the gap greater."*
>
> —(Julianne Malveaux, *USA Today*, June 22, 2001)

Write an essay that argues your position on Malveau's claim about the gap in internet access.

The Planning/Prewriting Process

What follows is an example of the prewriting process that addresses the given prompt.

1. Reread the prompt and highlight important terms, ideas, etc.
2. *Take a position.* Agree "it is one of the many things that have made the gap greater."
3. *My topic is:* Internet is one cause of the widening gap between the haves and the have-nots.
4. *My thesis statement is:* I agree with Julianne Malveaux when she states that access to the Internet has widened the gap between the haves and the have-nots.
5. *I will develop my argument using:*
   —personal anecdote
   — specific examples of the gap (at least three)
   — statistics and facts that I can remember from the news, and other sources
6. The *specifics I will use to support my assertion are*:
   (Make certain examples are introduced, discussed, and linked to my thesis.)
7. I will use the *inductive* technique to develop my argument.
8. I will *end my argument* with the image of a single child with her nose against a window peering into a room filled with children using computers. The child outside is not alone. Behind her are many, many others, and they all look as if they are growing more and more anxious and angry at being left outside.

This planning took about 10 to 12 minutes to develop. Based on this planning, writing the essay is easy. As a class assignment or as personal practice, you would:

- Write your first draft
- Have the initial argument checklist completed by one of your peers
- Complete your second draft
- Complete the revision activity either by yourself or with a member of your peer reading group

If you have practiced this process throughout the year or semester, when the AP English Language exam rolls around, you will find this kind of writing second nature to you.

Rapid Review

- Argument can be ethical, emotional, or logical.
- Inductive reasoning forms generalizations.
- Deductive reasoning reaches conclusions based on given premises.
- A premise is a proven proposition or one that is taken for granted.
- A syllogism is the format of a formal argument:
  — All A is C.
  — B is A.
  — Therefore, B is C.
- Logical fallacies are intended or unintended errors in reasoning.
- Rhetorical fallacies are used to manipulate the audience.
- Read editorials and ads to try to locate any fallacies that may be present.
- Do practice exercises with induction and deduction and analogy.
- All argument has a rhetorical context: the writer, the occasion, and the audience.
- When reading arguments, locate judgments and find supporting evidence.
- Be certain to recognize and to separate fact from interpretation.
- Evaluate the argument according to the given rubrics.
- When writing an argument, make certain to:
  — address the prompt
  — take a position
  — state your thesis
  — develop your position with evidence

CHAPTER **10**

Comprehensive Review—Synthesis

IN THIS CHAPTER

Summary: Examine the synthesis purpose and process, including the prompt.

Key Ideas

○ Practice with reading and evaluating different types of texts from various mediums, including graphics.
○ Work with summary, paraphrase, and inference.
○ Learn different approaches to incorporating sources into the text of your essay.

Some Basics

What Is the Synthesis Essay?

Synthesis is the process in which you, as the writer, develop a thesis and, in the course of developing this thesis,

- you investigate a variety of sources, both print and visual;
- you choose which of these sources to include in your presentation;
- you respond to these sources and discuss how they relate to your position on the topic.

Note: A well-respected and experienced Advanced Placement English instructor, Jodi Rice, uses the following example to clarify the idea of *synthesis:* You're having a dinner party, and you consult two recipes you've been given and use bits of each to create your own, new dish. You let your dinner guests know that you invented the dish, but that you used and combined recipes from your grandmother and from the newspaper. You don't take credit for those two recipes, but you <u>do</u> take credit for what you did with them.

In the case of the AP Language exam, you only have time to write a first draft, and it must be clear, organized, logical, and thoughtful. In developing each of your major points, make certain to:

- Relate it to the thesis/claim
- Use specific examples (personal and otherwise)
- Use selected sources to support the major point
- Incorporate sources into the development of your point by using
  — Attribution and introduction of cited sources
  — Transitions
  — Mix of direct quotations, summary, and paraphrases

A Few Comments Before Beginning

Your AP Language class, as well as other courses across the curriculum, has taught you how to conduct, evaluate, and present research. You most likely have completed at least one research paper that required you to develop a thesis on a particular subject; to find, read, and annotate outside sources related to the topic; to determine which of the sources to use in support of your thesis; to incorporate these sources into your research paper; and to appropriately cite your sources.

If you've written this type of paper before, whether brief or lengthy, you're well on your way to being able to compose a successful synthesis essay.

The synthesis essay also requires you to be familiar with both **analysis** and **argument**. Because of this, we strongly urge you to review Chapters 5, 6, 8, and 9. Those skills needed to develop a successful essay of analysis or argument are requisites for composing a **synthesis** essay.

This chapter briefly reviews strategies and provides you with practice activities specifically related to writing the synthesis essay as it would most probably appear on the AP English Language exam.

Let's begin.

Note: We will use the synthesis prompt and sample essay from the Diagnostic Master exam (Chapter 3) as the basis for the following review segments.

Strategies

Strategy 1: Critical Reading of Texts

A word about the texts: The several texts you will be given for the synthesis prompt will be related to the topic, and you can be assured that each text has been evaluated and judged to be appropriate, of acceptable quality, and representing several points of view.

Critical reading of texts specifically for the synthesis essay demands that you determine the following:

- Purpose/thesis
- Intended audience
- Type of source (primary, secondary)
- Main points
- Historical context
- Authority of the author
- How the material is presented
- Type of evidence presented
- Source of the evidence
- Any bias or agenda
- How the text relates to the topic
- Support or opposition toward the thesis

Practice with Critical Reading

Our example: Here is a text provided in the Diagnostic Master exam's synthesis essay.

Source E

Broder, John M., "States Curbing Right to Seize Private Homes." *New York Times*, February 21, 2006.

The following passage is excerpted from an article published in the *New York Times*.

> "Our *opposition* to eminent domain is *not across the board*," he [Scott G. Bullock of the Institute for Justice] *said*. "It has an *important but limited role in government planning* and the building of roads, parks, and public buildings. What *we oppose* is eminent domain *abuse for private development*, and we are encouraging legislators to curtail it."
>
> *More neutral observers expressed concern that state officials*, in their zeal to protect homeowners and small businesses, *would handcuff local governments* that are trying to revitalize dying cities and fill in blighted areas with projects that produce tax revenues and jobs.
>
> "It's fair to say that many states are on the verge of seriously overreacting to the Kelo *decision*," said John D. Echeverria, executive director of the Georgetown Environmental Law and Policy Institute and an authority on land-use policy. "*The danger is that some legislators* are going to *attempt to destroy* what is a significant and sometimes painful but essential *government power*. The extremist position is a *prescription for economic decline* for many metropolitan areas around the county."

Our writer's critical reading of the passage provides the following information:

1. Thesis: ". . . What we oppose is eminent domain abuse for private development, and we are encouraging legislators to curtail it."
2. Intended audience: generally educated readers
3. Main points:
   A. qualified opposition to eminent domain
   B. opposed to eminent domain for private development
   C. acknowledges that there are those who see their position as handcuffing local officials
   D. Echeverria says, "The danger . . . " He fears legislation could destroy essential government power.

4. <u>Historical context:</u> 2006 in response to *Kelo* decision
5. <u>How material is presented:</u> Thesis + expert's direct quotation + acknowledgment of opposition + expert's direct quotation
6. <u>Type of evidence presented:</u> direct quotations of experts in the field
7. <u>Source of evidence:</u> expert opinions
8. <u>Any bias or agenda:</u> both sides of issue are presented
9. <u>How text relates to the topic:</u> specific statements for and against eminent domain
10. <u>Support or not for thesis:</u> one quotation supports a qualifying position: "I can empathize with the home owners affected by the recent 5:4 Supreme Court decision." The other quotation could be used to recognize those who would oppose it.

Note: This is a process that does not necessarily require that every point be written out. You could easily make mental notes of many of these items and jot down only those that you think you could use in your essay. You may prefer to annotate directly on the text itself.

Practice

Now, you complete a critical reading of another text from the Master exam on eminent domain.

Source C

Kelo v. New London. U.S. Supreme Court 125 S. Ct. 2655.
The following is a brief overview of a decision by the U.S. Supreme Court in 2005.

> Suzette Kelo, et al. v. <u>City of New London</u>, et al., <u>*125 S. Ct. 2655*</u> *(2005), more commonly* Kelo v. New London, *is a land-use law case argued before the <u>United States Supreme Court</u> on <u>February 22, 2005</u>. The case arose from a city's use of <u>eminent domain</u> to condemn privately owned real property so that it could be used as part of a comprehensive redevelopment plan.*
>
> *The owners sued the city in Connecticut courts, arguing that the city had misused its eminent domain power. The power of eminent domain is limited by the <u>Fifth</u> and <u>Fourteenth Amendments to the United States Constitution</u>. The Fifth Amendment, which restricts the actions of the federal government, says, in part, that "private property [shall not] be taken for public use, without just compensation"; under Section 1 of the Fourteenth Amendment, this limitation is also imposed on the actions of <u>U.S. state</u> and local governments. Kelo and the other appellants argued that economic development, the stated purpose of the Development Corporation, did not qualify as public use.*
>
> *The Supreme Court's Ruling: This 5:4 decision holds that the governmental taking of property from one private owner to give to another in furtherance of economic development constitutes a permissible "public use" under the Fifth Amendment.*

1. Purpose/thesis: _____

_____

2. Intended audience: _____

3. Main points: _____

_____

4. Historical context: _____

5. How material is presented: _____

6. Type of evidence presented: _____

_____

7. Source of evidence: _____

8. Any bias or agenda: _____

9. How text relates to topic: _____

_____

10. Support or opposition for my thesis: _____

What Types of Visual Texts Can I Expect on the AP Language Exam?

You can expect to encounter a variety of visual sources on the AP Language exam. They may include:

- Editorial cartoons (*Note:* Often editorial cartoons are referred to as political cartoons.)
- Charts and graphs
- Posters
- Advertising
- Paintings
- Photographs

As with the steps involved in the critical reading of written material, visuals also require critical analysis. The following are steps you should consider when faced with a visual text:

- Identify the subject of the visual.
- Identify the major components, such as characters, visual details, and symbols.
- Identify verbal clues, such as titles, taglines, date, author, and dialogue.
- Notice position and size of details.
- Does the visual take a positive or negative position toward the issue?
- Identify the primary purpose of the visual.
- Determine how each detail illustrates and/or supports the primary purpose.
- Does the author indicate alternative viewpoints?

What Follows Is a Sample Critical Reading of an <u>Editorial Cartoon</u> Taken from the Master Exam

One type of text that could be used for the synthesis essay prompt on the AP English Language exam is the editorial cartoon. No, AP Language has not turned into a history or journalism course. But, it does recognize the variety of texts that can be created to advance or illustrate a particular thesis. The editorial cartoon does in a single- or multiple-frame presentation what would take hundreds of words in an essay, editorial, and so forth. It is a visual presentation of a specific point of view on an issue.

> *Note:* Even though the synthesis essay prompt may include editorial cartoon, or charts, or surveys, you are not required to use any of them. Your choice of texts depends on your purpose.

When dealing with an editorial cartoon, here are the specific steps to consider that are adapted from the critical reading of a visual.

- Identify the subject of the cartoon.
- Identify the major components, such as characters, visual details, and symbols.
- Identify verbal clues, such as titles, taglines, date, cartoonist, and dialogue.
- Notice position and size of details within the frame.
- Does the cartoon take a positive or negative position toward the issue?
- Identify the primary purpose of the cartoon.
- Determine how each detail illustrates and/or supports the primary purpose.
- Does the cartoonist indicate alternative viewpoints?

Notice that an editorial cartoon assumes the reader is aware of current events surrounding the specific issue. So, we recommend you begin to read a newspaper or news magazine regularly and/or watch a daily news program on TV. Even listening to a five-minute news summary on the radio as you drive to and from errands or school can give you a bit of background on what's happening in the world around you.

Example: Source D, editorial cartoon
The following editorial cartoon appeared in an Omaha, Nebraska, newspaper.

Jeff Koterba, *Omaha World Herald*, NE

1. <u>Subject of the cartoon:</u> eminent domain.
2. <u>Major components:</u> one chicken, one cow in a barnyard.
3. <u>Verbal clues:</u> Print size and form indicates the chicken is very excited, even panicked, while the cow is calm and unimpressed.
4. <u>Position and size of details:</u> The chicken and cow are drawn mostly to scale and perspectives with the chicken taking center stage.
5. <u>Position of the cartoonist:</u> Sees fears surrounding eminent domain as overexaggerated.

6. <u>Primary purpose of the cartoon:</u> Ridicule those who believe that all is lost if eminent domain remains in effect.

7. <u>How details illustrate the primary purpose:</u> Size and form of print indicates the chicken's state of mind. The sigh of the calmly chewing cow indicates its recognition of the chicken's silly warning. The chicken's last warning that says the cow is a threatening monster is just wrong and over the top.

8. <u>Indication of alternative viewpoints:</u> Yes, both sides are indicated.

As pointed out previously, each of these steps is important in understanding an editorial cartoon, but it is not necessary that you write out each of them every time you come across one in the newspaper, and so forth. Most of the analysis is done quickly in your mind, but when you are practicing techniques and strategies, it is most beneficial to write out, just as our writer did, each of the previous eight steps.

Practice critically reading editorial cartoons that you find in newspapers and news magazines. You might even try a few included in your history textbook.

Strategy 2: Selecting Sources

Once you've carefully read the prompt, critically read each of the given texts, and decided on your claim, you must choose which of the sources you will use in your essay. This choice is dependent on your answers to the following:

- What is your purpose?
- Is the text background information or pertinent information?
- Does the source give new information or information that other sources cover?
- Is this information that will add depth to the essay?
- Does this text reflect the viewpoints of any of the other texts?
- Does this text contradict the viewpoints of any of the other texts?
- Does the source support or oppose your claim?

Our writer has to make some important decisions about the seven texts provided in the Master synthesis essay prompt. As the writer answers each of the previous questions, he or she will decide which texts to use in the essay.

<u>My purpose:</u> to qualify the support and opposition to eminent domain
<u>Background information:</u> *Constitution* (Source A) *Kelo* decision (Source C)
<u>Pertinent information:</u> *60 Minutes* (Source B), Broder (Source E), Survey (Source G)

A helpful technique to answer the next several questions is to construct a quick chart that incorporates all of the sources at once. The following is a sample of such a chart.

SOURCE	TYPE OF INFO	ADDS DEPTH	REFLECTS VIEWS OF OTHER TEXTS	SUPPORT OF CLAIM
A	Primary and covered by Sources C and E	Yes	No	Yes and no
B	Covered by Sources C–G	Yes	Yes	Yes
C	Covered by Sources A, D, E	Yes	Yes, Sources D, G	Yes and no
D	Covered by Sources A, C	Not really	Yes, Sources A, C	Yes and no
E	Covered by Sources B, F, G	Yes	Yes, Sources B, F, G	Yes and no
F	Covered by Sources B, E, G	Not really	Yes, Sources B, E, G	Yes and no
G	Covered by Sources B–F	Yes	Yes, Sources B–F	Yes

There certainly is a great deal of information to gather and consider. The good news is that the more practice you have with this process, the more quickly you will be able to complete the task. Writing the answers to the previous questions for each of the given texts is a good practice technique for you. But, when it comes to a timed writing situation, you will be annotating the given texts as you read them and jotting down brief notes that reflect the type of thinking our writer performed previously. You will NOT have time to write answers to each question for each text. But, you WILL be thinking about them as you read and as you plan.

Practice responding to these questions using editorials, letters to the editor, and editorial cartoons that revolve around current events issues in which you have an interest. Don't ignore your school and local newspapers, and columnists in news magazines and newspapers. **Become an informed reader and citizen!**

After carefully considering each of the given texts, our reader has decided to eliminate both editorial cartoons because neither seems to add much depth. The other five sources can be used to develop a position.

Strategy 3: Choosing Which Parts of the Selected Texts to Use

Pay no attention to those texts you have eliminated. For those sources you have chosen to include in your essay, do the following:

- Review the notes/highlights on each of your chosen passages.
- Ignore those items you have not annotated.
- Determine if each excerpt contributes to the development of your thesis.
    — Identify the major point each will support.
    — Does it strengthen your position or not (if not, ignore it)?
    — How much of the excerpt will you use?
    — Why have it in your essay?
    — What comments can you make about it?

For example: You might construct a chart such as the following:

SOURCE:	A	B	C	E	G
	–Use all of excerpt	–City ¶ 1	–ID Kelo case ¶ 1	–Bullock ".": 1st line in title	–Survey ID
	–Use in Intro	–Background ¶ 1	–Summary in ¶3	–Echeverria".": Line 1, ¶3	–Major result lines 1 & 2
		–1st "." ¶ 2			
		–Mayor's position"." ¶7			
		–Blighted ¶8			

Our writer now has a clear idea of what part(s) of each text to use. The next task is to plan the essay. The following are some planning notes:

INTRO: *Background*
Basic prompt info
My room when grandmother visits
My position—qualify

POINT 1: Kelo *decision* + *Saleets (oppose current ruling)*
     Saleets' mayor (supports ruling)
     My comments
POINT 2: *Broder = Bullock & Echeverria (both qualify and for ruling)*
     Survey

With this brief outline in mind, our writer knows where to place each of the chosen excerpts. If this were a class situation that allotted time for prewriting plans, more details would be possible when constructing the outline.

Note: Our writer chose to jot down a brief outline, but could have chosen to plan the essay in a number of different ways, such as:

- Mapping
- Charting

As we stated earlier in this chapter, for the AP English Language exam, you only have time to write a first draft, and it must be clear, organized, logical, and thoughtful. In developing each of your major points, make certain to:

- Relate it to the thesis/claim
- Use specific examples (personal and otherwise)
- Use selected sources to support the major point
- Incorporate sources into the development of your point
  — Attribution and introduction of cited sources
  — Transitions
  — Mix of direct quotations, summary, and paraphrases

A Note About Summary, Paraphrase, and Inference

No doubt you have been constructing summaries, paraphrases, and inferences as you learned the techniques of close reading and research. As a quick review, here are the definitions of these processes and an example of each. If you have any further questions, we strongly recommend you ask your instructor for clarification and further examples and/or practice.

Summary

If you want to summarize a text, you read closely and locate those key words and/or phrases that enable you to <u>reduce the piece into its essential point</u>(s).

  Example: The previous *New York Times* article by Broder

Number of words in given text: 175

Number of key words underlined: 47

<u>Summary based on the key words and phrases:</u> *For many, the debate about eminent domain centers around opposing local governments using it to seize private property for private development or supporting eminent domain because cities face economic disaster without this necessary power.* (34 words)

Comments: The writer has whittled the original down by more than 73 percent to its essential point.

Practice this strategy on newspaper or magazine articles that you read regularly.

Note: Many online databases provide abstracts of longer articles when you perform a search. You might want to seek these out and read them to see how they are constructed to emphasize only the main points of the articles (Jodi Rice).

Paraphrase

To paraphrase a given text or part of a text, you transpose the original material into your own words. This will probably be close to the number of words in the original. In most cases, you need to cite the original.

Example: The first paragraph in the previous Source C

Paraphrase: Kelo v. New London *is an eminent domain case that was presented to the U.S. Supreme Court in February of 2005. The argument centered around New London using the power of eminent domain to seize private property so that it could be sold and used in the redevelopment of a section of this city (Source C).*

Comments: The original contains 67 words and two sentences, and the 54-word paraphrase is also two sentences long. Our writer has eliminated specific court numbers and the day of the month and combined several phrases into briefer and more direct ones. **Because this background on the *Kelo* case is NOT common knowledge and because our writer is NOT a recognized expert in this field, a citation is necessary.**

Practice this technique on sections of your own course textbooks and on newspaper or magazine articles you read regularly. You might also try to paraphrase the Master exam synthesis prompt itself, both the introduction and the assignment.

Inference

An inference is the process of drawing a conclusion based on specific material. By carefully considering the important information provided in the text, the reader reaches a conclusion or makes a judgment.

Example: Source B given in the synthesis essay prompt

Inference: *Considering the amount of time given to the Saleets as compared to the mayor of their town, one could conclude that* 60 Minutes *is more inclined to side with the homeowners over the local government in this eminent domain confrontation.*

Comments: Seven out of the ten paragraphs in this interview are positively related to the Saleets or their problem. The rhetorical question and answer given by the voiceover in paragraph five is indicative of the position of *60 Minutes*, and the diction used to describe both sides of the issue is more favorable toward the position of the Saleets.

Practice making inferences based on editorials or letters to the editor that you find in your local newspapers. Go a step further. Take a close look at ads you find in the magazines you read regularly and draw some conclusions about their purpose, their intended audience, and the specific way the ads are presented. Remember, you must be able to support each of your inferences from specifics found in the text itself.

Strategy 4: Incorporating Sources into the Text of Your Essay

Let's be realistic. The synthesis essay is not just a list of direct quotations from sources related to the topic. Once you have chosen your passages, you need to place them appropriately and interestingly within the actual text of your essay in the order that you've planned to best support your thesis/claim.

Just how do you do this? You could select from among the following techniques:

Direct quotation—full citation provided at beginning of the sentence

> *John Broder, in his February 21, 2006,* New York Times *article titled "States Curbing Right to Seize Private Homes," quotes Scott G. Bullock of the Institute for Justice: "Our opposition to eminent domain is not across the board . . . What we oppose is eminent domain abuse for private development, and we are encouraging legislators to curtail it."*

Direct quotation—citation placed outside the text

> *In a* 60 Minutes *interview presented on July 4, 2004, Jim Saleet, a homeowner being adversely affected by the current eminent domain policy, stated, "The bottom line is this is morally wrong . . . This is our home . . . We're not blighted. . . . This is a close-knit, beautiful neighborhood" (Source E).*

Paraphrase of and direct quotation from the third paragraph—citation placed outside of the text

> *John D. Echeverria, an authority on land-use policy, sees a danger arising from legislatures doing away with many of the powers of eminent domain. For the Director of the Georgetown Environmental Law and Policy Institute, if this policy change takes place across the country, there is a real danger that many urban areas will experience "economic decline" (Source E).*

Combination of direct quotation and paraphrase—citation provided outside of text; note the use of the ellipsis

> *In 2005, a 5–4 Supreme Court decision in the* Kelo v. New London *case ruled that ". . . the government taking of property from one private owner to give to another in furtherance of economic development constitutes a permissible 'public use' under the Fifth Amendment" (Source C).*

Notice that each of the examples integrates the source material into the text. The information is not just plopped down on the page. Take a close look at how our writer integrates the second example into the following paragraph in his essay.

> *Contrary to what the Court sees as "permissible public use" (Source C), I believe that a government taking a person's home or business away and allowing another private individual or company to take it over goes against the idea of our private property rights. A good example of this is the situation in Lakewood, Ohio, where the mayor wants to condemn a retired couple's home in order to make way for a privately owned, high-end condominium and shopping mall. As Jim Saleet said in his interview with* 60 Minutes *presented on July 4, 2004, "The bottom line is this is morally wrong . . . This is our home . . . We're not blighted. . . . This is a close-knit, beautiful neighborhood." The Saleets, who have paid off their mortgage, should be allowed to remain there as long as they want and pass it on to their children. Here, individual rights should prevail.*

Comments: Our writer uses the sources to establish negative feelings toward the current policy. The writer then refers to the *Kelo* decision in a summary and proceeds to introduce the context of the Saleet reference with the transition phrase, "A good example of this is . . ." Cohesiveness is achieved by referring to Source C, which was previously cited in the essay. The actual quotation is incorporated into the text with an introductory dependent clause. Two related sentences follow that reemphasize the writer's own position.

Practice: As you read, become aware of HOW professional writers incorporate sources into their writing. Use these as models to practice incorporating outside sources into your own sentences and/or essays.

> *Note:* You might want to take a close look at reviews of movies and books. In many cases, you will find they include direct quotations from the dialogue of the film or passages from the book.

Strategy 5: Writing the Conclusion

Our writer has used each of the excerpts in the body of the essay, EXCEPT for the survey information. Although this number is quite important, it does not fit into the development of the body paragraphs. Therefore, the writer decides to incorporate this survey result into the conclusion. It will contribute to a strong final statement. Following are three different ways to use the survey.

Direct quotation—citation after sentence

> *68% of survey respondents said that they "favored legislative limits on the government's ability to take private property away from owners . . ." (Source G).*

Direct quotation—citation within sentence

> *According to a survey conducted by CNN on July 23, 2005, 66% of those responding said "never" to the question, "Should local governments be able to seize homes and businesses?"*

Paraphrase—citation outside sentence

> *In recent polls conducted by both the* Washington Times *and CNN, over 60% said no when asked if local governments should be able to take over private homes and businesses (Source G).*

Carefully consider how this sentence is incorporated into the concluding paragraph.

> *Ultimately, I have to agree with the large majority of people who responded to recent polls conducted by both the* Washington Times *and CNN. When asked if local governments should be able to take over private homes and businesses, over 60% said "no" (Source G). But, I will have to be open to the possibility that public use and the greater good may, in some cases, be the only viable solution to a complicated problem.*

Comments: The source material is sandwiched between two effective sentences. The first presents our writer's position and leads the reader to the cited excerpt employed to make the point. The last sentence begins with the word "But," which indicates that the writer is qualifying the cited sources in this paragraph and throughout the essay.

Final Comment

Remember, you MUST establish a position, and each source you choose to use MUST support and develop your position.

Rapid Review

- Establish a position on the issue.
- Critically read all given texts and any introductory material provided.
- Annotate your sources using the critical reading guidelines.
- Select appropriate sources to support your position and purpose.
- Choose appropriate excerpts from each of the selected sources that can help develop the thesis.
- Summarize, paraphrase, and draw inferences from selected material.
- Make certain you properly cite each source you incorporate into the essay.
- Construct a conclusion that clearly states a strong final point.
- Proofread.

STEP **5**

Build Your Test-Taking Confidence

Practice Exam 1
Practice Exam 2

PRACTICE EXAM 1

ANSWER SHEET FOR MULTIPLE-CHOICE QUESTIONS

The multiple choice section of the exam will have 45 questions.

- 22–28 will be related to close-reading skills.
- 18–24 will be related to writing skills.

1. _____	16. _____	31. _____
2. _____	17. _____	32. _____
3. _____	18. _____	33. _____
4. _____	19. _____	34. _____
5. _____	20. _____	35. _____
6. _____	21. _____	36. _____
7. _____	22. _____	37. _____
8. _____	23. _____	38. _____
9. _____	24. _____	39. _____
10. _____	25. _____	40. _____
11. _____	26. _____	41. _____
12. _____	27. _____	42. _____
13. _____	28. _____	43. _____
14. _____	29. _____	44. _____
15. _____	30. _____	45. _____

I did ☐ did not ☐ finish all the questions in the allotted 1 hour.

I had _____ correct answers. I had _____ incorrect answers. I left _____ blank.

I have carefully reviewed the explanations of the answers, and I think I need to work on the following types of questions:

The current AP English Language exam divides the multiple choice section of the exam into "Reading" and "Writing" categories with separate texts for each type. However, for our purposes, each of the texts in the practice exam contains both "Reading" and "Writing" questions.

PRACTICE EXAM I
ADVANCED PLACEMENT ENGLISH LANGUAGE

Section I

Total Time—1 hour

Carefully read the following passages and answer the questions that follow.

Questions 1–10 are based on the following passage excerpted from Charles Dickens's *Pictures from Italy* (1846).

Magnificently stern and sombre are the streets of beautiful Florence; and the strong old piles of building make such heaps of shadow, on the ground and in the river, that there is another and different city of rich forms and fancies, always lying at our feet. Prodigious palaces, constructed for defence, with small distrustful windows heavily barred, and walls of great thickness formed of huge masses of rough stone, frown, in   5
their old sulky state, on every street. In the midst of the city—in the Piazza of the Grand Duke, adorned with beautiful statues and the Fountain of Neptune—rises the Palazzo Vecchio, with its enormous overhanging battlements, and the Great Tower that watches over the whole town. In its court-yard—worthy of the Castle of Otranto in its ponderous gloom—is a massive staircase that the heaviest wagon and the stoutest team   10
of horses might be driven up. Within it, is a Great Saloon, faded and tarnished in its stately decorations, and mouldering by grains, but recording yet, in pictures on its walls, the triumphs of the Medici and the wars of the old Florentine people. The prison is hard by, in an adjacent court-yard of the building—a foul and dismal place, where some men are shut up close, in small cells like ovens; and where others look through   15
bars and beg; where some are playing draughts, and some are talking to their friends, who smoke, the while, to purify the air and some are buying wine and fruit of women-vendors; and all are squalid, dirty, and vile to look at. "They are merry enough, Signor," says the Jailer. "They are all blood-stained here," he adds, indicating, with his hand, three-fourths of the whole building. Before the hour is out, an old man, eighty years   20
of age, quarrelling over a bargain with a young girl of seventeen, stabs her dead, in the market-place full of bright flowers; and is brought in prisoner, to swell the number.

Among the four old bridges that span the river, the Ponte Vecchio—that bridge which is covered with the shops of Jewellers and Goldsmiths—is a most enchanting feature in the scene. The space of one house, in the center, being left open, the view   25
beyond is shown as in a frame; and that precious glimpse of sky, and water, and rich buildings, shining so quietly among the huddled roofs and gables on the bridge, is exquisite. Above it, the Gallery of the Grand Duke crosses the river. It was built to connect the two Great Palaces by a secret passage; and it takes its jealous course among streets and houses, with true despotism: going where it lists, and spurning every obstacle   30
away, before it.

1. The purpose of the passage is to
   A. condemn the squalor of Florence
   B. entice visitors to Florence
   C. praise the Grand Duke
   D. present the dichotomy existing in Florence
   E. reveal the author's worldliness

2. The primary rhetorical strategy used by the author is
   A. narration
   B. description
   C. analysis
   D. process
   E. argument

3. In developing his purpose, the author uses all of the following rhetorical devices except:
   A. spatial organization
   B. metaphor and simile
   C. comparison and contrast
   D. imagery
   E. chronological order

4. Which of the following lines contains an example of paradox?
   A. line 17
   B. lines 18–19
   C. lines 4–5
   D. lines 26–27
   E. line 29

5. The most probable function of the selected detail which focuses on the murder of the young girl by the old man (20–22) is
   A. to emphasize the brutality of the citizens
   B. to establish a tone of pathos
   C. to criticize the city's government
   D. to warn visitors about the dangers of the city
   E. to emphasize the contrasts evident in the city

6. The abrupt shift caused by a lack of transition between paragraphs 1 and 2 serves to do all of the following except:
   A. reemphasize the unexpected nature of murder
   B. reinforce the idea that there is no connection between the two paragraphs
   C. reinforce the element of contrast
   D. reinforce the author's style
   E. immediately whisk the reader to a place of safety away from the murder scene

7. What can be inferred from the following details taken from the passage
   — "small distrustful windows" (4)
   — "walls of great thickness" (5)
   — "enormous overhanging battlements" (8)
   — "secret passage" (29)
   A. Florence was not architecturally sound.
   B. Florence was designed to protect its artwork.
   C. Florence had experienced both warfare and intrigue.
   D. Florence was unsuited for habitation.
   E. Florence was preparing for war.

8. Lines 11–22 contain examples of which of the following rhetorical device?
   A. antithetical images
   B. anecdotal evidence
   C. parallel structure
   D. denotation
   E. inversion

9. If one were building a house of horrors, which of the following would be best suitable as a model or inspiration?
   A. Piazza of the Grand Duke (6–7)
   B. Fountain of Neptune (7)
   C. Palazzo Vecchio (8)
   D. Ponte Vecchio (23)
   E. Gallery of the Grand Duke (28)

10. The tone of the passage can best be described as
    A. somber and distant
    B. reportorial and appreciative
    C. respectful and dispassionate
    D. satirical and angry
    E. melancholy and reflective

Questions 11–20 are based on the following passage from Margaret Atwood's "Origins of Stories" (1989).

Our first stories come to us through the air. We hear voices.   1

Children in oral societies grow up within a web of stories; but so do all children.   2
We listen before we can read. Some of our listening is more like listening in, to the
calamitous or seductive voices of the adult world, on the radio or the television or in our
daily lives. Often it's an overhearing of things we aren't supposed to hear, eavesdropping
on scandalous gossip or family secrets. From all these scraps of voices, from the
whispers and shouts that surround us, even from ominous silences, the unfilled gaps in
meaning, we patch together for ourselves an order of events, a plot or plots; these, then,
are the things that happen, these are the people they happen to, this is the forbidden
knowledge.

We have all been little pitchers with big ears, shooed out of the kitchen when the   3
unspoken is being spoken, and we have probably all been tale-bearers, blurters at the
dinner table, unwitting violators of adult rules of censorship. Perhaps this is what writers
are: those who never kicked the habit. We remained tale-bearers. We learned to keep
our eyes open, but not to keep our mouths shut.

If we're lucky, we may also be given stories meant for our ears, stories intended for   4
us. These may be children's Bible stories, tidied up and simplified and with the vicious
bits left out. They may be fairy tales, similarly sugared, although if we are very lucky
it will be left in. In any case, these tales will have deliberate, molded shapes, unlike
stories we have patched together for ourselves. They will contain mountains, deserts,
talking donkeys, dragons; and, unlike the kitchen stories, they will have definite
endings. We are likely to accept these stories being on the same level of reality as the
kitchen stories. It's only when we are older that we are taught to regard one kind of
story as real and the other kind as mere invention. This is about the same time we're
taught to believe that dentists are useful, and writers are not.

Traditionally, both the kitchen gossips and the readers-out-loud have been mothers   5
or grandmothers, native languages have been mother tongues, and the kinds of stories
that are told to children have been called nursery tales or old wives' tales. It struck me
as no great coincidence when I learned recently that, when a great number of prominent
writers were asked to write about the family member who had the greatest influence
on their literary careers, almost all of them, male as well as female, had picked their
mothers. Perhaps this reflects the extent to which North American children have been
deprived of the grandfathers, those other great repositories of story; perhaps it will come
to change if men come to share in early child care, and we will have old husbands' tales.
But as things are, language, including the language of our earliest-learned stories, is a
verbal matrix, not a verbal patrix . . .

11. One reason Atwood gives for the presence of
    stories in children's lives is
    A. scandalous gossip
    B. family secrets
    C. supernatural influences
    D. listening
    E. radio and television

12. The close association between the reader and
    the author is immediately established by
    A. a first person, plural point of view
    B. placing the reader into a family situation
    C. using accessible diction and syntax
    D. being emotional
    E. appealing to the child in the reader

13. The last sentence of paragraph 2, "From all these scraps . . ." to "forbidden knowledge," contains all of the following except:
    A. parallel structure
    B. a periodic sentence
    C. prepositional phrases
    D. a compound-complex sentence
    E. an ellipsis

14. The phrase "forbidden knowledge" in the last sentence of the second paragraph can best be categorized as
    A. a paradox
    B. a biblical allusion
    C. hyperbole
    D. antithesis
    E. understatement

15. According to the author, the writer is like a child because
    A. "We are likely to accept these stories being of the same level of reality as the kitchen stories" [paragraph 4]
    B. ". . . we are taught to regard one kind of story as real . . ." [paragraph 4, next to last line]
    C. "We remained tale-bearers" [paragraph 3]
    D. "We will have old husbands' tales" [paragraph 5]
    E. ". . . the kinds of stories that are told to children have been called nursery tales . . ." [paragraph 5]

16. A careful reading of the last two paragraphs of the excerpt can lead the reader to infer that
    A. society does not value the storyteller
    B. women should be the storytellers
    C. storytelling should be left to children
    D. men can never be storytellers
    E. the author is a mother herself

17. The predominant tone of the passage is best stated as
    A. scathingly bitter
    B. sweetly effusive
    C. reverently detailed
    D. wistfully observant
    E. aggressively judgmental

18. The author makes use of which of the following rhetorical strategies?
    A. narration and description
    B. exposition and persuasion
    C. process and analysis
    D. anecdote and argument
    E. cause and effect

19. A shift in the focus of the passage occurs with which of the following?
    A. "If we're lucky" [paragraph 4]
    B. "Perhaps this is what writers are . . ." [paragraph 3]
    C. "Traditionally, . . ." [paragraph 5]
    D. "Perhaps this reflects the extent to which North American children have been deprived of the grandfathers . . ." [paragraph 5]
    E. "But as things are, language, including the language of the earliest-learned stories . . ." [paragraph 5]

20. The primary purpose of the passage is to
    A. plead for men to tell more stories
    B. criticize censorship
    C. idealize children
    D. analyze storytelling
    E. look at the sources of storytelling

Questions 21–30 are based on the following passage from "The American Dream and the American Negro," James Baldwin's debate with William F. Buckley at The Cambridge Union Society at Cambridge University in 1965.

This debate was between arch conservative William F. Buckley, the editor of the National Review, *and James Baldwin, an African American playwright, essayist and poet. The topic was, "That the American dream has come at the expense of the American Negro." Below is an excerpt from Baldwin's famous speech.*

. . . One of things the white world does not know, but I think I know, is that black people are just like everybody else. We are also mercenaries, dictators, murderers, liars. We are human, too. Unless we can establish some kind of dialogue between those people who enjoy the American dream and those people who have not achieved it, we will be in terrible trouble. This is what concerns me most. We are sitting in this room and we are all civilized; we can talk to each other, at least on certain levels, so that we can walk out of here assuming that the measure of our politeness has some effect on the world.   1

I remember when the ex-Attorney General, Mr. Robert Kennedy, said it was conceivable that in 40 years in America we might have a Negro President. That sounded like a very emancipated statement to white people. They were not in Harlem when this statement was first heard. They did not hear the laughter and bitterness and scorn with which this statement was greeted. From the point of view of the man in the Harlem barber shop, Bobby Kennedy only got here yesterday and now he is already on his way to the Presidency. We were here for 400 years and now he tells us that maybe in 40 years, if you are good, we may let you become President.   2

Perhaps I can be reasoned with, but I don't know—neither does Martin Luther King—none of us knows how to deal with people whom the white world has so long ignored, who don't believe anything the white world says and don't entirely believe anything I or Martin say. You can't blame them.   3

It seems to me that the City of New York has had, for example, Negroes in it for a very long time. The City of New York was able in the last 15 years to reconstruct itself, to tear down buildings and raise great new ones, and has done nothing whatever except build housing projects, mainly in the ghettoes, for the Negroes. And of course the Negroes hate it. The children can't bear it. They want to move out of the ghettoes. If American pretensions were based on more honest assessments of life, it would not mean for Negroes that when someone says "urban renewal" some Negroes are going to be thrown out into the streets, which is what it means now.   4

It is a terrible thing for an entire people to surrender to the notion that one-ninth of its population is beneath them. Until the moment comes when we, the Americans, are able to accept the fact that my ancestors are both black and white, that on that continent we are trying to forge a new identity, that we need each other, that I am not a ward of America, I am not an object of missionary charity, I am one of the people who built the country—until this moment comes there is scarcely any hope for the American dream. If the people are denied participation in it, by their very presence they will wreck it. And if that happens it is a very grave moment for the West.   5

21. The thesis is which sentence in the first paragraph?
    A. 1
    B. 3
    C. 4
    D. 5
    E. 6

22. The primary audience for this speech is
    A. readers of the *New York Times* and the *London Times*
    B. William S. Buckley
    C. Cambridge students and the Cambridge Union Society
    D. Cambridge University class in world politics
    E. Cambridge University History faculty

23. Which of the following best describes Baldwin's exigence for this piece?
    A. the need to confront the cultural bias toward black Americans
    B. a distrust of William F. Buckley and his political viewpoints
    C. the need to get publicity for his newest novel
    D. the desire to advocate for equal rights for black Americans
    E. the desire to win the debate

24. Which of the following best identifies Baldwin's purpose?
    A. to win the debate
    B. to show how inadequate conservatives are when dealing with race relations
    C. to call for a rebellion on the part of black Americans
    D. to convince the audience of the dire consequences of refusing to afford black Americans equal partnership in the promise that is America.
    E. to build support for the civil rights movement in the United States

25. In paragraph 2, the speaker employs which of the following rhetorical strategies to further develop his thesis?
    A. cause/effect
    B. comparison/contrast
    C. description
    D. process
    E. definition

26. The primary rhetorical strategy employed in paragraph 2 introduces the audience to Baldwin's sense of
    A. history
    B. optimism
    C. inevitability
    D. humility
    E. irony

27. In context, paragraphs 2, 3, and 4 could be used to support which of the following claims about the writer's tone?
    A. His tone when discussing white Americans is condescending.
    B. His tone when discussing the situation of black Americans is bitter and ominous.
    C. He tone is beseeching when discussing what white Americans can do when dealing with the black population.
    D. He adopts a reverent, admiring tone when dealing with racial equality.
    E. He adopts a detached, impersonal tone when addressing the situation of black Americans.

28. In the third paragraph, Baldwin introduces Martin Luther King, Jr., into his argument primarily to
    A. question the effectiveness of the methods King uses
    B. underscore his own involvement in the civil rights movement
    C. affirm the righteousness of the civil rights movement
    D. emphasize the complexity and difficulty that black Americans have dealing with what white Americans say and what they do
    E. encourage civil rights activists to follow the example set by Martin Luther King, Jr.

29. The final paragraph is both a warning and a condemnation that is based primarily on which of the following rhetorical devices?
A. metaphor
B. juxtaposition
C. parallel structure
D. hyperbole
E. allusion

30. A primary purpose of Baldwin's switching between first, second, and third person when referring to himself is to
A. connect with the audience and its own history
B. prosecute white America for its treatment of blacks
C. motivate his audience to sympathize with black Americans
D. advocate for required sensitivity training in all American schools
E. emphasize that blacks are individuals and a part of all that makes up America: its history, its promise, its triumphs, its failures

Questions 31–40 are based on "Making the World Safe for Stupidity," by Leonard Pitts, Jr., which appeared in the *Chicago Tribune* on May 30, 2000.

So here's the question: How stupid are you?   1

Let's say on a scale of 1 to 10, how stupid do you figure?   2

Yes, I know I'm being awfully rude. It's just that lately I find myself deeply annoyed   3
at the way your feeblemindedness—and more importantly, mine—are considered a
foregone conclusion by the people who make and market the stuff we buy.

I refer you to the fine print of an automotive ad I saw the other day on television.   4
Doesn't matter which one, because they're all the same. The computer-enhanced image
shows the car performing some can't-be-done feat—driving up a wall, let's say—and the
text at the bottom invariably admonishes: "Professional driver on closed course. Please
do not attempt."

Whew. Glad they told me. Otherwise, I might have tried to drive my minivan to the   5
observation deck of the Empire State Building.

I wrote a column about cautions like this a couple of years ago. "Idiot warnings,"   6
I called them, as in, those warnings that would insult Homer Simpson's intelligence,
much less the intelligence of a couple of smart cookies like you and me. It wasn't a car
ad that set me off that time, but a flimsy toy hard hat whose makers found it necessary
to tell buyers that it provided no protection against head injury.

My rant resonated with readers, many of whom sent in idiot warnings of their own.   7
Like a bread-pudding container that says, "Product will be hot after heating." Or the
iron that cautions, "Do not iron clothes on body." Or a chain saw that admonished,
"Do not attempt to stop chain with your hands."

Wait, there's more: 8
- How a windshield sunshade that says, "Don't operate vehicle with shade in
  place?"
- The Christmas lights that say, "For indoor or outdoor use only."
- The sleep aid that says, "Warning: may cause drowsiness."
- *Or my personal favorite, the Superman costume that wants you to know, "This
  costume will not enable wearer to fly."*

One imagines some guy perched on the roof, wearing his costume with the big "S"   9
on his chest, fists thrust out before him and getting ready to fly. Just before he jumps, a
move that would clearly improve the gene pool, he reads the warning and frowns.

Don't get me wrong. I understand why people who make stuff find it necessary to   10
insult the intelligence of those who buy it. In these litigious days, it's not inconceivable
that a corporation might wind up paying a multimillion-dollar judgment to, say, some
doofus who didn't realize that a sleep aid might make you sleepy or a Halloween
costume purchaser who hurts himself trying to fly.

So corporate America covers its hindquarters by making the world safe for stupidity.   11
But it occurs to me that in the process, corporate America also does profound damage
to the human species.

Follow me on this. Remember what you learned in biology about Charles Darwin's   12
theory of natural selection? It says, in essence, that the strong survive. Not only that,
but they pass their strength down the genetic line.

The problem is that now, thanks to idiot warnings, the weak survive, too. This in   13
turn allows them to pass their weakness down as well. I mean, did anyone stop to think
that maybe the guy who put on the Superman suit and went up to the roof was actually

meant to leap off? Then he reads that warning and, instead of liquefying himself against the pavement, he survives. To procreate.

Stupidity, it seems obvious to me, is spreading like kudzu.[1]   14

In the face of this national emergency, I offer two proposals: First, that we away, now   15 and forever, with idiot warnings. Second, that the federal government supply every man, woman, and child in this country . . . a Superman suit.

I know it sounds harsh, but it's the only way.   16

---

[1] kudzu is an invasive species of climbing vine that overwhelms the surrounding vegetation.

31. The exigence for Pitts's column is most probably
   A. frustration with the dumbing down of ads and warning labels
   B. anger toward the advertising world
   C. seeing consumers take warning labels too seriously
   D. one too many warning labels
   E. a desire to seek revenge on corporations he sees as paternalistic

32. The thesis is located in which paragraph?
   A. 1
   B. 2
   C. 3
   D. 11
   E. 16

33. Which rhetorical strategy does Pitts primarily use to support his thesis?
   A. comparison/contrast
   B either/or alternatives
   C. cause/effect
   D. exemplification
   E. narration

34. The tone of the essay can best be described as
   A instructive
   B. sarcastic
   C. exhortative
   D. congratulatory
   E. pensive

35. Which of the following paragraphs does NOT help develop the tone of the essay?
   A. 5
   B. 6
   C. 10
   D. 11
   E. 12

36. The function of the rhetorical questions used throughout the essay is to
   A. win the involvement and favor of his audience
   B. lead the audience through a series of accusations
   C. introduce each new claim
   D. transition to a different time frame
   E. strengthen his portrayal of corporate America

37. The primary audience for this column is most likely
   A. advertising agencies
   B. retail salespeople
   C. the average consumer
   D. injury attorneys
   E. corporations

38. Which of the following is not included in the creation of Pitts' primary purpose?
   A. to chide the stupidity of the American consumer
   B. to criticize corporations' opinions about the American consumer
   C. to offer a valid, universal solution to stupid ads and warnings
   D. to advocate for laws prohibiting unneeded warnings
   E. to make readers aware of the corporate world's dumbing down of the American consumer

39. The writer uses which of the following organizational patterns to develop his line of reasoning?
   A. deduction
   B. familiar to unfamiliar
   C. induction
   D. chronological
   E. unfamiliar to familiar

40. The writer has decided NOT to use the following sentence to begin paragraph 12.

I believe humanity is rapidly going downhill, and if you remember your high school days, you'll agree with me.

Which of the following would NOT be a reason for his decision?

A. A transition is already in place.
B. The writer has already involved the reader.
C. The second sentence lets the reader know the reference is to high school.
D. The logic of the argument needs clarification.
E. The sentence may lead the reader to think that a new subject is being introduced.

Questions 41–45 are based on the passage written by poet John Ciardi who was a long time member of the staff of the now extinct literary weekly, *The Saturday Review* (1964).

1   The middle drawer of an average desk may be described as a sliding box, about two and a half inches deep and about two and a half feet square, beginning with a pencil rack and ending in oblivion. Such, at least, are the estimated dimensions and the obvious organization of the antique but average desk at which I sit [*The Saturday Review*] when I am sitting there, which I do only irregularly, and only as the spirit moves me.

2   The average pencil rack with which this average middle drawer begins was designed to hold the pencils that lie scattered across the desk top. The remaining cavern, for whatever purpose it was designed, is the oblivion file.

3   Moved by what might be called an obscure impulse (to obscure my average reluctance to get to work), I recently fell to taking inventory of my average pencil rack and came up with the following itemization: two red pencils (unsharpened), one black grease pencil, one ball point and one fountain pen (both broken), one mailing sticker that had curled up into a small tube and which I unrolled to find that I had once printed on it with some care my social security number (032-10-1225), one purchaser's receipt for a money order in the amount of the opening night of *The Rise of Arturo Ui*, one second-best (therefore $7.15) theater ticket stub (R108), one letter opener, one spool of J. & P. Coats black thread (15 cents, 125 yards, number 60, origin and purpose unknown), one dentist's tool (broken, but obviously useful for picking things out of things if I had anything of that sort to pick related things out of), two nail files, one pair of cuff links, one metal pill box (empty, origin and purpose unknown), one glass marble (probably a souvenir of a visit from Ben), one four-for-a-quarter-while-you-wait-press-the-button photo taken, as I recall, at, then, Idlewilde (JFK) Airport and showing Jonnel and me looking at one another in some sort of fond but unsubstantiated pride, one twenty-cent stamp (1938 Presidential issue, James Garfield), two rubber bands, one pocket comb, a litter of paper clips, one 1889 quarter (to give to the kids for their collection as soon as I am sure they will not spend it on candy), one Canadian dime and one British halfpenny (to be given to them any time), one air-mail sticker, two six-penny nails, three thumb tacks, two match folders, one broken tie clip (probably repairable), one small screw driver (in case any small screws show up to be driven?), one pocket pack of Kleenex, one pair of paper scissors, one staple remover, assorted grit.

4   It was, I concluded in an average glow of identity with all mankind, an irreproachably average holding, and carried away by goodwill toward average man, I pulled the drawer wide to explore what lay beyond.

Let me forego itemization for a more shapen[1] thought. Can the years of man's life be   5
brought to mere inventory? Let any man look into his own average heart and desk for
his own average litters and so learn to describe himself to himself.

My one perhaps off-average accumulation consisted of about two pounds of   6
individually wrapped sugar cubes, a hoard I come by because the coffee I send out for,
and which I drink black and without sugar, always arrives with its quota of sugar
cubes, which I always think of saving for the kids until I always remember that they
eat too much sugar without my adding more, but which (to round out this month's
exercise in all-out sentence structure) I can never bring myself to throw away, their
average cavities and my more than average disorder notwithstanding, and because on
days when I am not cleaning out my middle desk drawer I can always play blocks
with them. There is always some way of not working.

---

[1] shapen: having a designated shape

41. Located in which paragraph, the thesis
indicates which organizational pattern for this
passage?
A. paragraph 1, deduction
B. paragraph 2, deduction
C. paragraph 4, induction
D. paragraph 5, induction
E. paragraph 6, induction

42. If one accepts that form follows function,
one may conclude that the third paragraph is
composed of only one sentence because
A. Ciardi is illustrating his control of syntax
B. it's the most important paragraph in the
passage
C. the complex content demanded a
complicated presentation
D. listing makes it easier to read
E. the contents of the drawer are observed and
noted in a single glance

43. Ciardi contrasts the topics and syntax of
paragraphs 3 and 6 with that of paragraph 4
and 5 primarily to
A. create a logical "nest" in which to place
personal thoughts about himself
B. explain the complexities of keeping a desk
drawer neat and useful
C. emphasize the difference between the
objective world and the world of ideas
D. provide specific examples of comments
given in paragraphs 1 and 2
E. suggest a method of keeping track of what
is superficial and what is meaningful

44. Which of the following rhetorical devices is not
used by Ciardi to develop the gentle
humor of the passage?
A. repetition of the word "average"
B. hyperbole
C. parenthetical comments
D. irony
E. metaphor

45. After carefully considering the thesis and
the logic involved in the organization of the
passage, the reader could best describe Ciardi's
purpose as
A. an inventory of his desk drawer
B. a description of his relationship with his
grandchildren
C. a self-reflection
D. an examination of his writing process
E. a nostalgic and whimsical memoir piece

END OF SECTION I

Section II

Total Time—2 hours

Question 1

Suggested Writing Time: 40 minutes

A new word has entered the American vocabulary: *affluenza*. A 1997 PBS documentary titled *Affluenza* introduced this new term and defined it: "n. 1. The bloated, sluggish, and unfulfilled feeling that results from efforts to keep up with the Joneses. 2. An epidemic of stress, overwork, waste, and indebtedness caused by dogged pursuit of the American Dream. 3. An unsustainable addiction to economic growth."

Since then, scholars, journalists, political leaders, artists, and even comedians have made America's ever-increasing consumption the subject of dire warnings, academic studies, social commentary, campaign promises, and late-night TV jokes.

Carefully read the following sources (including any introductory information). **Then, in an essay that synthesizes at least three of the sources, take a position that supports, opposes, or qualifies the claim that Americans are never satisfied. They are constantly wanting new things and are never content with what they have. There is a superabundance of "stuff," and Americans have lost their sense of meaning. As Sheryl Crow's 2002 lyrics state, *"it's not having what you want. It's wanting what you've got."***

Make certain that you take a position and that the essay centers on your argument. Use the sources to support your reasoning; avoid simply summarizing the sources. You may refer to the sources by their letters (Source A, Source B, etc.) or by the identifiers in the parentheses below.

- Source A (*U.S. Constitution*)
- Source B (*60 Minutes*)
- Source C (*Kelo* decision)
- Source D (Koterba, editorial/political cartoon)
- Source E (Broder)
- Source F (Britt, editorial/political cartoon)
- Source G (CNN and American Survey)

- Provide evidence from at least three of the provided sources to support the thesis. Indicate clearly the sources used through direct quotation, paraphrase, or summary. Sources may be cited as Source A, Source B, etc., or by using the description in parentheses.
- Explain the relationship between the evidence and the thesis.
- Demonstrate an understanding of the rhetorical situation.
- Use appropriate grammar and punctuation in communicating the argument

Source A
Aristotle's *Nicomachean Ethics*

> *Certainly the future is obscure to us, while happiness, we claim, is an end and something in every way final. . . . If so, we shall call happy those among living men in whom these conditions are, and are to be fulfilled.*
>
> *Happiness is desirable in itself and never for the sake of something else. But honor, pleasure, reason, and every virtue we choose indeed for themselves, but we choose them also for the sake of happiness, judging that by means of them we shall be happy. Happiness, on the other hand, no one chooses for the sake of these, nor, in general, for anything other than itself. Happiness, then, is something final and self-sufficient.*
>
> *He is happy who lives in accordance with complete virtue and is sufficiently equipped with external goods, not for some chance period but throughout a complete life.*
>
> *To judge from the lives that men lead, most men seem to identify the good, or happiness, with pleasure: which is the reason why they love the life of enjoyment. The*

mass of mankind are evidently quite slavish in their tastes, preferring a life suitable to beasts.

With regard to what happiness is (men) differ, and the many do not give the same account as the wise. For the former think it is some plain and obvious thing, like pleasure, wealth, or honor. They differ, however, from one another—and often even the same man identifies it with different things, with health when he is ill, with wealth when he is poor.

Source B
The Declaration of Independence
From the opening paragraph of The Declaration of Independence.

We hold these Truths to be self-evident, that all Men are created equal, that they are endowed by their Creator with certain unalienable Rights: that among these are Life, Liberty, and the Pursuit of Happiness. That to secure these Rights, Governments are instituted among Men, deriving their just Powers from the Consent of the Governed . . .

Source C
Utilitarianism, written by John Stuart Mill, an eighteenth-century British philosopher, in 1863. Available at http://www.utilitarianism.com/mill2.htm.
The following is an excerpt from Chapter 2 entitled "What Utilitarianism Is."

. . . The creed which accepts as the foundation of morals, Utility, or the Greatest Happiness Principle, holds that actions are right in proportion as they tend to promote happiness, wrong as they tend to produce the reverse of happiness. By happiness is intended pleasure, and the absence of pain; by unhappiness, pain, and the privation of pleasure. . . .

. . . no intelligent human being would consent to be a fool, no instructed person would be an ignoramus, no person of feeling and conscience would be selfish and base, even though they should be persuaded that the fool, the dunce, or the rascal is better satisfied with his lot than they are with theirs. They would not resign what they possess more than he for the most complete satisfaction of all desires which they have in common with him. If they ever fancy they would, it is only in cases of unhappiness so extreme, that to escape from it they would exchange their lot for almost any other, however undesirable in their own eyes. A being of higher faculties [humans] requires more to make him happy, is capable probably of more acute suffering, and certainly accessible to it at more points, than one of the inferior type [animals]: but in spite of these liabilities, he can never really wish to sink into what he feels to be a lower grade of existence. . . . Whoever supposes that this preference takes place at a sacrifice of happiness—that the superior being, in anything like equal circumstances, is not happier than the inferior—confounds two very different ideas, of happiness and content. It is indisputable that the being whose capacities of enjoyment are low, has the greatest chance of having them fully satisfied; and a highly endowed being will always feel that any happiness which he can look for, as the world is constituted, is imperfect. But he can learn to bear its imperfections, but only because he feels not at all the good which those imperfections qualify. It is better to be a human being dissatisfied than a pig satisfied; better to be Socrates dissatisfied than the fool satisfied. And if the fool, or the pig, are of different opinion, it is because they only know their own side of the question. The other party to the comparison knows both sides.

Source D
Cartoon by Jim Sizemore
Available at http://www.cartoonstock.com/blowup.asp?imageref=jsi0087&artist=Sizemore, +Jim&topic=consumerism.
This cartoon appeared in a recent issue of *The New Yorker*.

"Something is missing."

Source E
O'Neill, Jesse H. *The Golden Ghetto: The Psychology of Affluence*, The Affluenza Project: Milwaukee, Wisconsin, 1997.
The following is adapted from passages in Jesse H. O'Neill's book and from the mission statement of The Affluenza Project founded by O'Neill. http://www.affluenza.com.

> *The malaise that currently grips our country comes not from the fact that we don't have enough wealth, but from a terrifying knowledge that has begun to enter our consciousness that we have based our entire lives, our entire culture and way of being on the belief that "just a little bit more" will finally buy happiness.*
>
> *Although many people in our culture are beginning to question the assumptions of the American Dream, we still live in a time of compulsive and wasteful consumerism.*
>
> *Statistics to consider:*
>
> - *Per capita consumption in the United States has increased 45 percent in the past twenty years.*
> - *During the same period, quality of life as measured by the index of social health has decreased by roughly the same percentage.*
> - *The average working woman plays with her children forty minutes a week— and shops six hours.*
> - *Ninety-three percent of teenage girls list shopping as their favorite pastime.*

Source F

Lapham, Lewis. *Money and Class in America: Notes and Observations on Our Civil Religion*, Grove Press: New York, 1988.

The following is a passage from Mr. Lapham's text.

I think it fair to say that the current ardor of the American faith in money easily surpasses the degrees of intensity achieved by other societies in other times and places. Money means so many things to us—spiritual as well as temporal—that we are at a loss to know how to hold its majesty at bay. . . .

Henry Adams in his autobiography remarks that although the Americans weren't much good as materialists they had been "so deflected by the pursuit of money" that they could turn "in no other direction." The natural distrust of the contemplative temperament arises less from the innate Philistinism than from a suspicion of anything that cannot be counted, stuffed, framed or mounted over the fireplace in the den. Men remain free to rise or fall in the world, and if they fail it must be because they willed it so. The visible signs of wealth testify to an inward state of grace, and without at least some of these talismans posted in one's house or on one's person an American loses all hope of demonstrating to himself the theorem of his happiness. Seeing is believing, and if an American success is to count for anything in the world it must be clothed in the raiment of property. As often as not it isn't the money itself that means anything; it is the use of money as the currency of the soul.

Against the faith in money, other men in other times and places have raised up countervailing faiths in family, honor, religion, intellect and social class. The merchant princes of medieval Europe would have looked upon the American devotion as sterile stupidity; the ancient Greek would have regarded it as a form of insanity. Even now, in the last decades of a century commonly defined as American, a good many societies both in Europe and Asia manage to balance the desire for wealth against the other claims of the human spirit. An Englishman of modest means can remain more or less content with the distinction of an aristocratic name or the consolation of a flourishing garden; the Germans show to obscure university professors the deference accorded by Americans only to celebrity; the Soviets honor the holding of political power; in France a rich man is a rich man, to whom everybody grants the substantial powers that his riches command but to whom nobody grants the respect due to a member of the National Academy. But in the United States a rich man is perceived as being necessarily both good and wise, which is an absurdity that would be seen as such not only by a Frenchman but also by a Russian. Not that the Americans are greedier than the French, or less intellectual than the Germans, or more venal than the Russians, but to what other tribunal can an anxious and supposedly egalitarian people submit their definitions of the good, the true and the beautiful if not to the judgment of the bottom line?

Source G

"Wealth" written by Andrew Carnegie,[1] published in *North American Review*, CCCXCI, June 1889. Available at http://facweb.furman.edu/~benson/docs/carnegie.htm.

The following is excerpted from the article by Andrew Carnegie.

The problem of our age is the proper administration of wealth, so that the ties of brotherhood may still bind together the rich and poor in harmonious relationship. The conditions of human life have not only been changed, but revolutionized, within the past few hundred years. In former days there was little difference between the dwelling, dress, food, and environment of the chief and those of his retainers.

The Indians are today where civilized man then was. When visiting the Sioux, I was led to the wigwam of the chief. It was just like the others in external appearance, and even within the difference was trifling between it and those of the poorest of his braves. The contrast between the palace of the millionaire and the cottage of the laborer with us today measures the change which has come with civilization.

This change, however, is not to be deplored, but welcomed as highly beneficial. It is well, nay, essential for the progress of the race, that the houses of some should be homes for all that is highest and best in literature and the arts, and for all the refinements of civilization, rather than that none should be so. Much better this great irregularity than universal squalor. Without wealth there can be no Maecenas.[2] The "good old times" were not good old times. Neither master nor servant was as well situated then as today. A relapse to old conditions would be disastrous to both—not the least so to him who serves—and would sweep away civilization with it. But whether the change be for good or ill, it is upon us, beyond our power to alter, and therefore to be accepted and made the best of. It is waste of time to criticize the inevitable.

[1] Late nineteenth-century American capitalist and philanthropist
[2] Patron of the arts in ancient Rome

Question 2

(Suggested time 40 minutes. This question counts as one-third of the total score for Section II.)

In her 2007 essay, "Two Years Are Better Than Four," Liz Addison responds to conservative historian Rick Perlstein's comment that "college as America used to understand it is coming to an end." Read the passage carefully. Then, in a well-developed essay analyze the rhetorical choices Addison makes to develop her argument about the community college in America.

In your response you should do the following:

- Respond to the prompt with a thesis that analyzes the writer's rhetorical choices.
- Select and use evidence to develop and support your line of reasoning.
- Explain the relationship between the evidence and your thesis.
- Demonstrate an understanding of the rhetorical situation.
- Use appropriate grammar and punctuation in communicating your argument.

Two Years Are Better Than Four   1

Oh, the hand wringing. "College as America used to understand it is coming to an end," bemoans Rick Perlstein and his beatnik friend of fallen face. Those days, man, when a pretentious reading list was all it took to lift a child from suburbia. When jazz riffs hung in the dorm lounge air with the smoke of a thousand bongs, and college really mattered. Really mattered?

Rick Perlstein thinks so. It mattered so much to him that he never got over his four   2
years at the University of Privilege. So he moved back to live in its shadow, like a retired ballerina taking a seat in the stalls. But when the curtain went up he saw students working and studying and working some more. Adults before their time. Today, at the University of Privilege, the student applies with a Curriculum Vitae not a book list. Shudder.

Thus, Mr. Perlstein concludes, the college experience—a rite of passage as it was meant it to be—must have come to an end. But he is wrong. For Mr. Perlstein, so rooted in his own nostalgia, is looking for himself—and he would never think to look for himself in the one place left where the college experience of self-discovery does still matter to those who get there. My guess, reading between the lines, is that Mr. Perlstein has never set foot in an American community college.

3

The philosophy of the community college, and I have been to two of them, is one that unconditionally allows its students to begin. Just begin. Implicit in this belief is the understanding that anything and everything is possible. Just follow any one of the 1,655 road signs, and pop your head inside—yes, they let anyone in—and there you will find discoveries of a first independent film, a first independent thought, a first independent study. This college experience remains as it should. This college brochure is not marketing for the parents—because the parents, nor grandparents, probably never went to college themselves.

4

I left school hurriedly at sixteen. Thomas Jefferson once wrote, "Everybody should have an education proportional to their life." In my case, my life became proportional to my education. But, in doing so, it had the good fortune to land me in a community college and now, from that priceless springboard, I too seek admission to the University of Privilege. Enter on empty and leave with a head full of dreams? How can Mr. Perlstein say college does not matter anymore?

5

The community college system is America's hidden public service gem. If I were a candidate for office I would campaign from every campus. Not to score political points, but simply to make sure that anyone who is looking to go to college in this country knows where to find one. Just recently, I read an article in *The New York Times* describing a "college application essay" workshop for low-income students. I was strangely disturbed that those interviewed made no mention of community college. Mr Perlstein might have been equally disturbed, for the thrust of the workshop was no different to that of an essay coach to the affluent. "Make Life Stories Shine," beams the headline. Or, in other words, prove yourself worldly, insightful, cultured, mature, before you get to college.

6

Yet, down at X.Y.C.C. it is still possible to enter the college experience as a rookie. That is the understanding—that you will grow up a little bit with your first English class, a bit more with your first psychology class, a whole lot more with your first biology, physics, chemistry. That you may shoot through the roof with calculus, philosophy, or genetics. "College is the key," a young African-American student writes for the umpteenth torturous revision of his college essay, "as well as hope." Oh, I wanted desperately to say, please tell him about community college. Please tell him that hope can begin with just one placement test.

7

When Mr. Perlstein and friends say college no longer holds importance, they mourn for both the individual and society. Yet, arguably, the community college experience is more critical to the nation than that of former beatnik types who, lest we forget, did not change the world. The community colleges of America cover this country college by college and community by community. They offer a network of affordable future, of accessible hope, and an option to dream. In the cold light of day, is it perhaps not more important to foster students with dreams rather than a building takeover?

8

I believe so. I believe the community college system to be one of America's uniquely   9
great institutions. I believe it should be celebrated as such. "For those who find it
necessary to go to a two-year college," begins one University of Privilege admissions
paragraph. None too subtle in its implication, but very true. For some students, from
many backgrounds, would never breathe the college experience if it were not for the
community college. Yes, it is here that Mr. Perlstein will find his college years of self-
discovery, and it is here he will find that college does still matter.

Question 3

In his essay "The Wilderness Idea," Wallace Stegner states the following.

> *Without any remaining wilderness we are committed wholly, without chance for even
> momentary reflection and rest, to a headlong drive into our technological termite-life,
> the Brave New World of a completely man-controlled environment.* (1960)

Write a well-constructed essay that supports your position on Stegner's statement about
conservation of wildernness.

- Respond to the prompt with a defensible thesis that relates to the prompt.
- Select and use evidence to develop and support the line of reasoning.
- Explain the relationship between the evidence and the thesis.
- Demonstrate an understanding of the rhetorical situation.
- Use appropriate grammar and punctuation in communicating the argument.

END OF SECTION II

ANSWER KEY

1. D	16. A	31. A
2. B	17. D	32. C
3. E	18. B	33. D
4. A	19. C	34. B
5. E	20. E	35. E
6. B	21. A	36. A
7. C	22. C	37. C
8. A	23. A	38. C
9. C	24. D	39. A
10. B	25. B	40. D
11. D	26. E	41. D
12. A	27. B	42. E
13. E	28. D	43. A
14. B	29. C	44. B
15. C	30. E	45. C

Explanations of Answers to the Multiple-Choice Section

The Dickens Passage

1. **D.** The very first sentence indicates the author's purpose. Here, the reader is told directly that Florence is both fanciful and somber, rich and stern.

2. **B.** This selection is based on a quite specific description of Florence and an area within the city. To correctly answer this question, the student needs to be familiar with the different types of rhetorical strategies.

3. **E.** The reader is brought from the general street scene to a specific prison and then to a specific scene outside the prison. Metaphors, similes, and imagery are found throughout the selection, such as "small cells like ovens," "distrustful windows." Contrast and comparison are provided with such phrases as "faded and tarnished Great Saloon" placed next to the "walls which record the triumphs of the Medici." The passage does *NOT* follow a specific timeline.

4. **A.** The test taker needs to know the definition of paradox and must be able to recognize it in a given text. Here, smoke is being used to purify the air even though it is in itself a pollutant.

5. **E.** Dickens is not warning people away from Florence, nor is he criticizing its government. What the text and its selection of details do is to reinforce the idea of Florence being a city of contrast (youth and age, life and death, bright flowers and squalid prisons).

6. **B.** There is no support from a close reading of the text that will allow you to defend choice B, which sees no connection between the two scenes described. Obviously both reveal aspects of Florence. Both are descriptive, with the second paragraph containing the selective contrast with the first paragraph.

7. **C.** Distrustful and secret are indicative of "intrigue," and building thick walls and huge battlements points to the need for protection from aggression. No other choice provides these same inferences.

8. **A.** A close look at each of the selected lines reveals opposites being placed side by side. This is the nature of antithesis.

9. **C.** The Palazzo Vecchio is described using such terms as "ponderous gloom," "faded" and "tarnished" and "mouldering." These are evocative of a place that is creepy and frightening. None of the other choices projects these qualities.

10. **B.** Even though there are images that could be interpreted as melancholy, reflective, or respectful, no other pair of words is appropriate in characterizing the overall impact of the descriptions of Florence other than B. This passage reads like a travel book that provides the traveler with places to see accompanied by interesting details.

The Atwood Passage

11. **D.** Although you might be inclined to accept A, B, or E as possible correct choices, you should be aware that these are specific things the child hears. Each of these would cancel the other out, because they would be equally valid. Choice C is nowhere to be found in the selection. Therefore, the appropriate choice is D, listening.

12. **A.** The very first word of the selection is "Our." This immediately links the writer and the reader. Both are vested with this choice of pronoun.

13. **E.** If you look carefully, you find examples of all of the choices except E. An ellipsis is punctuation comprising three periods. You find none in this sentence. Its function is to notify the reader that a piece of the text has been omitted.

14. **B.** The question makes reference to wanting or seeking something not permitted, such as Adam and Eve being warned not to eat of the forbidden fruit from the tree of knowledge. The other choices are simply not appropriate to the relationship between *forbidden* and *knowledge*.

15. **C.** This is a rather easy question. The entire third paragraph supports this idea.

16. **A.** The answer is clearly supported in the last sentence of paragraph 4. That which is immediately practical and helpful in a very tangible way is the more valuable.

17. **D.** Words, phrases used, and specific details given in this passage support the adjective "wistful" (paragraphs 3 and 4). She is observant throughout the passage as she provides details of the child acquiring her stories. The writer's wistfulness is reiterated in the last paragraph as she states her yearning for men to share in the language of storytelling.

18. **B.** The only choice that presents two strategies actually present in the text is B. The entire passage employs exposition to support the author's purpose. Even the final paragraph, which attempts to persuade, uses exposition to strengthen the appeal to have men welcomed into the language of storytelling. (If you are not crystal clear about the terminology used in the choices, this may be one of those questions you choose to skip, because it can be time consuming trying to determine the correct choice.)

19. **C.** The abruptness of "Traditionally," provides no real connection with the previous paragraph or the previous sentence. It is an obvious break that grabs the reader's attention and leads him or her to Atwood's point.

20. **E.** Throughout the passage, Atwood is taking a close look at the beginnings of storytelling. Although she does attempt to persuade us of the need to encourage men to tell their stories, this is not the primary purpose of the piece. It is important to also notice that the title is a clue to this answer.

The American Dream and the American Negro

21. **A.** The third sentence of paragraph 1 provides a clear, defensible assertion and provides the reader with an idea of the line of reasoning. Each of the other paragraphs develop and support that assertion.

22. **C.** Remember to always read introductory material. In this case, the reader is told when and where this debate took place. With that in mind, the initial audience is Cambridge students and the members of the debate society that invited him.

23. **A.** Each of the five choices is most likely part of the basis for Baldwin agreeing to debate Buckley. However, the only choice that specifically references cultural bias toward black Americans is choice **A.** He tells us in the first paragraph: *That this is what concerns me most.*

24. **D.** Of course Baldwin wants to in this debate. That's the purpose of debating. However, the purpose of this particular argument is to convince his audience of the situation of black Americans. Choices B and C are not a part of the argument as Baldwin presents it. It can be inferred that in developing his argument, Baldwin hopes to build support for the civil rights movement in the U.S. (E). But this is not the primary purpose as given in paragraph 1.

25. **B.** Throughout his presentation, Baldwin provides example after example of what white America thinks and does about racial equality and what black Americans actually think and experience. The last paragraph does use cause/effect (A), but it is not the primary rhetorical strategy for the entire passage.

26. **E** Baldwin's reporting of the RFK comment and the reaction of the residents of Harlem is an example of situational irony. What RFK and white America believed was the message was not what Harlem heard; it was just the opposite.

27. **B.** Baldwin develops his ominous and bitter tone throughout the passage. He does this using irony/sarcasm, comparison/contrast, historical examples, and a final "grave" prediction. None of the other choices is supported with diction, syntax, or logic.

28. **D.** MLK, Jr. was an internationally known civil rights leader and a world-renowned religious thinker. Referring to King, Baldwin emphasizes the difficulty of dealing with and explaining the current differences between the perceptions of white versus black Americans.

29. **C.** The second sentence of the last paragraph of 78 words is constructed primarily using parallel structure. The force of this concluding paragraph is entirely dependent on this one sentence.

30. **E.** This audience is British; it is primarily white and well-educated. Baldwin's presentation is not trying to connect these people with their history, nor is he prosecuting white America or motivating or advocating to this group. What he is doing is developing a case that black Americans are individuals with all that is associated with that idea and must be treated as such.

Making the World Safe for Stupidity

31. **A.** Remember that exigence is that event that gives the writer a kick in the butt to begin to write, to go to the computer. It is what ignites the writer's engine. The exigence for Pitts' essay is most probably his frustration with "stupid" ads. The *advertising world* (B) and *warning labels* (D) are too general for this essay, and C and E are not part of this passage.

32. **C.** After carefully reading the given paragraphs, the reader can only conclude that the thesis is located in paragraph 3. The author clearly states his defensible assertion and provides are clear indication of the organization that will be presented in support of the thesis. The other paragraphs support that thesis.

33. **D.** Most of the paragraphs in the body of the essay are examples that relate to the thesis. None of the other rhetorical strategies is used as the primary method of developing the thesis.

34. **B.** Remember that sarcasm mocks or ridicules an individual or group by using such devices as hyperbole, humor, verbal irony. In paragraph after paragraph, Pitts employs these devices to illuminate and criticize current ads and warnings and the corporations that create them.

35. **E.** Paragraph 12 is purely informative, referring to the previous paragraph and anticipating the point made in the final section of his column.

36. **A.** As with many rhetorical questions, these are used primarily to get the audience involved. Each question assumes the reader will respond, and this leads to Pitts' comments and examples. The other choices do not describe this purpose.

37. **C.** Given the types of examples Pitts cites, the use of rhetorical questions, and the concluding paragraphs, this essay is aimed at the average reader/consumer.

38. **C.** A, B, D, and E can all be included in the primary purpose of Pitts's column, which is to make readers aware of the corporate world's dumbing down of the American consumer. The recommendation made in choice C is not. Pitts' recommended solution is neither valid nor universal. It's probably just "stupid."

39. **A.** Deduction moves from general to the specific, and induction (C) moves from specific to general. In this essay, the writer provides the general (thesis) at the beginning of the column and proceeds to cite specific after specific example.

40. **D.** Considering both the previous paragraph and tis paragraph, the reader is already aware of the points made in choices A, B, C, E. There is no need to add the extra words that could easily lead to confusion.

John Ciardi's Desk Drawer

41. **D.** The rhetorical question in the fifth paragraph (*Can the years of man's life be brought to mere inventory?*) leads into the thesis: *Let any man look into his own average heart and desk for his own average litters and so learn to describe himself to himself.* Here the author presents his assertion, and provides a clear idea of the organization of the material that will be used to support/illustrate this assertion. Paragraphs 1 and 2 act as an introduction to the description of the drawer's contents. Paragraph 6 continues the content inventory with a couple of personal comments.

42. **E.** This almost breathless description of the contents of a desk drawer is structured to give

the reader the feeling of taking a deep breath and reciting everything that is seen in one gulp of air. Without the period, you are conditioned to keep going and going and. . . . It's rushed and everything is seen clumped into the whole. Size is not everything (B), just as syntax (A) isn't the reason for this paragraph (form follows function). This is not the stereotypical list (D), and it does not contain a rundown of complicated items (C).

43. **A.** Paragraphs 3 and 6 present inventories that are described objectively with little or no personal comments. Paragraphs 4 and 5 are just the opposite—personal commentaries. The power of these two paragraphs rests in their placement between objective lists. The contrast and comments are emphasized. The drawer's contents are not cited in paragraphs 4 and 5 (B) nor are examples of the general comments made in paragraphs 1 and 2 (D). The objective world and the world of ideas are not discussed (C), nor does the author recommend methods to deal with what is superficial versus what is real (E).

44. **B.** There is no way to avoid the repetition of "average" throughout the passage. The two longest paragraphs contain numerous examples of parentheticals. Irony is easily located in the parentheticals in paragraph 3, and metaphors are used in paragraphs 2, 3, and 6 metaphor. Hyperbole is not to be found anywhere in the passage; understatement, yes; hyperbole, no.

45. **C.** *Let any man look into his own average heart and desk for his own average litters and so learn to describe himself to himself.* This thesis clearly states what Ciardi's purpose is. The first, second, and third paragraphs illustrate the "litters" with paragraphs four and five presenting the author's self-reflection.

Sample Student Essays

Rubric for the Synthesis Essay

THESIS = 1 Point
- **1 pt.** Addresses the prompt with a thesis that makes it clear HOW the thesis will be developed.
- **0 pts.** Merely repeats the prompt, or statement is vague, avoids taking a position, or presents only an obvious fact.

DEVELOPMENT WITH EVIDENCE = 4 Points
- **4 pts.** With references to at least three of the given sources, the writer presents support for the thesis explaining the relationships between the evidence and the thesis.
- **3 pts.** With references to at least three of the given sources, the development may be uneven, limited; there may be minor errors or weak links between thesis and support.
- **2 pts.** With references to at least three of the given sources, the development repeats, oversimplifies, or misinterprets cited references; points made are not supported by the text.
- **1 pt.** With references to two or fewer of the given sources, the writer merely summarizes the referenced sources, or references to the text are not clear or relevant; provides little or no commentary that links the source to the thesis.
- **0 pts.** May lack a thesis; or presents irrelevant or too few references to the text in support of a clear thesis; or does not address the prompt; or writes about something totally unrelated to the prompt.

Note: Writing that lacks grammatical or syntactical control that interferes with a clear presentation of ideas cannot earn a 4.

SOPHISTICATION (Complexity and Style) = 1 Point
- **1 pt.** (sophistication of thought or development of complex argument) Writer develops the thesis with nuanced explanation of evidence; and/or recognizes and discusses a broader context; and/or recognizes and engages with opposition; and/or makes strong, convincing rhetorical choices in developing the thesis; and/or prose is especially convincing or appropriate.
- **0 pts.** Oversimplifies complexities of the text or the thesis; and/or diction and/or syntax does not enhance the presentation; and/or may overuse sweeping generalizations.

Student A

Affluenza. This new word created only nine years ago aptly describes the pervasive illness in American society and culture that involves our obsession with wealth and possessions. Symptoms include stress, a hollow feeling of still not having enough to be happy, credit and debt, and depression-ridden withdrawals when the dream becomes a nightmare.

The justification for our gluttony is, as some would say in its defense, written into our Declaration of Independence. "We hold these Truths to be self-evident . . . the unalienable right to life, liberty, and the pursuit of happiness" they shout. "We have the unalienable rights of freedom to buy everything to make ourselves happy, and we'll live with it!" The Enlightenment ideals of the 18th century have been tweaked to fit those of Bergdorf-Goodman and eBay.

In a country where we have no national religion, we did find something that tied us 3
together. Money quickly became our national religion, with the wealthy as its priests.
Rockefeller and Carnegie were our first high priests. Social Darwinists to the core, they
lived and preached the power of copper, gold, oil, commerce, and wealth from their
glittering towers, and the plebian masses ate the crumbs left over, hoping to become
a member of the clergy some day. "This change, however, is . . . welcomed as highly
beneficial," cries the high priest Carnegie. "Much better this great irregularity than
universal squalor" (Source G).

But, is it much better? As pictured in a recent *New Yorker* cartoon, when a rich man 4
and woman lie in bed surrounded by paintings, lamps, sculptures, and other luxurious
odds and ends, and say to each other, "Something is missing," it is indicative of the fact
that they and we don't begin to realize how deep a truth this is (Source D). What they
are missing is a meaning, an intimacy, a happiness in their lives. That can't be found in a
four-poster bed with lavish objet d'art encroaching from all sides.

Perhaps the worst thing about affluenza is the way it is taught to the children of 5
today. According to statistics provided by Jesse H. O'Neill's *The Golden Ghetto: The
Psychology of Affluence*, most working mothers play with their children forty minutes a
week. They SHOP six hours a week (Source E). The family is replaced by shopping bags
strewn across the bed. No wonder ninety-three percent of teenage girls list shopping as
their favorite hobby. They can't go to the beach without designer bikinis. They can't
listen to music without an iPod, and it <u>must</u> be accessorized!

We hold these truths to be self-evident: money buys <u>things</u>, no more, no less. It 6
can't replace people, or love, or nature, or travel to places where they just don't worship
<u>things</u> as much as we do. It's time for America to wake up and stop smelling the designer
perfume and ink on the greenbacks. There's no cure for affluenza but ourselves.

Student B

In a world in which material possessions are looked upon as treasures to be collected 1
and guarded, the thought of being content with what one has is considered a prehistoric
myth. America, the main culprit, has been infected by what PBS calls "affluenza." This
"disease" has crept into American homes causing "an epidemic of stress, overwork, waste,
and indebtedness." [introduction to prompt] The claim that Americans are never satisfied
holds much validity and gains more validity as the economy continues to flourish.

As the economy continues to grow and produce objects in which Americans can 2
become infatuated, one can only see America's affluenza infection worsening. A recent
cartoon in which a husband and wife peer over their bed sheets into a vast room ridden
with trinkets and stuffed with mere junk, one can only agree with the claim that
Americans value "stuff" too much (Source D). The cartoon described ends with a witty
comment, "Something is missing." This cartoon is a clear satirical look at what America
has become. Although the room is already stuffed with belongings, the couple feels that
something is missing, showing that Americans are never happy with what they have.

To be happy is one thing, but to buy happiness is something completely different.   3
Yet, Americans have fallen into the trap of widespread consumerism. O'Neill states
that "we have based . . . our entire culture . . . on the belief that 'just a little bit more'
will finally buy happiness" (Source E). He, then, continues on to provide statistics
showing that "93% of teenage girls list shopping as their favorite pastime." It is a sad
reality that what we have is never good enough; that, hopefully, a new pair of shoes
will bring happiness for at least a day or two. America's future, its youth, are the ones
with the most serious infection of affluenza, and as time ticks on that infection only
continues to grow.

Happiness has been a goal of America since its creation, *The Declaration of*   4
Independence states that Americans have the "unalienable" rights: life, liberty, and the
pursuit of happiness (Source B). Although we continue to pursue happiness, American's
idea of happiness has taken a drastic turn. Our idea of happiness in today's standards is
to be rich, and have anything and everything we want. Our days are consumed with the
prospect of reaching happiness. Money is what drives us to work extra hours, but what
will that money buy us? Not happiness, but simply objects—objects that may bring us
happiness for a day or so, but will never satisfy us in the long run.

America's affluenza infection has become a widespread epidemic. Society has become   5
infatuated with purchases and gifts in hopes of finding happiness. Americans are truly
never satisfied with what they have. As America continues to buy, the affluenza only
roots itself deeper into our society and into our future.

Note: For our purposes, scoring comments will be followed by one of three letters to
indicate one of the three areas used in the AP English Language rubric for the rhetorical
analysis essay. Thesis = (A), Evidence/Commentary = (B), Sophistication = (C)

Rating the Student Essays: Affluenza

Student A
This is a high-range essay for the following reasons:

- The essay opens dramatically, immediately catching the reader's attention. It creatively
  defines the term and implies the argument to follow. (A)
- The writer establishes a tone and voice through diction and allusion: *shout, tweaked,
  Bergdorf,* and *eBay.* (C)
- The writer illustrates the argument by presenting an extended analogy. (B)
- Following a rhetorical question that serves as a transitional device, the writer adeptly
  incorporates and comments on one of the sources. (B and C)
- Personal examples and strong details and images continue to support and develop the
  writer's position. (B and C)
- The writer employs proper citation guidelines. (B and C)
- The conclusion is especially effective because it enforces the opening, leaves the reader
  with the essence of the argument, and presents the writer's thesis as a parting comment.
  (B and C)

Student B

This is a mid-range essay for the following reasons:

- The writer states a position on Americans being afflicted with affluenza: "The claim that Americans are never satisfied holds much validity and gains more validity as the economy continues to flourish." (A)
- The writer recognizes and addresses the demands of the prompt. (B)
- The writer properly integrates transitions. (B and C)
- Varied sentence structure is evident in the analysis. (C)
- The development is organized into an orderly presentation. (B)
- The essay presents a clear thesis in the next-to-last paragraph: "Money is what drives us to work extra hours, but what will that money buy us? Not happiness, but simply objects—objects that may bring us happiness for a day or so, but will never satisfy us in the long run." (A)
- The analysis of the writer's sources is brief, leaving the reader looking for more development. (B)

Rubrics for the Rhetorical Analysis Essay

THESIS = 1 Point

- **1 pt.** Addresses the prompt with a thesis that makes it clear HOW the thesis will be developed.
- **0 pts.** Merely repeats the prompt, or statement is vague, avoids taking a position, or presents only an obvious fact.

DEVELOPMENT WITH EVIDENCE = 4 Points

- **4 pts.** With specific references to the text, the writer develops the thesis with conclusions and inferences that are the result of explaining the relationship between what the author says and what the rhetorical strategy does.
- **3 pts.** Development may be uneven, limited; there may be minor instances of description rather than analysis; there may be minor errors or weak links between thesis and support.
- **2 pts.** Development repeats, oversimplifies, or misinterprets cited references; may misinterpret or misunderstand the chosen rhetorical strategies; points made are not supported by the text.
- **1 pt.** Merely summarizes the text, or references to the text are not clear or relevant; merely restates points made in the text.
- **0 pts.** May lack a thesis; or presents irrelevant or too few references to the text in support of a clear thesis; or does not address the prompt; or writes about something totally unrelated to the prompt.

Note: Writing that lacks grammatical or syntactical control that interferes with a clear presentation of ideas cannot earn a 4.

SOPHISTICATION (Complexity and Style) = 1 Point

- **1 pt.** (sophistication of thought or development of complex argument) Writer develops the thesis with nuanced explanation of evidence; and/or recognizes and discusses a broader context; and/or recognizes and engages with opposition; and/or makes strong, convincing rhetorical choices in developing the thesis; and/or prose is especially convincing or appropriate.
- **0 pts.** Oversimplifies complexities of the text or the thesis; and/or diction and/or syntax do not enhance the presentation; and/or may overuse sweeping generalizations.

Addison Passage—Student A

Author Liz Addison wrote an essay in 2007 called "Two Years Are Better Than Four." In this essay she uplifts community colleges as a response to Rick Perlstein's comment that "college as America used to understand it is coming to an end." Addison first undermines Perlstein's idea of the American college experience, provides a background of her own experience with higher education, and illustrates a hypothetical situation to show where her loyalties lie in order to persuade the reader that attending community college is a valid option for education. 1

Within the first two paragraphs of her essay Addison states ". . . Rick Perlstein thinks so. It mattered so much to him that he never got over his four years at the University of Privilege." In referring to Perlstein's academic institution as "The University of Privilege" in a sarcastic manner she highlights Perlstein's pigeonholed perspective on education, thus undermining his statements on college. In doing this, Addison is targeting a major portion of her audience, those who do not have access to prestigious universities and great wealth. She communicates to them that prestigious institutions and the experiences that come with them are not the only option. Considering Addison attended community college she is able to present information from a different viewpoint than Perlstein, whose viewpoint stems from a place of privilege. 2

Following Addison's statements about "The University of Privilege," she shifts from 3rd person point of view to 1st person point of view and tells a personal anecdote about herself and her experience with higher education. Through this personal anecdote Addison reveals that she was not a high-performing student in high school. This gives her credibility as well as providing an example of the benefits and the beauty of community college: She reveals that community college provides anyone with the chance to obtain an education, even those who did not have the best academic track record. This provides comfort to those of her audience that may not be the best students and assuages their fears about attending college. 3

Later, Addison provides a hypothetical situation in which she was a political candidate to appeal to her audience's emotions and show she has their best interest at heart. Addison explains "If I were a candidate for office I would campaign from every campus. Not to score political points, but simply to make sure that anyone who is looking to go to college in this country knows where to find one." With this statement, Addison assures her audience, young students that may be concerned about their education, that she cares about them and wants to help them access educational opportunities and feel secure in the future that lies ahead of them. This encourages her audience to believe her assertions about community college and trust in her judgment. 4

In sum, Addison contradicts the notion that a privileged university experience is the only university experience, provides personal input on her college experience, and creates a hypothetical scenario to convince young students that community college is a valid option for education and might be the right option for them. 5

Addison Passage—Student B

In her 2007 essay, Liz Addison responds to Rick Perlstein's comment that "college as America used to understand it is coming to an end." In her essay, "Two Years Are Better Than Four," she aims to prove him wrong. By appealing to students, making comparisons, and uncrediting Perlstein, Addison proves that Community Colleges are just as important as the "University of Privilege." 1

Addison readily tears down Perlstein's judgement from the beginning of her essay. She uses words like "bemoan" and "shudder" to create a humorous and sarcastic exaggeration to Perlstein's view. She creates an argument that Perlstein is doing nothing but trying to relive that time that "mattered so much to him." She writes, "Mr. Perlstein, so rooted in his own nostalgia, is looking for himself—and he would never think to look for himself in the one place left where the college experience of self-discovery does still matter to those who get there." Her bold statements introduce Community College and tear down credibility from Perlstein. She paints him as a man who is biased for the beatnik days, and who couldn't relate to the modern idea of college. Later, she claims that Perlstein is wrong, without hesitation. She knows that what came before her bold claim was enough to uncredit Perlstein as a source. She further discredits Perlstein by making him seem entitled. She uses "University of Privilege" several times in her piece, and each time creating a snobby and entitled tone. By the time she gets into the main topic of her essay, she has completely reduced Perlstein's once credible character to shambles. 2

As Addison introduces Community College as an option, she openly reaches out to students in her writing. "The philosophy of the community college, and I have been to two of them, is one that unconditionally allows its students to begin. Just begin." She then continues by explaining just how common they are, and how anyone can visit. "Just follow any one of the 1,655 road signs, and pop your head inside—yes, they let anyone in—and there you will find discoveries. . . ." By adding such a high number and reiterating that Community Colleges let anyone in, she informs the reader that Community College is a common and accepting substitute to a University. She continues and writes to show students that she is on their side, and wishes them the best in life. "Oh, I wanted to desperately to say, please tell him about community college. Please tell him that hope can begin with just one placement test." Addison wants the students reading her essay to succeed, and is trying to inform them about a cheaper alternative than a University. 3

She further makes her argument by alluding to one of the Founding Fathers. "Thomas Jefferson once wrote, 'Everybody should have an education proportional to their life.'" She then relates the quote to herself, making a personal connection to the reader. She wants them to know that not all success is as a "University of Privilege"; they can start at a Community College. 4

Addison makes an argument for the worth of Community College by making bold comparisons. She claims that "the community college system is American's hidden public service gem." She defends this comparison by explaining how these colleges "offer a network of affordable future, of accessible hope, and an option to dream." She continues 5 to fight that community college, while not widely known as an option, is still one of the best there is. "I was strangely disturbed that those interviewed made no mention of community college." She wants it to be known that Community College, a diamond in the rough, is affordable to those with a low income. "This college brochure is not marketing for the parents—the parents, nor grandparents, probably never went to college themselves."

Note: For our purposes, scoring comments will be followed by one of three letters to indicate one of the three areas used in the AP English Language rubric for the rhetorical analysis essay. Thesis = (A), Evidence/Commentary = (B), Sophistication = (C)

Rating Student Sample A

This is a high-range essay for the following reasons:

- Clear thesis stated with relevant reference to the prompt (paragraph one) (A)
- Line of reasoning clearly established using transitions and internal references to the argument (paragraph 2: "Within the first two paragraphs . . . ;" paragraph 3: "Following Addison's statements about . . . ;" paragraph 4: Later . . . ") (B)
- Body paragraphs consistently developed with relevant evidence and meaningful commentary relating both to the thesis (paragraph 2 in reference to "privilege") (B)

Rating Student Sample B

This is a mid-range essay for the following reasons:

- An acceptable thesis statement (paragraph one) (A)
- A formulaic introductory paragraph (B)
- Body paragraphs present evidence in support of the thesis, but do not follow the line of reasoning presented in thesis (B)
- Paragraphs tend toward summary with little commentary (B)
- Final paragraph primarily summary (B)

Rubrics for the Argument Essay

THESIS = 1 Point

- **1 pt.** Addresses the prompt with a thesis clearly, takes a position, and makes it clear HOW the thesis will be developed.
- **0 pts.** Merely repeats the prompt, or statement is vague, avoids taking a position, or presents only an obvious fact.

DEVELOPMENT WITH EVIDENCE = 4 Points

- **4 pts.** The writer presents support for the thesis clearly explaining the relationships between the evidence and the thesis.
- **3 pts.** The development may be uneven, limited, incomplete; there may be minor errors or weak links between thesis and support.

- **2 pts.** The development repeats, oversimplifies, or misinterprets cited evidence; points made are not supported by the text.
- **1 pt.** The writer provides little or no commentary that links the evidence to the thesis.
- **0 pts.** May lack a thesis; or presents irrelevant or too few references to the text in support of a clear thesis; or does not address the prompt; or writes about something totally unrelated to the prompt.

Note: Writing that lacks grammatical or syntactical control that interferes with a clear presentation of ideas cannot earn a 4.

SOPHISTICATION (Complexity and Style) = 1 Point

- **1 pt.** (sophistication of thought or development of complex argument) Writer develops the thesis with nuanced explanation of evidence; and/or recognizes and discusses a broader context; and/or recognizes and engages with opposition; and/or makes strong, convincing rhetorical choices in developing the thesis; and/or prose is especially convincing or appropriate.
- **0 pts.** Oversimplifies complexities of the text or the thesis; and/or diction and/or syntax does not enhance the presentation; and/or may overuse sweeping generalizations.

Stegner Passage—Student Sample A

Wallace Stegner writes in an essay, "Without any remaining wilderness we are committed wholly, without chance for even momentary reflection and rest, to a headlong drive into our technological termite-life, the Brave New World of a completely man-controlled environment." This excerpt attempts to convey that humankind is on a direct path to a highly mechanical and technological world; one that is ideal in man's quest for scientific and technological dominance over nature. According to Stegner, man has neglected to stop and smell the proverbial patch of roses. The idea that humankind aims at ultimately dominating the earth with its technological advances can be tenable. However, Stegner's argument is fallacious because people DO pause to observe and introspect.

Humans have been in constant search of enlightenment in the world since time immemorial. Like all other organisms, man tends to innovate in order to better adapt to his natural surroundings. As time progresses, man develops more and better ways to survive. From the days of the Enlightenment, to the Scientific Revolution, to the Industrial Revolution, and to the computerized world of today, humankind has persistently been pursuing ways to analyze and control his environment. During the

Enlightenment, natural philosopher Francis Bacon developed the scientific method as a set process which experiments ought to follow. His methodology has been adhered to since then in experimentation throughout the world. Using this method, Benjamin Franklin experimented with a kite in a storm and discovered electricity. Other thinkers utilized Franklin's findings and developed ways to use new energy sources. One concept has led to another and another, eventually arriving at our highly evolved world today.

These advances serve to benefit man's survival, which is why Stegner sees humans as heading for a man-controlled environment. To relieve nature-related hardships, man seeks ways to make things more comfortable for himself. For instance, air-conditioning was invented to control temperature. Another example of man controlling his environment can be found in the area of transportation: automobiles, trains, airplanes, ships, etc. Man is naturally slow, and to adapt himself to the large world, he creates machines to do the transporting. All of the inventions in the world today demonstrate attempts mankind has made in order to survive and to make life more "livable," and in these efforts, man controls nature.

Though Stegner's case that humanity's focus on dominating their environment can be defended, his idea that people ignore the need to rest for reflection is erroneous. While scientific and technological advancement is a commanding aspect of humankind, it is not as if history, art and culture do not exist. These facets of human society contribute to introspection. We create art to express modes of self-examination. Musicians, painters, sculptors, poets, and other artists concentrate on reflecting about man and his world. We study history as a method of introspection, and, in so doing, we essentially examine our past and reflect on it. There exist in this world goals other than the desire to control nature with technology. Humans are not "committed wholly, without chance for even momentary reflection and rest," to dominate the globe.

While Stegner's concept of humanity's desire to attain dominance over nature contains truth, his notion that people do not focus on anything else is false. Yes, humans do possess the tendency to explore and conquer. However, humans do not exclude all else in life. We are not always in pursuit of scientific and technological accomplishment. We are also seekers of cultural, artistic and philosophical achievement.

Stegner Passage—Student Sample B

Wallace Stegner wrote that, "Without any remaining wilderness we are committed   1
wholly, without chance for even momentary reflection and rest, to a headlong drive into
our technological termite-life, the Brave New World of a completely man-controlled
environment." It seems that in writing this, Stegner expresses his concern for the receding
forests and other wilderness areas, along with the extinction of the species that populate
them. His concern is quite justified, for as we use our natural resources, we destroy those
species that we now share this planet with.

It has long been known that unlike the other species of the Earth, the one known   2
as Homo Sapiens does not adapt well to its environment. Instead, this species adapts the
environment to it, and the Devil take anything that stands in its way. Homo Sapiens
cannot bear the fierce winters of New England or the hot summers of the Caribbean,
so it chops down trees to build houses. It does this without the slightest concern for the
other species that call the forest home. Many terrible injuries have been dealt to the eco-
system of this planet because of the lack of concern Homo Sapiens has shown. Holes in
the ozone layer, which let terrible amounts of ultra-violet radiation bombard the earth.
The constant growth of the Sahara Desert, and the destruction of the rainforests are
painful examples of Homo Sapiens' ignorance, painful not just to other species, but to
Homo Sapiens itself. It seems as though Homo Sapiens does not realize that when all
the trees are gone, there will be no oxygen left for anyone. Hopefully before that atrocity
is carried out, for it is almost sure that it will be, Homo Sapiens will figure out how to
adapt very quickly.

When Stegner wrote of a "completely man-controlled environment," he is talking of a   3
world where our species has destroyed the wilderness or at least bent it totally to our will.
He writes of a world with cities, inhabited "termite-like" by reflective Homo Sapiens, the
size of which no one has ever seen, most likely with rampant air pollution. Let us hope
that we are not one day forced, as in "Lost in Space," to seek out other planets to live
on because ours is taking its last breath. This is one possibility; Stegner is warning us to
change our ignorant ways before it is too late, and he certainly has the right idea. For, if
we don't, we will have truly become exactly like our hated enemy, the virus.

Note: For our purposes, scoring comments will be followed by one of three letters to indicate one of the three areas used in the AP English Language rubric for the rhetorical analysis essay. Thesis = (A), Evidence/Commentary = (B), Sophistication = (C)

Rating Student Sample A

This is a high-range essay for the following reasons:

- Effectively covers the points made by Stegner in his statement (B)
- Clearly takes a position regarding Stegner's statement (A)
- Thoroughly develops the argument with specific examples and historical references (paragraphs 2 and 3) (B and C)
- Indicates and discusses the fallacy of Stegner's statement (paragraphs 4 and 5) (B and C)
- Good topic adherence (B)
- Thorough development of the points of the writer's argument (B and C)
- Mature voice, diction, and syntax (C)

This high-range essay was written by a student who is both confident and well-versed and one who has balanced the presentation with scientific and introspective illustrations in support of the argument.

Rating Student Sample B

This is a mid-range essay for the following reasons:

- Clearly understands Stegner's statement and the demands of the prompt (A and B)
- Creative voice is present (C)
- An interesting objectification of humanity (paragraph 2—"Homo Sapiens") (B)
- Strong conclusion (B and C)
- Linkage between man's destruction of the wilderness and its consequences needs further development (B)
- Development of the argument needs further support (B)
- A few syntactical errors (C)
- Lacks needed transitions (C)

This student writer has a definite opinion to which he or she gives a strong voice. Although there is a strong, clear opening and conclusion, the body paragraphs containing the argument need further development.

PRACTICE EXAM 2

ANSWER SHEET FOR MULTIPLE-CHOICE QUESTIONS

The multiple choice section of the exam will have 45 questions.

- 20–25 will be related to close reading/analysis.
- 20–25 will be related to the rhetorical situation.

1. _____	16. _____	31. _____
2. _____	17. _____	32. _____
3. _____	18. _____	33. _____
4. _____	19. _____	34. _____
5. _____	20. _____	35. _____
6. _____	21. _____	36. _____
7. _____	22. _____	37. _____
8. _____	23. _____	38. _____
9. _____	24. _____	39. _____
10. _____	25. _____	40. _____
11. _____	26. _____	41. _____
12. _____	27. _____	42. _____
13. _____	28. _____	43. _____
14. _____	29. _____	44. _____
15. _____	30. _____	45. _____

I did ☐ did not ☐ finish all the questions in the allotted 1 hour.

I had _____ correct answers. I had _____ incorrect answers. I left _____ blank.

I have carefully reviewed the explanations of the answers, and I think I need to work on the following types of questions:

The current AP English Language exam divides the multiple choice section of the exam into "Reading" and "Writing" categories with separate texts for each type. However, for our purposes, each of the texts in the practice exam contains both "Reading" and "Writing" questions.

PRACTICE EXAM 2
ADVANCED PLACEMENT ENGLISH LANGUAGE

Section I

Total Time—1 hour

Carefully read the following passages and answer the questions that follow.

Questions 1–9 are based on the following passage from Annie Dillard, *What an Essay Can Do* (1988).

In some ways the essay can deal in both events and ideas better than the short story can, because the essayist—unlike the poet—may introduce the plain, unadorned thought without the contrived entrances of long-winded characters who mouth discourses. This sort of awful evidence killed "the novel of idea." (But eschewing it served to limit fiction's materials a little further, and likely contributed to our being left with the short story of scant idea.) The essayist may reason; he may treat of historical, cultural, or natural events, as well as personal events, for their interest and meaning alone, without resort to fabricated dramatic occasions. So the essay's materials are larger than the story's.

The essay may deal in metaphor better than the poem can, in some ways, because prose may expand what the lyric poem must compress. Instead of confining a metaphor to half a line, the essayist can devote to it a narrative, descriptive, or reflective couple of pages, and bring forth vividly its meanings. Prose welcomes all sorts of figurative language, of course, as well as alliteration, and even rhyme. The range of rhythms in prose is larger and grander than that of poetry. And it can handle discursive idea, and plain fact, as well as character and story.

The essay can do everything a poem can do, and everything a short story can do—everything but fake it. The elements in any nonfiction should be true not only artistically—the connections must hold at base and must be veracious, for that is the convention and the covenant between the nonfiction writer and his reader. Veracity isn't much of a drawback to the writer; there's a lot of truth out there to work with. And veracity isn't much of a drawback to the reader. The real world arguably exerts a greater fascination on people than any fictional one; many people at least spend their whole lives there, apparently by choice. The essayist does what we do with our lives; the essayist thinks about actual things. He can make sense of them analytically or artistically. In either case he renders the real world coherent and meaningful; even if only bits of it, and even if that coherence and meaning reside only inside small texts.

1. Which rhetorical technique does the author employ to focus the reader's attention on the specific topic of the passage?
   A. use of parallel structure
   B. identifying herself with her audience
   C. beginning each paragraph with the same subject
   D. use of passive voice
   E. use of anecdote

2. Based on a careful reading of the first paragraph, the reader can conclude that the author blames the death of the "novel of idea" on
   A. real life and situations
   B. simplicity
   C. appeal to philosophy
   D. reliance on historical data
   E. artificiality

3. The primary rhetorical strategy the author uses to develop the first paragraph is
   A. process
   B. narration
   C. description
   D. cause and effect
   E. definition

4. Near the end of the third paragraph, Dillard states, "The essayist does what we do with our lives; the essayist thinks about actual things. He can make sense of them analytically or artistically." The most probable reason for the author choosing to write two separate sentences rather than constructing a single, longer sentence using a listing, is
   A. to reinforce cause and effect
   B. both subjects are of equal importance, although separate processes
   C. to create a parallel situation
   D. to contrast the two ideas
   E. to highlight the criticism of fictional writing

5. The primary rhetorical strategy the author uses to develop the second paragraph is
   A. contrast and comparison
   B. narration
   C. argument
   D. description
   E. analogy

6. In terms of her position on her subject, the author can best be categorized as
   A. an adversary
   B. a critic
   C. an advocate
   D. an innovator
   E. an artist

7. An example of parallel structure is found in which of the following lines taken from the passage?
   A. "But eschewing it served to limit fiction's materials a little further, and likely contributed to our being left with the short story of scant idea."
   B. "The essay may deal in metaphor better than the poem can, in some ways, because prose may expand what the lyric poem must compress."
   C. "The elements in any nonfiction should be true not only artistically—the connections must hold at base . . ."
   D. ". . . that is the convention and the covenant between the nonfiction writer and his reader."
   E. "In either case he renders the real world coherent and meaningful; even if only bits of it, and even if that coherence and meaning reside only inside small texts."

8. The contrast between the short story writer and the essayist is based on which of the following?
   A. reflection
   B. presentation
   C. fundamental reality
   D. content
   E. clarity of purpose

9. The tone of the passage can best be described as
   A. impartial and critical
   B. condescending and formal
   C. candid and colloquial
   D. clinical and moralistic
   E. confident and informative

Questions 10–22 are based on the following passage from Herman Melville's *Moby Dick* (1851).

Nantucket! Take out your map and look at it. See what a real corner of the world it occupies; how it stands there, away off shore, more lonely than the Eddystone lighthouse. Look at it—a mere hillock, and elbow of sand; all beach, without a background. There is more sand there than you would use in twenty years as a substitute for blotting paper. Some gamesome wights* will tell you that they have to plant weeds there, they don't grow naturally; they import Canada thistles; they have to send beyond seas for a spile† to stop a leak in an oil cask; that pieces of wood in Nantucket are carried about like bits of the true cross in Rome; that people there plant toadstools before their houses, to get under the shade in summer time; that one blade of grass makes an oasis, three blades a day's walk in a prairie; that they wear quicksand shoes, something like Laplander snowshoes; that they are so shut up, belted about, every way inclosed, surrounded, and made an utter island of by the ocean, that to their very chairs and tables small clams will sometimes be found adhering, as to the backs of sea turtles. But these extravaganzas only show that Nantucket is no Illinois.

Look now at the wondrous traditional story of how this island was settled by the red-men. Thus goes the legend. In olden times an eagle swooped down upon the New England coast, and carried off an infant Indian in his talons. With loud lament the parents saw their child borne out of sight over the wide waters. They resolved to follow in the same direction. Setting out in their canoes, after a perilous passage they discovered the island, and there they found an empty ivory casket,—the poor little Indian's skeleton.

What wonder, then, that these Nantucketers, born on a beach, should take to the sea for a livelihood! They first caught crabs and quahogs in the sand; grown bolder, they waded out with nets for mackerel; more experienced, they pushed off in boats and captured cod; and at last, launching a navy of great ships on the sea, explored this watery world; put an incessant belt of circumnavigations round it; peeped in at Behring's Straits; and in all seasons and all oceans declared everlasting war with the mightiest animated mass that has survived the flood; most monstrous and most mountainous! That Himmalehan, salt-sea Mastodon, clothed with such portentousness of unconscious power, that his very panics are more to be dreaded than his most fearless and malicious assaults!

And thus have these naked Nantucketers, these sea hermits, issuing from their ant-hill in the sea, overrun and conquered the watery world like so many Alexanders; parceling out among them the Atlantic, Pacific, and Indian oceans, as the three pirate powers did Poland. Let America add Mexico to Texas, and pile Cuba upon Canada; let the English overswarm all India, and hang out their blazing banner from the sun; two thirds of this terraqueous globe are the Nantucketer's. For the sea is his; he owns it, as Emperors own empires; other seamen having but a right of way through it. Merchant ships are but extension bridges; armed ones but floating forts; even pirates and privateers, though following the sea as highwaymen the road, they but plunder other ships, other fragments of the land like themselves, without seeking to draw their living from the bottomless deep itself. The Nantucketer, he alone resides and riots on the sea; he alone, in Bible language, goes down to it in ships; to and fro ploughing it as his own

1

2

3

4

---

* wights: human beings
† spile: a small plug

special plantation. *There* is his home; *there* lies his business, which a Noah's flood would not interrupt, though it overwhelmed all the millions in China. He lives on the sea, as prairie dogs in the prairie; he hides among the waves, he climbs them as mountain goats climb the Alps. For years he knows not the land; so that when he comes to it at last, it smells like another world, more strangely than the moon would to an Earthsman. With the landless gull, that at sunset folds her wings and is rocked to sleep between billows; so at nightfall, the Nantucketer, out of sight of land, furls his sail, and lays him to his rest, while under his very pillow rush herds of walruses and whales.

10. The controlling analogy of the passage is
   A. Nantucket to Illinois
   B. sea to land
   C. Noah to Nantucket
   D. moon to Earthsman
   E. legends to reality

11. The purpose of the last sentence of the first paragraph is to
   A. change subjects
   B. reinforce the importance of the geography of Nantucket
   C. switch the focus of the audience
   D. change the narrator's point of view
   E. emphasize the grandeur of Nantucket

12. The most probable reason for repeating and italicizing "*There*" in the middle of paragraph 4 at the beginning of two main clauses in the same sentence is to
   A. force the reader to look for an antecedent
   B. sound poetic
   C. provide a break in a long, complicated sentence
   D. emphasize the sense of place
   E. indicate sympathy for the plight of the Nantucketer

13. The shift in the focus of the piece occurs in which line?
   A. The first sentence of paragraph 2
   B. The first sentence of paragraph 3
   C. The first sentence of paragraph 4
   D. The third sentence in paragraph 4
   E. The last sentence

14. In the first paragraph, Melville uses which of the following rhetorical choices to emphasize Nantucket's uniqueness?
   A. Parallel structure
   B. Anecdote
   C. Periodic sentence
   D. Generalization
   E. Argument

15. Melville retells the Native American legend of how the island was settled in order to
   A. have his audience identify with the Native American population
   B. make the passage seem like a parable
   C. contrast with the reality of the Nantucketers
   D. bring a mythic quality to the subject
   E. highlight the plight of the Nantucketers

16. The development of paragraph 3 is structured around
   A. spatial description
   B. selection of incremental details
   C. central analogy
   D. parallel structure
   E. paradox

17. The passage's argument and line of reasoning are based on
   A. definition
   B. cause and effect
   C. analysis
   D. process
   E. analogy

18. One may conclude from the information contained in paragraph 3 that "Himmalehan, salt-sea Mastedon" refers to
   A. the ocean
   B. the whale
   C. the power of nature
   D. Biblical vengeance
   E. emperors

19. The purpose of the passage is most probably to
A. encourage people to settle on Nantucket
B. use Nantucket as a model of ecological conservation
C. honor the indomitable spirit of the Nantucketers
D. plead for the return of Nantucket to the Native Americans
E. present a nostalgic reminiscence of the writer's birthplace

20. Melville uses *thus* twice in this passage: once in the second paragraph to begin the Native American legend about the island being settled. All of the following are reasons for using *thus* in the first sentence of paragraph 4 except
A. to begin a comparative legend with the Nantucketers settling the sea
B. to balance the first part of the passage with the second part
C. to indicate a kind of cause and effect relationship
D. to reinforce the formality of his presentation
E. to further connect the inhabitants to the island and its legends

21. The subtle humor of the first paragraph is dependent upon
A. paradox
B. hyperbole
C. juxtaposition
D. irony
E. ad hominem argument

22. The last sentence of the passage continues the analogy between
A. reality and illusion
B. night and day
C. man and animal
D. gull and walrus
E. sea and land

Questions 23–31 are based on the following passage from "Tell Me a Story" (2005) by Roger Rosenblatt.

In the *Sunday New York Times Book Review*, there was an interesting article by   1
Rachael Dinadio about the novelist V.S. Naipaul, who spoke of the necessity of writing
nonfiction because, he said, "If you spend your life just writing fiction, you're going
to falsify your material." He implied that without nonfiction, a grasp of the truth is
incomplete.

Events in publishing seem to support this. *The Atlantic Monthly* has cut back on   3
fiction. Publishers avidly seek nonfiction that promises a big, quick sale rather than
serious novels in part because the market beckons but also because of the wider idea
Naipaul was getting at: Where does the truth of experience lie—in what you see in the
real world or in what you make up?

There are some kinds of literature to which the question does not apply   3
Autobiographical novels about coming of age, such as Joyce's *Portrait of the Artist as a
Young Man* or Baldwin's *Go Tell It on the Mountain*. Both novels decorate the facts of
the author's young manhood with invented names, places and thoughts to make sense
of reality, the deeper sense that only dreams can unearth.

But if the truth is what you're after, you have to define the terms. An essay question: 4
Compare and contrast *The Perfect Storm*, nonfiction, with *Moby Dick*"—fiction to a
tee—two first-rate tales of terror and obsession at sea and of the stubborn pursuit of
men for profit.

Yet, we will remember Captain Ahab long after we've forgotten *The Perfect Storm* not   5
because Ahab was believably real, but because he was not.

Truth is preposterous both in fiction and in fact. Which really happened, the events   6
of 9/11 or Wells's *War of the Worlds*? Much less significantly, which was harder to
believe, last year's Red Sox or the musical *Damn Yankees*? For me I can tell you which
was harder to take.

The test of endurance has to do with the quality of the story. The choice in and of   7
writing is not Naipaul's, it seems to me, is the story worth telling, whether it happened
or it didn't.

When a child asks, tell me a story, he's not asking for fact or fiction, just something   8
wonderful. Both creationists and scientists are single-mindedly devoted to great stories,
Adam, Eve, God and Satan, no more or less than frogs, birds, apes and us. The stories
are not to be confused in the classroom. But when it comes to individual truth, neither
story falsifies the material.

In his autobiographical novel, *Manchild in the Promised Land*, Claude Brown offers   9
a way to see fiction and nonfiction as both factual and fanciful as the truth is itself. In
a story about growing up in the hell of Harlem in the 1960's, Brown leaves us stunned
equally with belief and disbelief.

"You might see someone get cut or killed," he writes in the novel's last lines. "I could   10
go out on the street, and I would see so much that when I came in the house I'd be
talking and talking. Dad would say, 'Boy, why don't you stop that lyin'. You know you
didn't see all that. You know you didn't see nobody do that.' But I knew I had.

23. The exigence for this TV essay was most probably
   A. Rosenblatt's love of a good argument
   B. an article by Rachael Dinadio in *The New York Times Book Review*
   C. a contractual agreement with PBS News Hour
   D. Rosenblatt's belief in the power of non-fiction
   E. a perceived need to defend the novelist V.S. Naipaul

24. The major rhetorical choice used to develop the thesis is
   A. cause/effect
   B. narration
   C. comparison/contrast
   D. definition
   E. exemplification

25. Which rhetorical appeal is not utilized by the writer?
   A. logos (reason)
   B. ethos (authority/credibility)
   C. pathos (emotion)
   D. timeliness
   E. commonality

26. What is the one assumption Rosenblatt does not make about his audience?
   A. They are college educated.
   B. They read both fiction and nonfiction.
   C. They find truths in works of fiction.
   D. They are interested in distinguishing fact from fiction.
   E. They recognize the intersection of fact and fiction in varied instances.

27. The line of reason of this essay is developed using
   A. most important to least important
   B. chronological
   C. logical/topical
   D. least familiar to most familiar
   E. spatial

28. The thesis is located in which paragraph?
   A. 1
   B. 2
   C. 4
   D. 5
   E. 8

29. Rosenblatt's purpose can best be stated as
   A. advocating for the superiority of fiction when considering the truth
   B. advocating for the superiority of nonfiction when considering the truth
   C. recommending the elimination of nonfiction from the canon of western literature
   D. recommending the elimination of fiction from the classroom
   E. a consideration of whether truth lies in truth or fiction

30. Considering the logic and coherence of the essay, the last two paragraphs, 9 and 10, should be placed
   A. as is
   B. before paragraph 8
   C. after 4
   D. before paragraph 3
   E. omitted

31. Which of the following claims is not made by Rosenblatt?
   A. Events in publishing seem to support the idea that without nonfiction, a grasp of the truth is incomplete.
   B. If you're after the truth, you have to define the terms.
   C. Both James Joyce and James Baldwin invent names, places, and thoughts in their autobiographical novels.
   D. Truth is preposterous both in fiction and in fact.
   E. The test of endurance has to do with the quality of the story.

Questions 32–41 are based on the following excerpt from "Automania" (2013) by Leah Napolin, noted playwright.

Not long ago I was driving westbound in the fast lane on my way into the city [1] when I noticed that something was wrong with one of the hazard-alert signs that are posted overhead every couple of miles. (Why is it, by the way, that the moment you get into the fast lane, like the express line at the supermarket, everything grinds to a halt?)

Should some tie-up occur—due, say, to a skid resulting in a disabled car on the [2] shoulder or a work crew fixing a pothole or widening a lane—these state-of-the-art signs display an electronic message: *Road Surface Slippery When Wet, Use Caution,* or it might say: *Delays From Exits 23 to 29.* If there's a problem at eastbound exit 23 and I've just passed exit 20, then I can get off at 21 and take the service road, avoiding the tie-up. (Why is it, by the way, that when you exit a highway where traffic is bumper to bumper onto a service road that's empty, within minutes the cars on the highway are moving briskly and the traffic on the service road stops?)

Sometimes, though, the sign displays the message *Volume.* This is by far the [3] worst message to encounter. Worse, even, than *shortcut.* You can't do anything about *Volume. Volume* means there are just too many of us out there at the same time, going places. On the other hand, the happiest message to see are the four words: *Normal Traffic Conditions Ahead.* As defined by the Department of Transportation, *normal* is a certain mix of cars able to maintain the 55 mph speed limit.

On this particular day, however, the sign isn't working properly and the first word [4] of the message has gone dark. Instead of Normal Traffic Conditions Ahead, the sign reads: *Traffic Conditions Ahead.* A blown fuse, perhaps? Not even the WCBS traffic helicopter has a clue.

It's possible that someone stalled in the middle lane. Or someone else who was [5] then cruising along very nicely, thank you, is now hobbling at ten miles an hour with a blown tire flapping off his rim. Something *is* happening, because there's a cluster of red brake lights in the distance. So, *Traffic Conditions Ahead* leaves me wondering and vaguely unsettled.

Next week, same time, I notice that the sign is still malfunctioning. Another [6] blown fuse? Computers down? Now, in addition to the word *Normal,* the word *Traffic* has also disappeared, and the sign reads: *Conditions Ahead.*

This is both mysterious *and* alarming. *Conditions* could be anything, not just the [7] usual pileups, breakdowns, stripped and abandoned cars, fender-benders, road work, police activity—but war, nuclear accidents, terrorist bombings, earthquakes, floods, madness, cancer, senility! All in wait around the next bend of the road.

A weekend passes, then it's time to head out onto the highway again. Everything [8] seems *normal,* although we have no clue what that means. *Traffic* is moving or not, as usual. *Conditions* are everywhere, and nothing we poor *Jerks* can do seems to help.

It's then I note with shock that the message on the sign is now almost obliterated. [9] Like the Cheshire cat that kept vanishing incrementally until nothing was left but its smile—the only word that remains on the sign is the last one: *Ahead.*

In a flash, I understand exactly what it means. What it's all about. Yes, here [10] is a message more Zen than existential, more Shakespearean than Freudian. "By indirection find direction out—" advises the Bard. A message to ponder while we aim ourselves purposefully—AHEAD. Just one cryptic word: AHEAD. Damn the torpedoes, full speed AHEAD. Just us and the infrastructure, collapsing endlessly around us. All lights green, all roads merging into one road and that one like an arrow, pointing—where? AHEAD.

32. The exigence for the writer's essay is most probably
- A. anger toward erratic drivers
- B. confusion about road signage
- C. fear of driving on highways
- D. frustration with traffic delays and signage
- E. frustration with the daily commute into the city

33. The thesis statement is found in paragraph
- A. 1
- B. 2
- C. 5
- D. 7
- E. 10

34. The essay's line of reasoning is developed by primarily using
- A. familiar to unfamiliar
- B. unfamiliar to familiar
- C. induction
- D. deduction
- E. question and answer

35. Which of the following is the predominant rhetorical strategy is used to support the thesis?
- A. exemplification
- B. cause/effect
- C. comparison/contrast
- D. description
- E. definition

36. What doesn't the writer assume about the primary audience for this essay?
- A. They are familiar with famous literary and historical figures and terms.
- B. They are inexperienced drivers.
- C. They often commute for business of pleasure.
- D. They have experienced traffic slowdowns.
- E. They want traffic signage to be accurate and clear.

37. The first paragraph primarily functions to
- A. introduce the rhetorical situation
- B. ask the central question of the essay
- C. introduce the writer to the reader
- D. provide the thesis
- E. illustrate the writer's anger

38. The writer is considering adding the following sentence to the end of paragraph 5:

Driving more defensively, I move from the fast lane into the middle lane.

Should the writer make this revision?
- A. Yes, because the reader wants to know what the driver does next.
- B. No, because it is off topic.
- C. No, because it doesn't really relate to the topic sentence of the paragraph.
- D. Yes. This sentence adds to the reader's understanding of the writer.
- E. No. This sentence adds nothing to the information in the paragraph and begs for an answer to what happens when the driver moves into the middle lane.

39. Which of the following best describes the rhetorical effect achieved by the parentheticals in paragraphs 1 and 2?
- A. an invitation into the mind of the writer
- B. further illustrates the context of the essay
- C. further develops the identity of the writer
- D. involvement of the audience in the rhetorical situation
- E. strengthens reader's confidence in the writer

40. What best describes the rhetorical purpose of the last paragraph?
- A. to indicate that the average highway driver is fed up
- B. to suggest that this condition will never change and to accept the inevitable
- C. to advocate for better maintenance of our highways
- D. to prosecute the failure of the nation's infrastructure
- E. to advocate for more and better public transportation

41. In paragraph 7, the writer uses which of the following rhetorical devices/strategies to emphasize the reality and ridiculousness of the situation?
- A. allusion and either/or alternative
- B. hyperbole and metaphor
- C. euphemism and parallelism
- D. personification and cause/effect
- E. exemplification and antithesis

Questions 42–45 are based on the speech delivered by Greta Thunberg at the UN Climate Action Summit on September 23, 2019.

This is all wrong. I shouldn't be standing here. I should be back in school on the other side of the ocean. Yet you all come to me for hope? How dare you! — 1

You have stolen my dreams and my childhood with your empty words. And yet I'm one of the lucky ones. People are suffering. People are dying. Entire ecosystems are collapsing. — 2

We are in the beginning of a mass extinction. And all you can talk about is money and fairytales of eternal economic growth. How dare you! — 3

For more than 30 years the science has been crystal clear. How dare you continue to look away and come here saying that you are doing enough, when the politics and solutions needed are still nowhere in sight. — 4

With today's emissions levels, our remaining CO_2 budget will be gone in less than 8.5 years. — 5

You say you "hear" us and that you understand the urgency. But no matter how sad and angry I am, I don't want to believe that. Because if you fully understood the situation and still kept on failing to act, then you would be evil. And I refuse to believe that. — 6

The popular idea of cutting our emissions in half in 10 years only gives us a 50 percent chance of staying below 1.5 C degrees, and the risk of setting off irreversible chain reactions beyond human control. — 7

Maybe 50 percent is acceptable to you. But those numbers don't include tipping points, most feedback loops, additional warming hidden by toxic air pollution or the aspects of justice and equity. — 8

To have a 67 percent chance of staying below a 1.5 C global temperature rise—the best odds given by the Intergovernmental Panel on Climate Change—the world had 420 gigatons of carbon dioxide left to emit back on January 1, 2018. Today that figure is already down to less than 350 gigatons. — 9

How dare you pretend that this can be solved with business-as-usual and some technical solutions. With today's emissions levels, that remaining CO_2 budget will be entirely gone in less than eight and a half years. — 10

There will not be any solutions or plans presented in line with these figures today. Because these numbers are too uncomfortable. And you are still not mature enough to tell it like it is. — 11

You are failing us. But the young people are starting to understand your betrayal. The eyes of all future generations are upon you. And, if you choose to fail us, I say we will never forgive you. We will not let you get away with this. Right here, right now is where we draw the line. The world is waking up. And change is coming, whether you like it or not. — 12

42. Greta wants to add a sentence to the beginning of paragraph 6 to set up her appeal to the world leaders to really care about the current climate situation and consequences. Which of the following choices best accomplishes this goal?
   A. Do you want your children and grandchildren to suffer the consequences of climate change?
   B. Have you been listening to us?
   C. I want to believe you will truly hear what I have to say.
   D. Has your country signed the climate accords?
   E. Will you take my message back home to your country?

43. In paragraph 4, which of the following versions of the first sentence best establishes the speaker's position on the main argument of her speech?
   A. Leave as is.
   B. For more than 30 years the science has been crystal clear, and you have ignored its findings.
   C. You have been ignoring what science has made crystal clear for more than 30 years.
   D. You do not listen.
   E. You must listen to us.

44. The writer wants to add the following sentence to the text to provide additional information that is appropriate to the purpose of her argument.

   Because I can't ignore what is happening to this planet, I started a school strike for climate awareness outside the Swedish Parliament, and this movement just led the largest climate strike in history that included an estimated 4 million people across 161 countries.

   Where would this sentence best be placed?
   A. at the beginning of paragraph 1
   B. at the end of paragraph 2
   C. at the beginning of paragraph 10
   D. at the end of paragraph 11
   E. at the end of paragraph 12

45. The speaker wants to add more information to the third paragraph to support the topic of the paragraph. All of the following pieces of evidence would help achieve this purpose except which one?
   A. Oyster seed[ling] production has plummeted by over 80% since 2005.
   B. Florida's coral reef is disintegrating.
   C. Ice-free summers in the Arctic Ocean can lead to the loss of an entire biome.
   D. A personal anecdote about the writer's sadness on the loss of her pet while she was at a speaking engagement.
   E. 99 percent of currently threatened species are at risk from human activities, primarily those driving habitat loss, introduction of exotic species, and global warming.

END OF SECTION I

Section II

Question 1

Suggested Writing Time: 40 minutes

Based on the Constitutional First Amendment guarantee of the right to freedom of speech, some citizens and citizen groups have used public burning of the American flag as a means of political expression. A proposed amendment to the *U.S. Constitution* states: "The Congress shall have the power to prohibit the physical desecration of the flag of the United States." Is desecrating the flag a legitimate form of expression guaranteed by the Constitution? Should the Constitution be amended to protect the flag?

Carefully read the following sources (including any introductory information). **Then, in an essay that synthesizes at least three of the sources, support your position on the claim that the U.S. flag should be protected with a constitutional amendment.**

Make certain that you take a position and that the essay centers on your argument. Use the sources to support your reasoning; avoid simply summarizing the sources. You may refer to the sources by their letters (Source A, Source B, etc.) or by the identifiers in the parentheses below.

- Source A (*U.S. Constitution*)
- Source B (*60 Minutes*)
- Source C (*Kelo* decision)
- Source D (Koterba, editorial/political cartoon)
- Source E (Broder)
- Source F (Britt, editorial/political cartoon)
- Source G (CNN and American Survey)

- Provide evidence from at least three of the provided sources to support the thesis. Indicate clearly the sources used through direct quotation, paraphrase, or summary. Sources may be cited as Source A, Source B, etc., or by using the description in parentheses.
- Explain the relationship between the evidence and the thesis.
- Demonstrate an understanding of the rhetorical situation.
- Use appropriate grammar and punctuation in communicating the argument.

Source A
From "The Bill of Rights," *The U.S. Constitution*.

Amendment I

Congress shall make no law respecting an establishment of religion, or prohibiting the free exercise thereof; or abridging the freedom of speech, or of the press; or the right of the people peaceably to assemble, and to petition the government for a redress of grievances.

Source B
The Proposed Amendment to the *U.S. Constitution* taken from *The Congressional Record*. Available at https://www.congress.gov/congressional-report/108thcongress/senate-report/334/1.

The full text of the amendment:

The Congress shall have power to prohibit the physical desecration of the flag of the United States.

Source C

Results of a survey conducted by *USA Today*, June 23–25, 2006, http://www.usatoday
.com/news/washington/2006-06-26-poll-results_x.htm.

> *Some people feel that the U.S. Constitution should be amended to make it illegal to
> burn or desecrate the American flag as a form of political dissent. Others say that the
> U.S. Constitution should not be amended to specifically prohibit flag burning or des-
> ecration. Do you think the U.S. Constitution should or should not be amended to
> prohibit burning or desecrating the American flag?*
>
> *Results based on 516 national adults in Form B:*
>
> | Date asked | Yes, amended | No, not | No opinion |
> |---|---|---|---|
> | *June 23–25, 2006* | 45% | 54% | 2% |

Source D

Two Supreme Court Decisions related to the desecration of the flag. Available at
http://www.firstamendmentcenter.org/speech/flagburning/overview.aspx?topic=
flag-burning_overview.

> *Texas v. Johnson, 491 U.S. 397 (1989), was a decision by the Supreme Court of the
> United States. The question the Supreme Court had to answer was: "Is the desecration
> of an American flag, by burning or otherwise, a form of speech that is protected under
> the First Amendment?" Justice William Brennan wrote the 5–4 majority decision in
> holding that the defendant's act of flag burning was protected speech under the First
> Amendment to the United States Constitution.*
>
> *The court held that the First Amendment prevented Texas from punishing the
> defendant for burning the flag under the specified circumstances. The court first found
> that burning of the flag was expressive conduct protected by the First Amendment. The
> court concluded that Texas could not criminally sanction flag desecration in order to
> preserve the flag as a symbol of national unity. It also held that the statute did not meet
> the state's goal of preventing breaches of the peace, since it was not drawn narrowly
> enough to encompass only those flag burnings that would likely result in a serious dis-
> turbance, and since the flag burning in this case did not threaten such a reaction.*
>
> *Subsequently, Congress passed a statute, the 1989 Flag Protection Act, making it a
> federal crime to desecrate the flag. In the case of United States v. Eichman, 496 U.S.
> 310 (1990), that law was struck down by the same five-person majority of justices as
> in Texas v. Johnson, 491 U.S. 397 (1989).*

Source E

Chief Justice William Rehnquist's dissenting opinion in the *Texas v. Johnson* (1989) case. Available at http://www.bc.edu/bc_org/avp/cas/comm/free_speech/texas.html.

In his dissenting opinion in Texas v. Johnson (1989), regarding Texas law against flag burning, the late Chief Justice William H. Rehnquist wrote,

The American flag, then, throughout more than 200 years of our history, has come to be the visible symbol embodying our Nation. It does not represent the views of any particular political party, and it does not represent any particular political philosophy. The flag is not simply another "idea" or "point of view" competing for recognition in the marketplace of ideas. Millions and millions of Americans regard it with an almost mystical reverence regardless of what sort of social, political, or philosophical beliefs they may have. I cannot agree that the First Amendment invalidates the Act of Congress, and the laws of 48 of the 50 States, which make criminal the public burning of the flag.

Rehnquist also argued that flag burning is "no essential part of any exposition of ideas" but, rather "the equivalent of an inarticulate grunt or roar that, it seems fair to say, is most likely to be indulged in not to express any particular idea, but to antagonize others."

Source F

"The case for flag-burning: An amendment banning it would make America less free." An editorial that appeared in the *Los Angeles Times*, June 27, 2006.

THERE ARE MANY ARGUMENTS AGAINST a proposed constitutional amendment to outlaw "the physical desecration of the flag of the United States." Let us count the ways in which the amendment, which is disturbingly close to the 67 votes required for Senate approval, is unworthy of that body's support:

- *It's a "solution" to a problem that doesn't exist. There has been no epidemic of flag-burning since the Supreme Court ruled in 1989 that destruction of Old Glory as a protest was symbolic speech protected by the 1st Amendment.*
- *As Sen. Mitch McConnell (R-Ky.) pointed out, "The First Amendment has served us well for over 200 years. I don't think it needs to be altered." Placing a no-flag-burning asterisk next to the amendment's sweeping guarantee of free speech is a mischievous idea, and it could invite amendments to ban other sorts of speech Americans find offensive.*

But the best argument against the flag amendment is the one some opponents are reluctant to make for fear of political fallout: It would make America less free.

Rare as flag-burning may be, a nation that allows citizens to denounce even its most sacred symbols is being true to what the Supreme Court in 1964 called the "profound national commitment to the principle that debate on public issues should be uninhibited, robust and wide-open, and that it may well include vehement, caustic, and sometimes unpleasantly sharp attacks on government and public officials."

In that decision, and in 1989, the court interpreted the free-speech protections of the First Amendment generously but correctly. The Senate, including Feinstein and fellow Democrat and Californian Barbara Boxer (who has opposed a flag-burning amendment in the past), should let those decisions be.

Source G

Congressional votes regarding proposed constitutional amendment regarding desecration of the flag. Available at http://en.wikipedia.org/wiki/Flag_Burning_Amendment#Congressional_votes.

The chronology of the House of Representatives' action upon the flag-desecration amendment running over a period of more than ten years:

Congress	Resolution(s)	Vote date	Yeas	Nays
104th Congress	House Joint Resolution 79	June 28, 1995	312	120
	Senate Joint Resolution 31	December 12, 1995	63	36
105th Congress	House Joint Resolution 54	June 12, 1997	310	114
106th Congress	House Joint Resolution 33	June 24, 1999	305	124
	Senate Joint Resolution 14	March 29, 2000	63	37
107th Congress	House Joint Resolution 36	July 17, 2001	298	125
108th Congress	House Joint Resolution 4	June 3, 2003	300	125
109th Congress	House Joint Resolution 10	June 22, 2005	286	130
	Senate Joint Resolution 12	June 27, 2006	66	34

Source H

Editorial cartoon by Clay Bennett, the *Christian Science Monitor*, Boston, July 4, 2006. Available at http://www.cagle.com/news/FlagBurning2/2.asp.

Clay Bennett, *Christian Science Monitor*, Boston 7/4/06

Source I

An excerpt from "The Star-Spangled Banner," an editorial by Todd Lindberg that appeared in the *Washington Times*, July 4, 2006. Available at http://washingtontimes.com/op-ed/20060703-102601-1107r.htm.

. . . *the last thing that a constitutional amendment banning flag-burning strikes me as is a slippery slope toward broader restriction on freedom of expression. There are two reasons for this.*

First, the flag is the flag; the only reason to accord it special status (if that's what you decide) is that it is, in fact, the singular national symbol. We are not even talking about a ban on burning red, white, and blue things, such as bunting, nor of suppressing the debate over whether banning the burning of the flag is a good thing. It's not hypocrisy but rather a pretty good philosophical point to say that the flag, as the symbol of the freedom to burn, baby, burn, is the one thing you shouldn't burn. For if you burn the freedom to burn, you have no freedom. For more on the danger that lies in this direction, see the collapse of the Weimar Republic in Germany.

On the other hand, the flag is not the freedom itself but its symbol. The freedom continues even if a particular flag is consumed in fire. To burn the flag is not to burn the only flag. There is no "the" flag, only flags; or if there is "the" flag, it is an idea of the flag and therefore beyond the reach of the flames.

Except that a perfectly acceptable way to dispose of a worn-out flag, according to the old Boy Scout manual Dad gave me, is by burning. The ceremony is to be at all times respectful and somber. Here, one reveres "the" flag by seeing to it that "a" flag gets decommissioned properly. So the symbolic content is always present. When someone burns a flag in protest, it's just not about the fire and the piece of cloth. The flag is indeed a symbol of a political community, and I'm not sure that political communities can get by without symbols.

The second reason I'm not worried about a slippery slope constricting expression once you ban flag-burning is that in the current environment, socially enforced restraints on expression are far broader and more important than legal restraints. In the case of flag-burning, if you do it now, most Americans will think you are an ingrate jerk, as noted above. But even if a constitutional amendment passes, no one is proposing the death penalty for flag-burning, nor life in prison. If you get busted, you can probably look forward to a few days in the clink, plus adulatory editorials in the New York Times.

So while I am not a great supporter of an amendment banning flag-burning, neither do I think that such an amendment would do harm if passed. If I were a member of the Senate, I would have voted for it. That's because as an elected officeholder, I would feel more solicitous of the national symbol, as perhaps befits someone who has chosen to hold office in accordance with the principles and procedures of the political community in question.

Question 2

(Suggested time 40 minutes. This question counts as one-third of the total score for Section II.)

Carefully read Chief Seattle's oration to Governor Isaac I. Stevens (1854), who had just returned from Washington, D.C., with orders to buy Indian lands and create reservations. In a well-written essay, identify Chief Seattle's purpose and analyze the rhetorical choices he uses to convey his purpose.

- Respond to the prompt with a defensible thesis that relates to the prompt.
- Select and use evidence to develop and support the line of reasoning.
- Explain the relationship between the evidence and the thesis.
- Demonstrate an understanding of the rhetorical situation.
- Use appropriate grammar and punctuation in communicating the argument.

. . . Yonder sky that has wept tears of compassion upon my people for centuries   1
untold, and which to us appears changeless and eternal, may change. Today is fair.
Tomorrow it may be overcast with clouds. My words are like the stars that never
change. Whatever Seattle says the great chief at Washington can rely upon with as
much certainty as he can upon the return of the sun. The White Chief says that Big
Chief at Washington sends us greetings of friendship and goodwill. This is kind of
him for we know he has little need of our friendship in return. His people are many.
They are like the grass that covers vast prairies. My people are few. They resemble the
scattering trees of a storm-swept plain. The great, and I presume—good White Chief
sends us word that he wishes to buy our lands but is willing to allow us enough to live
comfortably. This indeed appears just, even generous, for the Red Man no longer has
rights that he need respect, and the offer may be wise, as we are no longer in need of an
extensive country.

There was a time when our people covered the land as the waves of a wind-ruffled   2
sea cover its shell-paved floor, but that time long since passed away with the greatness
of tribes that are now but a mournful memory. I will not dwell on, nor mourn over, our
untimely decay, nor reproach my paleface brothers with hastening it as we too may have
been somewhat to blame.

Youth is impulsive. When our young men grow angry at some real or imaginary   3
wrong, and disfigure their faces with black paint, it denotes that their hearts are black,
and our old men and old women are unable to restrain them. Thus it was when the
white men first began to push our forefathers further westward. But let us hope that the
hostilities between us may never return. We would have everything to lose and nothing
to gain.

Our good father at Washington—for I presume he is now our father as well as   4
yours—our great and good father, I say, sends us word that if we do as he desires
he will protect us. But can that ever be? Your God is not our God! Your God loves
your people and hates mine. He folds his strong protecting arms lovingly about the
pale face—but he has forsaken his red children—if they really are his. Our God, the
Great Spirit, seems also to have forsaken us. Our people are ebbing away like a rapidly
receding tide that will never return. How then can we be brothers? We are two
distinct races with separate origins and separate destinies.

To us the ashes of our ancestors are sacred and their resting place is hallowed ground. 5
You wander far from the graves of your ancestors and seemingly without regret. Your
dead cease to love you and the land of your nativity as soon as they pass the portals of
the tomb and wander away beyond the stars. Our dead never forget the beautiful world
that gave them being . . . and often return to visit, guide, console, and comfort the
lonely hearted living.

It matters little where we pass the remnant of our days. They will not be many. The 6
Indians' night promises to be dark. Not a single star of hope hovers above his horizon.
Tribe follows tribe, and nation follows nation like the waves of the sea. It is the order of
nature, and regret is useless. Your time of decay may be distant, but it will surely come,
for even the white man whose God walked and talked with him as friend with friend,
cannot be exempt from the common destiny. We may be brothers after all. We will see.

And when the Last Red Man shall have perished, these shores will swarm with the 7
invisible dead of my tribe, and when your children's children think themselves alone,
they will not be alone. At night when you think your cities are deserted, they will
throng with the returning hosts that once filled them and still love this beautiful land.
The White Man will never be alone.

Let him be just and deal kindly with my people, for the dead are not powerless. 8

Question 3

During a recent presidential primary season, Andrew Yang, a presidential nomination candidate, proposed
creating a system that would allocate every American adult $1,000.00 a month. On his website, the "Freedom
Dividend," as Yang called it, "would put money into people's hands and keep it there. It would be a
continuous boost and support to job growth and the American economy . . . "

Carefully consider Andrew Yang's proposal. Then, write a well-developed essay in which you argue your
position on a guaranteed annual income.

In your response you should do the following:

- Respond to the prompt with a thesis that may establish a line of reasoning.
- Explain the relationship between the evidence and your thesis.
- Select and use evidence to develop and support your line of reasoning.
- Demonstrate an understanding of the rhetorical situation.

END OF SECTION II

ANSWER KEY

1. C	16. B	31. C
2. E	17. E	32. D
3. D	18. B	33. E
4. B	19. C	34. C
5. A	20. D	35. A
6. C	21. B	36. B
7. E	22. E	37. A
8. C	23. B	38. E
9. E	24. E	39. D
10. B	25. C	40. B
11. B	26. A	41. B
12. D	27. C	42. C
13. B	28. B	43. A
14. A	29. E	44. B
15. D	30. A	45. D

Explanations of Answers to the Multiple-Choice Section

The Annie Dillard Passage

1. **C.** Each paragraph opens with the words "the essay." With this repetition, Dillard guarantees that the reader's focus does not waver. It also provides the organizational framework of the passage. There is no passive voice present. (By the way, the previous sentence is an example of passive voice.) The author relates no personal narrative and does not identify herself with her audience.

2. **E.** In the first two sentences, the author blames "contrived entrances" for killing "the novel of idea." She supports this in the next to the last sentence in paragraph 1 by criticizing "fabricated dramatic occasions." Both of these examples point to the artificial construct of fiction.

3. **D.** The first paragraph contains two major cause-and-effect situations. The first is found in sentences 1–3, and the second is found in the last two sentences.

4. **B.** The first of the two sentences states what the essayist does: he thinks. The second sentence tells the reader *how* he thinks and writes. By writing two separate sentences, Dillard reinforces the equal importance of each of these points.

5. **A.** The second paragraph clearly develops its point through a contrast and comparison between prose and poetry. None of the other strategies is present in the paragraph.

6. **C.** Dillard's subject is the essay. Her position is one of unswerving allegiance to its form and function. Nowhere does she criticize the essay or the essayist, and nowhere does she discuss innovations or the changing of its form. Dillard **is** an artist. This classification, however, does not reveal her stance on the essay form.

7. **E.** Knowing the definition of parallel structure and being able to recognize it makes the choice of E an easy one. ("Even if . . . even if . . .")

8. **C.** Look carefully at sentences 1–3 of paragraph 3 and notice the author's use of the words "connections," "covenant," "veracity," and "truth." With this specific diction, the only appropriate choice is C.

9. **E.** The only choice that contains two adjectives that are *BOTH* applicable to the author's tone in this passage is E. The purpose of the essay is to inform/explain the function of the essay and the essayist. This, in itself, is the support for choosing E. The confidence is apparent in the writer's discussion of the other forms of literature.

The Herman Melville Passage

10. **B.** Throughout the passage, Melville builds his description on the comparison between items connected to the sea and those related to the land. Choices A and C are examples of this controlling analogy. D is another specific detail provided, and E is an example used by Melville to reinforce his description of the Nantucketer.

11. **B.** The entire paragraph centers on the geographic features using analogies, allusions, and factual data. There are no switches in subject, focus, or point of view (B, C, D). Grandeur (E) is not being described, rather the scarcity and hardships of this landscape.

12. **D.** Italics are used for very definite reasons. The purpose here is for emphasis. Melville wants to draw the reader back to the only other italicized word in the piece— *Nantucket*—the very first word of the passage.

13. **B.** Here, pronouns are very important. In paragraph 2, *this* refers the reader to paragraph 1, which is about the island. *These* in paragraph 4 refers to the previous paragraph, which is about the inhabitants of Nantucket. The last sentence of the passage, while quite moving, indicates, again, a reference to Nantucketers. However, *these* in the first sentence of paragraph 3 is a definite shift in focus from the island to its inhabitants.

14. **A.** The only choice appearing in the first paragraph is parallel structure, which is used throughout the listing of "extravaganzas" that Melville bestows on Nantucket. Many of the items in the listing begin with the word *that*.

15. **D.** Keeping in mind the central focus of the passage, Melville's retelling of the Native

American legend is not to highlight or focus on Native Americans, but to reinforce his attitude toward the Nantucketers, whom he perceives in mythic proportions. He compares them to Noah, to Alexander the Great, and to Emperors.

16. **B.** The question requires the reader to be aware of the consecutive details that build in size and importance: from the clam to the whale.

17. **E.** The entire passage develops Melville's opinion about both Nantucket and its inhabitants using analogies. For example, in paragraph 1, pieces of wood are "carried about like bits of the true cross." The entire second paragraph is a portrait built on a Native American legend. The last sentence of paragraph 3 employs an analogy comparing a "the mightiest animated mass" with "salt-sea Mastodon." Paragraph 4 compares Nantucketers to "Emperors," to "sea hermits," "so many Alexanders," etc. Any instance of the other choices is constructed using analogies.

18. **B.** The whale is a "mightiest animated mass." This can only refer to the largest creature in the sea. "Himmalehan" and "Mastadon" reinforce the power and size of the creature.

19. **C.** The tone, diction, syntax, and selection of detail all point to Melville's admiration of the fortitude, perseverance, and uniqueness of the Nantucketer.

20. **D.** In this question, the repetition balances the dual focus: the island and its inhabitants. The diction and syntax of this selection are not formal, but rather a grand folk myth of epic proportions.

21. **B.** Beginning with "There is more sand" and continuing to the end of the paragraph, Melville presents examples dependent upon extreme exaggeration.

22. **E.** The paragraph develops an extended analogy that compares the world of the sea to that of the land, such as sea to prairie, sailor to prairie dog. None of the other choices are valid in this context.

Tell Me a Story

23. **B.** Remembering the definition of exigence, the reader's best choice is the newspaper article Dinadio. The other choices contain either

information that is a misreading of the text (C, D) or an inference that is not appropriate (A).

24. **E.** Five of the essay's seven body paragraphs are developed using examples. The other choices do not apply to the organization and logic of the passage.

25. **C.** This is a well-developed essay that utilizes strategies and devices that appeal to common interests paragraphs 2, 8,10), reason (transitions, and examples), timeliness (paragraph 2), and credibility (cited examples, context) to present its argument.

26. **A.** The examples, context, organization all assume the reader is one or more of choices B, C, D, E. However, the writer does not assume any special education or background on the part of the reader.

27. **C.** Rosenblatt organizes his essay using examples that illustrate and support his thesis. The transitions and order of the examples, together with his comments are arranged logically and topically.

28. **B.** The thesis is located in the second paragraph. Here the writer asks a rhetorical question that clearly lays out his specific assertion with an indication of the organization of the argument.

29. **E.** Rosenblatt neither advocates (A, B) nor recommends (C,D) keeping or eliminating fiction or non-fiction. Instead, his essay presents his argument as to where truth resides.

30. **A.** Moving paragraphs 9 and 10 to any other spot in the essay would interfere with the argument's logic and clarity (B, C, D). Omitting these two paragraphs would alter and weaken the support of the thesis (E).

31. **C.** Each of paragraphs A, B, D, E illustrates and/or supports Rosenblatt's thesis. Choice C is just a detail used in support of the claim of paragraph 2.

Automania

32. **D.** Keeping the definition of exigence in mind, the event/situation that pushes the author to write "Automania" is first, foremost, and most immediate frustration with traffic

delays and signage. Choices A, B, C, and E are all included in and results of this initial frustration.

33. **E.** In a not too frequent situation, this passage's thesis statement is located in the final paragraph. The last two sentences state the writer's assertion about her frustration and present the final word that wraps up the previous paragraphs with their examples and narration. The other paragraphs provide the specific examples and comments that support and/or illustrate this thesis.

34. **C.** Induction is moving from specific to general. This essay, with its thesis located in the last paragraph, is a good example of this type of organizational pattern.

35. **A.** Except for paragraphs 1, 7, and 10, each of the other paragraphs support/illustrate the writer's assertion with examples.

36. **B.** With a careful reading of the essay of the essay, the reader can see that the impact of the writer's assertion and examples is based on all of the given assumptions except B. Although not necessary, the effect of the final paragraph is deepened if the reader knows who Shakespeare and Freud are and is familiar with the term *zen* (A).

37. **A.** In the first paragraph, the writer introduces the subject, context, and exigence to the reader. The other choices are not in this paragraph or are misreading.

38. **E.** The sentence that would precede it ends with the writer stating that she is *vaguely unsettled.* The logic and flow of the paragraph are interrupted with the introduction of how she is driving. The question arises: What does she do then? This question is out of context with the next paragraph.

39. **D.** These rhetorical questions are personal asides that beg for a response from the reader. The writer is letting the reader in on her private thoughts and invites the reader to respond.

40. **B.** Almost like the forever blinking of the time on the cable box, *AHEAD,* repeated four times, coupled with *endlessly* is the writer

suggesting to the reader that this problem will be forever and that "resistance is futile."

41. **B.** The list that follows the dash is a hyperbolic metaphor that is the world shattering opposite of the mundane highway minutiae the average highway commuter encounters. None of the other choices is supportable.

Greta Thunberg's UN Speech

42. **C.** Choices A, D, and E are not related to the topic, which is the speaker confronting the leaders not listening to what science is saying. B merely restates what is already in the paragraph. C makes the accusation, but leads to the glimmer of hope that the speaker addresses in the remainder of the paragraph.

43. **A.** This is a brief speech; therefore each word/phrase is important. Choices A and B basically repeat what is already in the paragraph. D and E do not add to the development of either the paragraphs topic nor the purpose of the argument. In this instance, it is best to leave things as they are.

44. **B.** A cause/effect rhetorical strategy is established with this sentence. The listing of negative factors leads to the speaker's actions, all of this part of the speaker setting the stage for the information that is to follow in support of her argument. The structure of this sentence demands a construction that indicates cause/effect. The placement of this sentence in any of the other paragraphs would not be logical.

45. **D.** Choices A, B, C, E are all statements of scientific facts related to mass extinction. A personal narrative about the sadness related to the loss of a pet is not specifically related to mass extinction.

Sample Student Essays

Rubrics for the Synthesis Essay

THESIS = 1 Point

- **1 pt.** Addresses the prompt with a thesis that makes it clear HOW the thesis will be developed.
- **0 pts.** Merely repeats the prompt, or statement is vague, avoids taking a position, or presents only an obvious fact.

DEVELOPMENT WITH EVIDENCE = 4 Points

- **4 pts.** With references to at least three of the given sources, the writer presents support for the thesis explaining the relationships between the evidence and the thesis.
- **3 pts.** With references to at least three of the given sources, the development may be uneven, limited; there may be minor errors or weak links between thesis and support.
- **2 pts.** With references to at least three of the given sources, the development repeats, oversimplifies, or misinterprets cited references; points made are not supported by the text.
- **1 pt.** With references to two or fewer of the given sources, the writer merely summarizes the referenced sources, or references to the text are not clear or relevant; provides little or no commentary that links the source to the thesis.
- **0 pts.** May lack a thesis; or presents irrelevant or too few references to the text in support of a clear thesis; or does not address the prompt; or writes about something totally unrelated to the prompt.

  Note: Writing that lacks grammatical or syntactical control that interferes with a clear presentation of ideas, cannot earn a 4.

SOPHISTICATION (Complexity and Style) = 1 Point

- **1 pt.** (sophistication of thought or development of complex argument) Writer develops the thesis with nuanced explanation of evidence; and/or recognizes and discusses a broader context; and/or recognizes and engages with opposition; and/or makes strong, convincing rhetorical choices in developing the thesis; and/or prose is especially convincing or appropriate.
- **0 pts.** Oversimplifies complexities of the text or the thesis; and/or diction and/or syntax do not enhance the presentation; and/or may overuse sweeping generalizations.

Synthesis Essay—Student A

Some were shocked. Others were indifferent. Still others were proud. What event   1
could cause such an array of emotions in so many different people? The burning of the
American flag. However, what seems to lead to even more controversy than the actual
burning of the flag is the legal ramifications of flag-burning—specifically, whether
or not it should be banned by the Constitution. Politicians in favor of such a law are
proposing a one-sentence amendment to the First Amendment to target the "desecration"
of the flag. But such an amendment is just not necessary.

Supreme Court Chief Justice William Rehnquist vehemently protested the burning   2
of the flag, stating, "Millions and millions of Americans regard it with an almost
mystical reverence." Indeed, quite true is that declaration, which matches the regard—in
the forms of laws which criminalize public flag-burning—of 48 states to such a symbol
(Source E). And, of course, the ultimate reflection of this point of view exists in the
very amendment causing such ruckus, which states, "The Congress shall have power to
prohibit the physical desecration of the flag of the United States" (Source B).

However, if Americans are in such cohesive opinion of flag-burning, or so it would   3
seem, why are some still setting fire to the beloved stars and stripes? Once again, we
return to the respected Chief Justice Rehnquist, who also states that "[The flag] does not
represent any particular political philosophy" (Source E). In a sense, this makes the flag
mutable enough to represent all things politically American, such as government officials
or even government policy. Such is the reasoning that the *Los Angeles Times* justified the
burning of the flag—as "attacks on government and public officials" (Source F). But,
other than a crowd's "distaste" at the politicians of America, another, more practical
explanation rights the burning of the flag: disposing it. According to Todd Lindberg,
the Boy Scout manual delineates a "ceremony" for getting the flag "decommissioned
properly. So the symbolic content is always present" (Source I). Such a respectful gesture
to a flag that has served its days seems almost shameful to ban.

Then, of course, arises the issue of freedom of speech. An opinion of Senator   4
McConnell of Kentucky finds that, "Placing a no-flag-burning asterisk next to the
amendment's sweeping guarantee of free speech . . . could invite amendments to ban
other sorts of speech" (Source F). Such a thought seems a little flawed in the snowball-
down-a-hill way, but the adage "power corrupts," no matter how trite, might still give
the idea enough fuel to scorch. However, Mr. Lindberg of the *Washington Times* proved
the hypocrisy of such an amendment best. A ban on "the symbol of the freedom to
burn, baby, burn," leaves a paradoxical taste in anyone's mouth. Limiting the freedom to
destroy freedom means, to Mr. Lindberg and many others, "you have no freedom."

But "burn, baby, burn" doesn't exactly sound like a right "of the people peaceably   5
to assemble," as stated in the First Amendment of the Constitution (Source A). Fire is
hardly a symbol of peace, and one could almost make the argument that burning the
flag is equivalent to yelling "fire!" in a crowded theater (almost, but not in the landmark
case of *Texas v. Johnson*). The justices of the Supreme Court ruled that the burning
of the flag caused neither "breaches of the peace" nor "a serious disturbance" (Source

D). Furthermore, United States v. Eichman voices the same opinion, thus, effectively eliminating the Flag Protection Act of 1989 (Source D). And, finally, to sooth the naysayers voicing opinions of a free-for-all burn, a 2006 *Los Angeles Times* editorial reports that "no epidemic of flag-burning" has occurred since such rulings. Indeed, flag-burning, as a freedom, fulfills all legal qualifications as an act of peaceful expression. No harm, no foul.

Ultimately, the voice of the people clearly decrees that an amendment to rid flag-burning is superfluous. The Supreme Court has already sanctioned flag-burning as a right in the penumbra of the First Amendment, and that Amendment, throughout its decade of existence, hasn't achieved the needed majority of Congress (Source G). But the sovereign of this state, the people, says it all. The 2006 poll in *USA Today* shows a minor, but significant 54 percent majority of the American public believing an amendment against flag-burning is unnecessary (Source C). Mr. Lindberg really did say it best in his own editorial: ". . . most Americans will think you are an ingrate jerk . . . But even if a constitutional amendment passes, no one is proposing the death penalty for flag-burning." Flag-burning is unpatriotic at best, but Americans have enough common sense not to use flag-burning as a favorite pastime without a law on their backs. 6

Synthesis Essay—Student B

Over the course of American history, political freedoms and inalienable rights have been the ultimate treasure of the American people. As a nation, we pride ourselves on our right to express our opinions without threat of punishment. From the Supreme Court ruling against the Alien and Sedition Acts to the current flag burning issue, free speech has been upheld. 1

In the cases of *Texas v. Johnson* and the *U.S. v. Eichman*, the Supreme Court has said that the act of desecrating the American flag is not illegal (Source D). This reliable source states that flag burning does not directly threaten anyone; in fact, a reference to the flag is amorphous. The flag is a symbol that takes billions of forms across the entire country. As stated in Source I, "There is no 'the' flag . . . it is an idea of the flag and therefore beyond the reach of the flames." An anti-flag burning amendment would be nebulous and would be incapable of addressing a specific act of flag desecration. 2

A survey taken by *USA Today* indicated that more than half of those Americans tallied do not want such an amendment added (Source C). The Constitution is a document for the people, by the people, and of the people; therefore, if an opinion is to matter, it should be the viewpoint of the people. They are the ones who need to abide by the laws and should have some say in their construction. 3

However, when Congress voted a series of six times, every single time there were more representatives for the amendment than were against it (Source G). There is a serious discrepancy between the people and their representatives. The author of Source F expresses his opinion on this matter, maintaining that if these representatives passed the amendment, it would severely restrict the freedoms that we as Americans have come to love. 4

The first amendment to the Constitution has clauses that are contradictory to the   5
proposed anti-flag burning amendment (Source A). The proposed amendment would
restrict the provided freedoms and would "prohibit the physical desecration of the flag
of the United States." Source F claims that the destruction of Old Glory as a protest was
symbolic speech protected by the First Amendment. Though the editorial may be biased,
the author makes a provocative argument. This country has been content with the First
Amendment. Why change it now? It may even create more of a problem. Telling someone
to do something often provokes him to do the opposite. When a child is told to refrain
from an action, the typical response is for the child to test the parent. Clay Bennet's
ironic editorial cartoon (Source H) reinforces this idea. It shows an American flag
marked with the quote, "do not desecrate." The cartoon mocks the idea of forbidding the
desecration of the flag and demonstrates that the amendment may not be taken seriously
and may possibly have the opposite effect from what it is trying to enforce.

It is apparent that the government and the people are currently undecided on the   6
issue. When it resurfaces, and it will, the representatives will be faced with a conundrum:
"yea" or "nay." Hopefully, the representatives will see the contradictions and turn down
the amendment for the good of the American people and their freedom.

Note: For our purposes, scoring comments will be followed by one of three letters to
indicate one of the three areas used in the AP English Language rubric for the rhetorical
analysis essay. Thesis = (A), Evidence/Commentary = (B), Sophistication = (C)

Rating the Student Essays

Student A
This high-range paper:

- Effectively introduces the argument and indicates the opposition in paragraph 1 (A)
- Opens with an interesting example of parallelism (B and C)
- Clearly establishes the writer's position against the amendment (B)
- Exhibits strong control of language: diction, syntax, transitions, rhetorical questions (C)
- Builds a cohesive and convincing argument against the amendment by effectively introducing, combining, and commenting on appropriate sources (B and C)
- Employs transitions to further the development of the points in the argument: *however, then, but, ultimately* (C)
- Creates mature concluding sentences in each paragraph that drive home the writer's position (B and C)
- Smoothly integrates and cites sources material (B and C)
- Presents a coherent, strong voice and tone (C)

Student B
This mid-range essay:

- Opening provides outside information to indicate the writer's position against the amendment (A)
- Incorporates and properly cites at least three sources to support the argument (B)

- <u>Adequately</u> comments on the synthesized material and includes <u>some</u> relevant outside information to reinforce the sources used (B)
- Indicates an understanding of the process of writing a synthesis essay (B)
- Demonstrates control of language through diction and syntax (C)
- Recognizes the bias in source material (B)
- Adds to the argument by creating an analogous situation: the child testing the parents (B)
- Indicates an understanding of tone and intent (B)

Rubrics for the Rhetorical Analysis Essay

THESIS = 1 Point

- **1 pt.** Addresses the prompt with a thesis that makes it clear HOW the thesis will be developed.
- **0 pts.** Merely repeats the prompt, or statement is vague, avoids taking a position, or presents only an obvious fact.

DEVELOPMENT WITH EVIDENCE = 4 Points

- **4 pts.** With specific references to the text, the writer develops the thesis with conclusions and inferences that are the result of explaining the relationship between what the author says and what the rhetorical strategy does.
- **3 pts.** Development may be uneven, limited; there may be minor instances of description rather than analysis; there may be minor errors or weak links between thesis and support.
- **2 pts.** Development repeats, oversimplifies, or misinterprets cited references; may misinterpret or misunderstand the chosen rhetorical strategies; points made are not supported by the text.
- **1 pt.** Merely summarizes the text, or references to the text are not clear or relevant; merely restates points made in the text.
- **0 pts.** May lack a thesis; or presents irrelevant or too few references to the text in support of a clear thesis; or does not address the prompt; or writes about something totally unrelated to the prompt.

Note: Writing that lacks grammatical or syntactical control that interferes with a clear presentation of ideas cannot earn a 4.

SOPHISTICATION (Complexity and Style) = 1 Point

- **1 pt.** (sophistication of thought or development of complex argument) Writer develops the thesis with nuanced explanation of evidence; and/or recognizes and discusses a broader context; and/or recognizes and engages with opposition; and/or makes strong, convincing rhetorical choices in developing the thesis; and/or prose is especially convincing or appropriate.
- **0 pts.** Oversimplifies complexities of the text or the thesis; and/or diction and/or syntax do not enhance the presentation; and/or may overuse sweeping generalizations.

Chief Seattle Passage—Student Sample A

In his oration to Governor Isaac I. Stevens, Chief Seattle attempts to convince the 1
whites that they should deal fairly with the Native Americans despite their inferior
status. Through the use of rhetorical strategies and devices like figurative language,
organization, diction, and tone, he appeals both to the pride and the reason of the
Governor, reminding him that, though weak, the Natives are not powerless.

Chief Seattle begins his oration in a friendly manner, appealing to the Governor and 2
the whites' pride while recognizing their superior status. He refers to the Governor as "the
great" and "the good White Chief" throughout the piece, hoping the governor will look
favorably on his subordinance despite the mocking that is hidden in his words. Seattle
takes responsibility for the plight of the Natives, another strategy that undoubtedly
makes him more respectable and admirable to the Governor, although he does not
necessarily believe his people are truly at fault. In yet another attempt to get or remain
on the Governor's "good side," Seattle says that the young Indian warriors' "hearts are
black," blaming them and not the whites for the warfare and distrust that characterizes
the Native American–American relationship. To increase his own credibility, Seattle uses
the simile "my words are like the stars that never change," once more emphasizing his
steadfastness and ability to work with the Americans. By presenting himself as inferior,
apologetic, responsible and respectful, Seattle attempts to win Stevens' favor.

In addition to promoting his own respectability, Seattle emphasizes differences 3
between his people and the Americans. Appreciating the Americans' "generosity" and
"friendship and goodwill," Seattle points out the differences between the two peoples in a
respectful manner. He calls the whites his "paleface brothers," but is certain to point out
that they believe in different supreme beings, have different customs, are "two distinct
races with separate origins and separate destinies." With rhetorical questions like "How
then can we be brothers?" Seattle suggests that the two peoples cannot intermingle
through no fault of their own. Instead of blaming the Americans, he implies that they are
just and kind and that the peoples' lack of friendship is just the way it's supposed to be.

Despite his calm, almost compromising attitude throughout his oration, Chief 4
Seattle does, at certain points, warn Governor Stevens of the power of his people. Short of
belligerent, these comments are often made in a manner that implies rather than openly
affirms Native American strength and lack of fear. With the emotional statement "Indians'
night promises to be dark," Seattle almost suggests that his people have nothing to lose if
the relationship with the Americans goes sour. They have already lost so much that they
will fight to the end. Seattle warns that "these shores will swarm with the invisible dead
of my tribe . . . the White Man will never be alone." Thus, he reminds Stevens that, even
though his people are but "the scattering trees of a storm-swept plain," they are strong—a

force to be reckoned with. In a respectful manner, he manages to threaten Stevens and clearly deliver his message that the tribe will not so easily be destroyed.

In addition to warning the Governor, acting respectfully and emphasizing the inherent differences between the two peoples, Chief Seattle gives a sense of the unfair treatment his tribe has suffered. In his oration so deeply saturated with figurative language, balanced sentences, carefully chosen diction, and hidden implications, the Chief conveys his message loud and clear. Though weak in number, his people are strong in heart; though inferior in legal status, his tribe is superior in customs and values. The governor may buy their land, but, Seattle reminds him, he may never buy their pride or their silence.

Chief Seattle Passage—Student Sample B

Chief Seattle, one of great speakers for the Native Americans, spoke out against Governor Stevens in an attempt to discourage the buying of more Indian land. His style which includes similes, rhetorical questions, and emotional diction, not only gets his point across, but warns and denounces the whites as well.

Right in the beginning, Seattle starts emotionally with "wept tears of compassion" to try to gain a sympathy for his people. Later on in the passage, he exclaims, "Your God is not our God!" and blatantly announces "Your God loves your people and hates mine." These harsh words obviously convey Chief Seattle's anger and disapproval.

To further increase the emotional appeal, Seattle employs rhetorical questions in an attempt to make the reader wonder and empathize. He states ". . . he will protect us. But can that ever be?" and "How then can we be brothers? We are two distinct races." Since this was addressed to Governor Isaac, what this did was it made the Governor question himself whether the buying of more Indian land and pushing the Indians west are right and moral. In addition, the rhetorical questions allow Chief Seattle to express his anger better.

The use of similes in this piece not only add a poetic touch, but also effectively describe the decrease in Native Americans and the increase in whites. He compares the invasive whites as "grass that covers vast prairies" while describing the disappearing Indians as "scattering trees of a storm-swept plain." The storm that swept through clearly also represents the whites that pushed the Native Americans westward or bought their land. By comparing the whites to grass that grows anywhere they want and as a storm, Chief Seattle subtly establishes the idea that whites are land-hungry and greedy.

In addition, the Chief denounces certain cultural aspects of whites through a series of antitheses. As he uses "To us the ashes of our ancestors are sacred . . . You wander . . . from the graves . . . without regret" and "your dead cease to love you . . . Our dead never forget the beautiful world," there seems to be a criticism of whites as loveless people who don't respect the dead. And, as a final warning, Chief Seattle says, "Your time of decay may be distant, but it will surely come . . ." As he tried to tell the whites that what they have done will eventually cause their demise.

In all, Chief Seattle's speech to Governor Isaac not only achieves his purpose of discouraging the actions of the whites, but warns and denounces the culture of the whites as well.

Note: For our purposes, scoring comments will be followed by one of three letters to indicate one of the three areas used in the AP English Language rubric for the rhetorical analysis essay. Thesis = (A), Evidence/Commentary = (B), Sophistication = (C).

Rating Student Sample A

This is a high-range essay for the following reasons:

- An immediate and clear indication of Seattle's purpose and attitude (A)
- Understanding and discussion of Seattle's attitude and purpose (paragraph 2) (B)
- Demonstration of a mature voice (C)
- Thorough and effective connection between texts and insights (last two sentences of paragraph 2) (B and C)
- Superior use of connective tissue—transitions and echo words ("in addition," "despite his calm," "acting respectfully," "winning favor") (B and C)
- Refers to a variety of rhetorical strategies and devices to support the writer's assertion (paragraph 3: rhetorical questions), (paragraph 3: cause and effect), (paragraph 4: details), (paragraph 4: figurative language) (B)
- Mature perceptions and insights (paragraph 2, sentence 2), (paragraph 4, sentence 2), (paragraph 5, next to last sentence) (C)
- Mature writing style (last sentence) (C)

This high-range essay indicates the clear voice of a mature writer and reader. Once the writer has committed to Seattle's purpose and attitude, the writer develops in each successive paragraph a supporting aspect of the stated purpose and/or attitude.

Rating Student Sample B

This is a mid-range essay for the following reasons:

- Concise, on-target development of prompt (A and B)
- Indicates an understanding of the oration (B)
- Makes intelligent points, but does not always develop them or defend them (paragraph 3, last sentence) (B)
- Each paragraph deals with a different strategy (paragraph 2: emotional details), (paragraph 3: rhetorical questions), (paragraph 4: simile), (paragraph 5: antithesis) (B)
- Good connective tissue (B and C)
- A few lapses in syntax and diction (paragraph 3, next to last sentence) (C)

This essay is indicative of a writer who understands both the passage and the prompt. There is an adequate analysis of the rhetorical strategies and devices present in the text, and the student reaches for unique insights (paragraph 4, last sentence). The lack of development of a couple of the cited points places this essay squarely in the mid-range.

Rubrics for Argument Essay

THESIS = 1 Point
- **1 pt.** Addresses the prompt with a thesis clearly, takes a position, and makes it clear HOW the thesis will be developed.
- **0 pts.** Merely repeats the prompt, or statement is vague, avoids taking a position, or presents only an obvious fact.

DEVELOPMENT WITH EVIDENCE = 4 Points
- **4 pts.** The writer presents support for the thesis clearly explaining the relationships between the evidence and the thesis.

- **3 pts.**   The development may be uneven, limited, incomplete; there may be minor errors or weak links between thesis and support.
- **2 pts.**   The development repeats, oversimplifies, or misinterprets cited evidence; points made are not supported by the text.
- **1 pt.**   The writer provides little or no commentary that links the evidence to the thesis.
- **0 pts.**   May lack a thesis; or presents irrelevant or too few references to the text in support of a clear thesis; or does not address the prompt; or writes about something totally unrelated to the prompt.

Note: Writing that lacks grammatical or syntactical control that interferes with a clear presentation of ideas cannot earn a 4.

SOPHISTICATION (Complexity and Style) = 1 Point

- **1 pt.**   (sophistication of thought or development of complex argument) Writer develops the thesis with nuanced explanation of evidence; and/or recognizes and discusses a broader context; and/or recognizes and engages with opposition; and/or makes strong, convincing rhetorical choices in developing the thesis; and/or prose is especially convincing or appropriate.
- **0 pts.**   Oversimplifies complexities of the text or the thesis; and/or diction and/or syntax does not enhance the presentation; and/or may overuse sweeping generalizations.

Yang Passage—Student A

During the recent pandemic, the Government supplied each family with $500 for each child. This was a great way to assist families during this predicament, as many parents were unable to work to provide for their families. Similarly, Andrew Yang proposed giving American adults $1000.00 a month. Yang's proposal is very efficient to assist those who need help with issues at home or help with jobs, but receiving money every month would cause a decrease in the economy that would not benefit America as well. Also, if this money gets into the wrong hands, there will be issues centered on drugs/crimes.   1

As we know, today around the world, there is a growing problem with the issue centered around COVID-19. As the number of victims continues to rise, hospital bills begin to rise as well. People around the world are unable to receive the treatment they need because of the huge pricing of hospitals. Prices in businesses as well have begun to rise. Water bottles, tissues, eggs, regular home goods that are usually cheaper have become extremely expensive due to this pandemic. Many parents are unable to go to work, and with their kids home, they need to support these homes and families. Yang's proposition is very helpful in this field. As each family's adults receives the money, they can support their families as well as help them stay healthy. The more people purchase the more there is in the growth of the American economy. There is a greater demand for toilet papers, water bottles, face masks, and food. The more production leads to more people buying which would, therefore, lead to the growth in the American economy.   2

Even though Yang states the proposition could be very handy for jobs, the problem is that if people see that they are receiving money without working, they may decide to not work again. Parents must teach their kids that to earn something in life, they have   3 to work for it. There is no easy way in life. If you don't work for it, you don't receive anything. Kids learn this both in school and at home. But, if the government starts handing money freely to every single American adult without actually earning it, kids will start to believe that they don't need to work to have a living when they grow up. Job growth may start to decline due to this proposition. Today, many kids follow the ideology of their parents. The way kids are brought up in homes, sets up how their life is going to be. If they see that their parents are depending on only the $1000.00 they receive every month, they're probably going to follow that pattern. Rather, Yang should propose giving it to them every 3 months. This would encourage people to continue to work which could, therefore, lead to a growth in the job industry.

Yang's proposition is helpful for those who live in poverty. In the United States, millions of Americans live in poverty. Many people have lost their homes due to being unable to pay for their taxes. This proposition will allow many people to have a new start in life. The money every month will set them up for a new beginning and assist them in getting the right education and allowing them to find new jobs that would set them up for the future. But, the money may also end up in the wrong hands. By giving $1000.00 to every American adult, some may use the money for wrongdoing like drugs and trafficking. The money should be given to those who need it, not to celebrities/famous people who have easier lives than others. Connected to this is a further problem with Yang's proposal. It is that he only states "American citizens." Many immigrants came to the United States for a new beginning but don't have the money to begin a new life. The money would benefit them as well. With this, they would be able to better assist their families while they search for a decent job. 4

Yang's proposal had both a good and a bad impact on America. This money may assist those caught up in national issues like the one we have now, as well as helping the poor, but there are setbacks. Since it benefits American citizens only, leaving non-citizens out, a large percentage of the population of the United States would remain outside of the American promise. 5

Yang Passage—Student B

Money is a valuable possession that is necessary throughout a person's life in a capitalist economy. Andrew Yang, a presidential nomination candidate, proposed creating a system called the "Financial Dividend" that entitles every American adult 1,000 dollars per month. Although money is beneficial to everyone and stimulates the economy, to give it away for free can be detrimental to humans because they will constantly be spoiled, and too many people would continuously spend the money on non-essential items. 1

Depending on the circumstance, Andrew Yang's policy may be good in a state of emergency, such as the current coronavirus. Money can help many with their everyday lives. It can help pay rent, groceries, and to utilities that are needed. Millions of Americans are unemployed and are facing an economic crisis because they need to 2 feed not only themselves, but their kids, too. This is why there already is financial aid such as Medicare, and Medicaid. Common sense would direct a person to believe that Americans would use the check in an efficient way; however, some Americans may take advantage of that money. Adults who aren't responsible may take the money for their personal pleasure.

Most Americans don't have the proper financial literacy to maintain their financial independence. As we see so very often, Americans, especially the middle class, are quick to spend rather than save and use their money as an asset. Yang argues that his policy "would put money into people's hands and keep it there"; however, too many Americans would see money as an opportunity to buy frivolous things such as a new video game or a new phone. Although some of these items could be an asset, such as a phone, it may not be necessary to buy at the time. A new phone or video game is not necessary every time a new one comes out. Instead, the money could be saved or used to invest in a business or stocks to create more money to plan for the future. Although this may seem like a reason to give people money, most people don't know how to manage and keep their money. Probably most people if given one million dollars; would return to their old habits in a couple of years because they don't know how to keep and grow that million.

3

There's a popular saying, "for much is given, much is expected." One could ask, "expected by whom or expected for whom?" For example, when children are "babied" and have everything done for most of their life, they are unintentionally spoiled and dependent on someone else. If people are constantly given money for free, they will believe that money is guaranteed and will develop a sense of entitlement to that continuous check. The American dream has always been to work hard to achieve your goals, follow your dreams. What separates the winners from losers is a work ethic. If a people don't earn what they have, they will take it for granted. In the case of money, they will keep spending. Instead of being a "continuous boost," the money given monthly would turn into a continuous cycle of paying bills and spending while little is saved or used in a wise way.

4

On one hand, a check for $1,000 per month could stimulate the economy in an economic crisis; however, if the country is stable and is not going through a pandemic or another type of crisis, the check is not needed. Money cannot benefit the American people if they don't have financial literacy.

5

Note: For our purposes, scoring comments will be followed by one of three letters to indicate one of the three areas used in the AP English Language rubric for the rhetorical analysis essay. Thesis = (A), Evidence/Commentary = (B), Sophistication = (C).

Rating Student Sample A

This is a high-range essay for the following reasons:

- Clear thesis stated with relevant reference to the prompt [paragraph one] (A)
- Line of reasoning clearly established using transitions and internal references to the argument [paragraph 2: "As we know . . . ;" paragraph 3: "Even though . . . ;" paragraph 4: Yang's proposition . . . ;" paragraph 5: "Yang's proposal had . . ."] (B and C)
- Body paragraphs consistently developed with relevant evidence and meaningful commentary relating both to the thesis and the development of the argument [specific examples used in paragraphs 1, 2, and 3] (B and C)
- Commentary that consistently discusses and references the complexity of the rhetorical situation and its relevance to world outside of the text. (B and C)

Rating Student Sample B

This is a mid-range essay for the following reasons:

- An acceptable thesis statement [paragraph one] (A)
- An awkward introductory paragraph (B)
- Body paragraphs present some evidence in support of the thesis with some commentary that helps develop the argument (B)
- Evidence and commentary is primarily in the form of generalizations (B)
- Weak final paragraph that primarily summarizes the introductory paragraph (B)

Appendixes

Glossary
Selected Bibliography
Websites

Abstract refers to language that describes concepts rather than concrete images.

Ad Hominem In an argument, an attack on the person rather than on the opponent's ideas. It comes from the Latin meaning "against the man."

Allegory a work that functions on a symbolic level.

Alliteration the repetition of initial consonant sounds, such as "Peter Piper picked a peck of pickled peppers."

Allusion a reference contained in a work.

Analogy a literary device employed to serve as a basis for comparison. It is assumed that what applies to the parallel situation also applies to the original circumstance. In other words, it is the comparison between two different items.

Analysis the process of taking apart a text by dividing it into its basic components for the purpose of examining how the author develops his/her subject.

Anecdote a story or brief episode told by the writer or a character to illustrate a point.

Annotate to make personal notes on a text in order to get a better understanding of the material. These notes can include questions, an argument with the author, acknowledging a good point, a clarification of an idea.

Antecedent the word, phrase, or clause to which a pronoun refers. The AP English Language and Composition exam often expects you to identify the antecedent in a passage.

Antithesis the presentation of two contrasting images. The ideas are balanced by word, phrase, clause, or paragraph. "To be or not to be . . ." "Ask not what your country can do for you, ask what you can do for your country . . ."

Argument a single assertion or a series of assertions presented and defended by the writer.

Attitude the relationship an author has toward his or her subject, and/or his or her audience.

Balance a situation in which all parts of the presentation are equal, whether in sentences or paragraphs or sections of a longer work.

Cacophony harsh and discordant sounds in a line or passage in a literary work.

Character those who carry out the action of the plot in literature. Major, minor, static, and dynamic are types of characters.

Claim rhetorically, a statement that asserts something is true; often works as the topic sentence in support of the thesis; primary point in support of an argument.

Colloquial the use of slang in writing, often to create local color and to provide an informal tone. *Huckleberry Finn* is written in a colloquial style.

Comic Relief the inclusion of a humorous character or scene to contrast with the tragic elements of a work, thereby intensifying the next tragic event.

Complexity the recognition and discussion of multiple ways elements of a text interact within the text and/or in relation to the given context.

Conflict a clash between opposing forces in a literary work, such as man vs. man; man vs. nature; man vs. god; man vs. self.

Connective Tissue those elements that help create coherence in a written piece. See Chapter 8.

Connotation the interpretive level of a word based on its associated images rather than its literal meaning.

Deduction the process of moving from a general rule to a specific example.

Denotation the literal or dictionary meaning of a word.

Dialect the re-creation of regional spoken language, such as a Southern dialect. Zora Neale Hurston uses this in such works as *Their Eyes Were Watching God*.

Diction the author's choice of words that creates tone, attitude, and style, as well as meaning.

Didactic writing whose purpose is to instruct or to teach. A didactic work is usually formal and focuses on moral or ethical concerns.

Discourse a discussion on a specific topic.

Ellipsis an indication by a series of three periods that some material has been omitted from a given text. It could be a word, a phrase, a sentence, a paragraph, or a whole section. Be wary of the ellipsis; it could obscure the real meaning of the piece of writing.

Epigraph the use of a quotation at the beginning of a work that hints at its theme. Hemingway begins *The Sun Also Rises* with two epigraphs. One of them is "You are all a lost generation" by Gertrude Stein.

Exigence a problem that needs to be addressed and which pushes the speaker to write or speak, why the author is writing.

Euphemism a more acceptable and usually more pleasant way of saying something that might be inappropriate or uncomfortable. "He went to his final reward" is a common euphemism for "he died." Euphemisms are also often used to obscure the reality of a situation. The military uses "collateral damage" to indicate civilian deaths in a military operation.

Euphony the pleasant, mellifluous presentation of sounds in a literary work.

Exigence a problem that needs to be addressed and that pushes the speaker to write or speak.

Exposition background information presented in a literary work.

Extended Metaphor a sustained comparison, often referred to as a conceit. The extended metaphor is developed throughout a piece of writing.

Figurative Language the body of devices that enables the writer to operate on levels other than the literal one. It includes metaphor, simile, symbol, motif, and hyperbole, etc.

Flashback a device that enables a writer to refer to past thoughts, events, or episodes.

Form the shape or structure of a literary work.

Hyperbole extreme exaggeration, often humorous, it can also be ironic; the opposite of understatement.

Image a verbal approximation of a sensory impression, concept, or emotion.

Imagery the total effect of related sensory images in a work of literature.

Induction the process that moves from a given series of specifics to a generalization.

Inference a conclusion one can draw from the presented details.

Invective a verbally abusive attack.

Irony an unexpected twist or contrast between what happens and what was intended or expected to happen. It involves dialogue and situation and can be intentional or unplanned. Dramatic irony centers around the ignorance of those involved, whereas the audience is aware of the circumstance.

Line of Reasoning in AP English Language, the arrangement of claims and the evidence that supports the thesis.

Logic the process of reasoning.

Logical Fallacy a mistake in reasoning (see Chapter 9 for specific examples).

Metaphor a direct comparison between dissimilar things. "Your eyes are stars" is an example.

Metonymy a figure of speech in which a representative term is used for a larger idea (*The pen is mightier than the sword*).

Monologue a speech given by one character (Hamlet's "To be or not to be . . .").

Motif the repetition or variations of an image or idea in a work used to develop theme or characters.

Narrator the speaker of a literary work.

Onomatopoeia words that sound like the sound they represent (hiss, gurgle, pop).

Oxymoron an image of contradictory terms (bittersweet, jumbo shrimp).

Pacing the movement of a literary piece from one point or one section to another.

Parable a story that operates on more than one level and usually teaches a moral lesson. (*The Pearl* by John Steinbeck is a fine example.)

Parody a comic imitation of a work that ridicules the original. It can be utterly mocking or gently humorous. It depends on allusion and exaggerates and distorts the original style and content.

Pathos the aspects of a literary work that elicit pity from the audience. An appeal to emotion that can be used as a means to persuade.

Pedantic a term used to describe writing that borders on lecturing. It is scholarly and academic and often overly difficult and distant.

Periodic Sentence presents its main clause at the end of the sentence for emphasis and sentence variety. Phrases and/or dependent clauses precede the main clause.

Personification the assigning of human qualities to inanimate objects or concepts. (Wordsworth personifies "the sea that bares her bosom to the moon" in the poem "London 1802.")

Persuasion a type of argument that has as its goal an action on the part of the audience.

Plot a sequence of events in a literary work.

Point of View the method of narration in a literary work.

Pun a play on words that often has a comic effect. Associated with wit and cleverness. A writer who speaks of the "grave topic of American funerals" may be employing an intentional or unintentional pun.

Reductio ad Absurdum the Latin for "to reduce to the absurd." This is a technique useful in creating a comic effect (see Twain's "At the Funeral") and is also an argumentative technique. It is considered a rhetorical fallacy, because it reduces an argument to an either/or choice.

Rhetoric refers to the entire process of written communication. Rhetorical strategies and devices are those tools that enable a writer to present ideas to an audience effectively.

Rhetorical Question one that does not expect an explicit answer. It is used to pose an idea to be considered by the speaker or audience. (François Villon [in translation] asks, "Where are the snows of yesteryear?")

Rhetorical Situation the context around which the author, subject, and audience are involved.

Sarcasm a comic technique that ridicules through caustic language. Tone and attitude may both be described as sarcastic in a given text if the writer employs language, irony, and wit to mock or scorn.

Satire a mode of writing based on ridicule, that criticizes the foibles and follies of society without necessarily offering a solution. (Jonathan Swift's *Gulliver's Travels* is a great satire that exposes mankind's condition.)

Says/Does a rhetorical analysis that observes/summarizes what the author says (content), plus discusses the purpose and/or effects of what the author presents (form + function).

Setting the time and place of a literary work.

Simile an indirect comparison that uses the word *like* or *as* to link the differing items in the comparison. ("Your eyes are like stars.")

SOAPStone an acronym for Speaker, Occasion, Audience, Purpose, Subject, and Tone.

Sophistication for the purposes of AP English, presenting a variety of insights or viewpoints while rhetorically analyzing a specific text or arguing a point of view.

SPACE CAT an acronym for Speaker, Purpose, Audience, Context, Exigence, Choices, Appeals, Tone.

Stage Directions the specific instructions a playwright includes concerning sets, characterization, delivery, etc.

Stanza a unit of a poem, similar in rhyme, meter, and length to other units in the poem.

Structure the organization and form of a work.

Style the unique way an author presents his ideas. Diction, syntax, imagery, structure, and content all contribute to a particular style.

Summary reducing the original text to its essential parts.

Syllogism the format of a formal argument that consists of a major premise, a minor premise, and a conclusion.

Symbol something in a literary work that stands for something else. (Plato has the light of the sun symbolize truth in "The Allegory of the Cave.")

Synecdoche a figure of speech that utilizes a part as representative of the whole. ("All hands on deck" is an example.)

Syntax the grammatical structure of prose and poetry.

Synthesis locating a number of sources and integrating them into the development and support of a writer's thesis/claim.

Theme the underlying ideas the author illustrates through characterization, motifs, language, plot, etc.

Thesis a statement that introduces the position/viewpoint/insight that will be developed throughout the entire presentation.

Tone the author's attitude toward his subject.

Transition a word or phrase that links one idea to the next and carries the reader from sentence to sentence, paragraph to paragraph. See the list of transitions in Chapter 8.

Understatement the opposite of exaggeration. It is a technique for developing irony and/or humor where one writes or says less than intended.

Voice can refer to two different areas of writing. The first refers to the relationship between a sentence's subject and verb (active voice and passive voice). The second refers to the total "sound" of a writer's style.

SELECTED BIBLIOGRAPHY

The following is a select listing of both fiction and nonfiction writers, past and present, whose works include: essays, news articles, novels, short stories, journals, biographies, histories, autobiographies, diaries, satire, and political treatises. Each of these writers presents ideas in original, thought-provoking, and enlightening ways. Our recommendation is that you read as many and as much of them as you can. The more you read, discuss, and/or analyze these writers and their work, the better prepared you will be for the AP English Language and Composition exam. And, there is another wondrous benefit. You will become much more aware of the marvelous world of ideas that surrounds you. We invite you to accept our invitation to this complex universe.

Personal Writing: Journals, Autobiographies, Diaries

Maya Angelou
Annie Dillard
Frederick Douglass
Lillian Hellman
Helen Keller
Martin Luther King, Jr.
Maxine Hong Kingston

Mary McCarthy
Samuel Pepys
Richard Rodriguez
May Sarton
Richard Wright
Malcolm X

Biographies and Histories

Walter Jackson Bate
James Boswell
Thomas Carlyle
Robert A. Caro
Bruce Catton
Winston Churchill

Shelby Foote
Doris Kearns Goodwin
David McCullough
George Trevelyan
Barbara Tuchman

Journalists and Essayists

Joseph Addison
Michael Arlen
Matthew Arnold
Francis Bacon
Russell Baker
Harold Bloom
David Brooks
G. K. Chesterton

Pauline Kael
Garrison Keillor
Charles Krauthammer
John McPhee
N. Scott Momaday
Anna Quindlen
John Ruskin
Paul Russell

Ta Nehisi Coates
Kenneth Clark
Joan Didion
Ross Douthat
Maureen Dowd
Nora Ephron
Anne Fadiman
William Hazlett
John Holt
Ellen Goodman

Marjorie Sandor
Susan Sontag
Richard Steele
Brett Stephens
Henry David Thoreau
Calvin Trillin
Eudora Welty
E. B. White
George Wills
Paul Zimmer

Political Writing and Satire

Hannah Arendt
Simone de Beauvoir
W. E. B. DuBois
William F. Buckley
Thomas Hobbes
Thomas Jefferson
John Locke
Machiavelli

John Stuart Mill
Sir Thomas More
Lincoln Steffens
Jonathan Swift
Alexis de Tocqueville
T. H. White
Tom Wolfe

Writers Known for Their Fiction and Nonfiction

Charlotte Perkins Gilman
Zora Neale Hurston
Norman Mailer

George Orwell
Virginia Woolf

Naturalists, Scientists, Adventurers

Edward Abbey
Rachel Carson
Charles Darwin
Loren Eisley
Stephen Jay Gould
William Least Heat-Moon

Verlyn Klinkenborg
Barry Lopez
Peter Matthiessen
Margaret Mead
Carl Sagan

Literally thousands of websites are, in some way, related to the study of college-level English. We are not attempting to give you a comprehensive list of all these websites. What we want to do is to provide you with a list that is most relevant to your preparation and review for the AP English Language and Composition exam. You can decide which websites may be of interest and/or offer you special benefits.

> *Note:* **These websites were available and online at the time this book was revised. Please be aware that we cannot guarantee that a site you choose to explore will be operating when you go to that URL.**

- Because this is an Advanced Placement exam you are preparing for, why not go to the source as your first choice: http://apcentral.collegeboard.com.
- McGraw Hill has several sites that can be very helpful as you work your way through the AP English Language course and prepare for the exam in May: www.mhpracticeplus.com
- Dogpile: www.dogpile.com is a good search engine that finds topics via categories and other search engines.
- Search.com is one of the newest and best search engines that accesses the biggest of the search engines available at www.search.com.
- Bowling Green University Writer's Lab: http://www.firelands.bgsu.edu/library/writing-lab.html is chock full of information.
- Purdue On-Line Writing Lab (OWL): https://owl.english.purdue.edu/owl/section/1/ is a helpful online writing center with a huge set of links.
- A+ Research and Writing: http://www.ipl.org/div/aplus/ is a comprehensive guide to writing research papers.
- A portal site that links to the best of library and research sites is available at www.libraryspot.com. It consists of three sections: libraries (academic, film, government, and so forth), reference desk (almanacs, biographies, dictionaries, and so forth), and reading room (books, journals, newspapers, magazines).
- www.americanrhetoric.com has political speeches and speeches from movies.
- For terms, exercises, tips, and rules from a primate with attitude, go to Grammar Bytes: http://chompchomp.com.
- Two useful sites that provide help with rhetorical and literary terms are: http://andromeda.rutgers.edu/~jlynch/terms/index.html and http://humanities.byu.edu/rhetoric/Silva.htm
- You can compare coverage of major events in newspapers from around the world at www.newseum.org/todaysfrontpages.
- A website that provides access to the world of arts and letters—including newspapers, literary magazines, and blogs—is: https://www.aldaily.com/.

Each of these websites will lead you to many more. Take the time to explore the various sites and make your own evaluations about their value to you. You might even decide to set up your own AP Language website, or chat room!

5 Steps to Teaching AP English Language and Composition

TEACHER'S MANUAL

Barbara Murphy

Endorsed College Board Consultant, AP English Language
and AP English Literature Instructor

*Thanks to Greg Jacobs, an AP Physics teacher at Woodberry Forest School in Virginia,
for developing the 5-step approach used in this teaching guide.*

Introduction to the *Teacher's Manual*

Since the AP English Language exam is the culminative evaluation tool for your students' high school English career, it would be wonderful if it could be truly representative of all that you have covered in the course. But it is only a 3-hour test. Therefore, it must of necessity be general, and it must be wide-ranging enough to provide equity and opportunity for every student who takes the exam. What the test makers assume about the students who take the AP exam is a common background of terminology and skills. *5 Steps to a 5: AP English Language and Composition* provides a resource for terminology and skills, exam clarification and explanation, and practice when needed.

Currently, teachers have no shortage of resources for the AP English Language class. No longer limited to just the teacher and the textbook, today's teachers can utilize online simulations, apps, computer-based homework, video lectures, and so on. In all probability, you will consider using many of these resources in your class. Even the College Board, itself, provides so much material related to the AP English Language exam that the typical teacher—and student— can easily become overwhelmed by an excess of teaching materials and resources.

As one of your major resources, this book is a vital asset for your class because it explains in straightforward language exactly what a student needs to know for the AP English Language exam and provides a review program students can use to review for the test. In addition to test prep, the text presents activities to introduce, develop, and enrich the skills on which the AP English Language course is based.

The 5 Steps of Teaching AP English Language

This *Teacher's Manual* will take you through the 5 steps in approaching and teaching AP English Language. These 5 steps are:

▶ **Prepare a strategic plan for the course**

▶ **Hold an interesting class every day**

▶ **Evaluate your students' progress**

▶ **Get students ready for the AP exam**

▶ **Become a better teacher every year**

What follows is a discussion of each of these steps, providing suggestions and ideas that have been successfully used by myself and other AP English Language instructors in our classes. Over the years, you may have developed a different course strategy, teaching activities, and evaluation techniques. That's fine; different things work for different teachers. But my hope is that you find in this *Teacher's Manual* materials and ideas that will be useful and beneficial to you and to your students.

STEP 1

Prepare a Strategic Plan for the Course

The Course and Exam Description (CED) developed by the College Board is available at https://apcentral.collegeboard.org/pdf/ap-english-language-and-composition-course-and-exam-description.pdf. You should use this as your course bible. It lays out a suggested scope and sequence for the AP English Language course. It also provides a comprehensive description and analysis of each of the four Big Ideas of the course.

The AP English Language CED is built around the four Big Ideas shown in the chart below. These four Big Ideas are briefly described in the chart and are correlated to the units of study found in the CED. The chart also shows how *5 Steps to a 5: AP English Language* can easily be used in conjunction with these Big Ideas. It correlates each of the Big Ideas to the chapters and pages in this book.

BIG IDEAS	UNITS OF THE CED	*5 STEPS TO A 5*
Rhetorical Situation (RHS): Individuals write within a particular situation and make strategic writing choices based on that situation.	1, 2, 4, 7, 8	Chapter 5, pp. 73–74, 100 (chart)
Claims and Evidence (CLE): Writers make claims about subjects, rely on evidence that supports the reasoning that justifies the claim, and often acknowledge or respond to other, possibly opposing, arguments.	1. 2. 3, 4, 6, 7, 9	Chapter 5, pp. 92–94
Reasoning and Organization (REO): Writers guide understanding of a text's lines of reasoning and claims through that text's organization and integration of evidence.	3, 4, 5	Chapter 5, pp. 94–95; Chapter 8, pp. 149–150, 154–155; Chapter 9, pp. 164–166; Chapter 10, pp. 170–173
Style (STL): The rhetorical situation informs the strategic stylistic choices that writers make.	5, 6, 7, 8	Chapter 8, pp. 131 (chart), 140–148

When I work with teachers in College Board workshops and Summer Institutes, my initial suggestion, especially for new instructors, is to stick with the suggested scope and sequence specified in the CED. But you may have a desire to approach the course in a different way. You may want to use a plan that centers the course thematically, or chronologically, or by the three types of essays in the AP exam (rhetorical analysis, argument, and synthesis). Whatever your choice, make certain your plan provides for the introduction to and development of the prescribed AP English Language goals and skills.

No matter what strategic plan you decide to use, allow time for review before the exam in May. Two to three weeks is an adequate prep time.

The following is an example of a course plan that centers on the three types of AP English Language exam essays: rhetorical analysis, argument, and synthesis. It is an alternative to using the scope and sequence in the CED. This plan is based on a four-quarter school year that has approximately 10 weeks per quarter. The class meets five times a week with 40 minutes per class. In planning for your class, it will be necessary to plan for miscellaneous "adventures" that absent students from the class.

You'll want to leave some time for review. Teachers usually plan on taking two to four weeks of cumulative review. And don't forget that once AP testing starts, your students will be busy with other exams. Schedule your review so that your last practice exam is in the last week of April—right before exams commence.

Scope and Sequence for AP English Language

1st Quarter (35–40 Classes)

Students should be introduced to the basics of rhetorical analysis, both in close reading and in writing. Particular attention and practice should center on the rhetorical strategies of exemplification, comparison/contrast, and cause/effect. Skills development will emphasize the thesis, annotation, rhetorical situation, and line of reasoning. *Throughout the entire course, students should be provided practice with syntax and organization.*

5 CLASSES: THESIS AND LINE OF REASONING

- Modeling
- Practice

10–15 CLASSES: THE RHETORICAL STRATEGY—EXEMPLIFICATION

- Close reading of professional essays that employ exemplification
- Practice with annotation and analysis
- Development of the thesis, rhetorical situation, and line of reasoning
- Student essay(s) using exemplification to develop and support a thesis
- Rhetorical analysis of a professional essay

10 CLASSES: THE RHETORICAL STRATEGY—COMPARISON/CONTRAST

- Close reading of professional essays that employ comparison/contrast
- Practice with annotation and analysis
- Development of commentary techniques in a rhetorical analysis essay
- Student essay(s) using comparison/contrast to develop and support a thesis
- Rhetorical analysis of a professional essay

10 CLASSES: THE RHETORICAL STRATEGY—CAUSE/EFFECT

- Close reading of professional essays that employ cause/effect
- Practice with annotation and analysis
- Development of techniques to embed evidence and commentary
- Student essay(s) using cause/effect to develop and support a thesis
- Rhetorical analysis of a professional essay

2nd Quarter (36–40 Classes)

The same general structure continues for each quarter. Students draw on the work of the previous quarter(s) and use the skills already introduced to further develop analysis and sophistication.

1–2 CLASSES: INTRODUCTION TO THE AP ENGLISH LANGUAGE EXAM

▶ General overview of sample multiple-choice questions

▶ Examination of samples of the three free-response questions (synthesis, rhetorical analysis, and argument)

25 CLASSES: 5 CLASSES FOR EACH OF THE FOLLOWING RHETORICAL STRATEGIES

▶ Classification

▶ Process

▶ Definition

▶ Description

▶ Narration

This follows the pattern already established in the first quarter—but only one student essay for each of the strategies (may not be possible, given time constraints). Work with tone and diction.

10–13 CLASSES: THE RHETORICAL STRATEGY—ARGUMENT

▶ Close reading of professional argument essays

▶ Further development of line of reasoning

▶ Applying skills to various media

▶ Evaluating sources and evidence

▶ Student essay(s) using argument to develop and support a thesis

▶ Rhetorical analysis of a professional essay

3rd Quarter (35–40 classes)

This is the time to pivot more directly toward the exam with in-class practice with multiple choice and the three types of essays in the exam: rhetorical analysis, argument, and synthesis.

5 CLASSES: FINISH WORK WITH ARGUMENT

▶ Student essay assignments

20–25 CLASSES: THE RHETORICAL STRATEGY—SYNTHESIS

▶ Close reading of professional essays that employ synthesis

▶ Choosing a topic to investigate

▶ Locating and evaluating appropriate resource texts

▶ Incorporating sources into the text

▶ Composing the synthesis essay

10 CLASSES: PREP FOR THE AP ENGLISH LANGUAGE EXAM

AP daily videos on YouTube and *5 Steps* practice exams are good sources for review.

4th Quarter

5 CLASSES: FINAL PREP FOR THE EXAM

This is an ideal time to address specific questions the students may have about the exam in general and specific doubts or weaknesses.

THE EXAM . . . AND BEYOND

The AP English Language exam is given in the first or second week of May.

Depending on specific district requirements and the number of days/weeks remaining in the school year, the remaining classes could include:

▶ Creative media projects

▶ Preparing college application essays

▶ Special-interest projects

Hold an Interesting Class Every Day

We all want to create a course and classroom activities that have our students looking forward to being part of a challenging and interesting class. This excitement is based on your offering a wide range of activities, opportunities, and strategies that will help students understand and internalize the goals of the course.

Beginning or Ending Your Class

Ensure every student speaks and writes every day. Breaking the intellectual and verbal silence in the first 5 minutes makes it more likely students will participate during the rest of the class. Here are a few suggestions:

▶ Begin class with an activity from the "5 Minutes to a 5" section of the Elite Edition, which provides 180 activities, each about 5 minutes or less, that are related to specific skills that make up the AP English Language and Composition course.

▶ Begin class with something silly, like having students get to know one another by making a "culinary" choice ("Hamburger or pizza?"), or go for something more pedagogically nutritious ("What are two words to describe your reactions to today's reading?" or "Read a sentence you'd like to talk about from today's text").

Encourage self-reflection as a habit, rather than an assignment. For example:

▶ Begin class with a 2-minute daily journal entry. This offers a type of intellectual warm-up exercise.

▶ End class with a brief response (2–4 minutes) to a concept introduced during the class. This could be in the form of a journal entry, a question or remark written on a Post-it, or a suggestion for a follow-up activity.

The *Elite Edition* of this book provides additional questions that can be used in your class. As noted earlier, it contains 180 activities and questions that require 5 minutes a day or less. While they are primarily intended to be used by students studying for the test, you can use these as daily warm-ups in your course. To do this, you will need the chart below, which organizes these questions and activities by unit.

UNIT	QUESTIONS/ACTIVITIES IN THE *ELITE EDITION*
Unit 1: Multiple Choice: Reading	Days 3–16, 23
Unit 2: Multiple Choice: Writing	Days 17, 21
Unit 3: Thesis	Days 30–34, 46–48, 65, 93, 137
Unit 4: Rhetorical Situation	Days 100–101
Unit 5: Claims and Evidence	Days 102–110, 131, 150–167
Unit 6: Reasoning and Organization	Days 74, 117, 118, 125–129

Providing the Basic Information

Aside from assigning students to read the basic information or overview of a topic found in your course text, you can have students watch brief videos provided by both the College Board and YouTube. Students can also work on activities in the *5 Steps to a 5: AP English Language and Composition* that are specifically related to a skill being addressed in class.

One of the most important techniques you can employ is *modeling*. Imagine your AP English Language students with their first essay assignment: "You are to write an analysis of Joan Didion's 'Why I Write.'" They could read about it in the textbook. They could just write. Or you could model for the class the process of writing a rhetorical analysis, argument, or synthesis essay. Your students can and will follow your lead. Modeling is a proven method for teaching skills. You can do this; your students will follow your lead.

Structuring the Full-Process Essay

The full-process essay set of activities, described below, is premised on prior instruction on the definition of the specific mode of discourse or rhetorical strategy under consideration. It also requires prior practice with close reading and analysis of several professionally written texts that are illustrative of that mode or strategy.

This is primarily a three-class set of activities (120 minutes) that culminates in a revised, well-organized, clear, and concise essay of between 500 and 800 words. All activities are completed in class except for the first and final drafts, which are written at home. The final draft is submitted with all writing activities attached in order.

Using this format, the first essay is the personal essay, which allows the student to practice using the mode or strategy within an accessible topic area. Essays 2 and 3 are rhetorical analysis essays based on a specific text with emphasis on a specific rhetorical strategy.

Technique for Writing the Full-Process Essay

DAY 1

▸ Locate and examine a controlling idea (area of inquiry).

▸ Decide on a preliminary topic (I'm interested in _____ related to the controlling idea).

▸ Create the preliminary claim, thesis, and assertion.

▸ Outline the major points to be included in the essay.

Using the preliminary activities as the basis, the student writes the first draft at home and brings two to three copies of the essay to the next class.

DAY 2

▸ The first draft is discussed and critiqued by the peer-group members.

▸ The writer does the prescribed activities related to revision (editing and proofreading).

▸ The writer responds to the comments of the peer group.

At home, the student writes the final draft based upon the work completed in his or her peer group and proofreads the final draft before bringing two to three copies of the finished essay to the next class.

DAY 3

▸ A member of the student's peer group reads the final draft aloud back to the writer.

▸ After it is read aloud, the student has a choice of either submitting the essay as is or making revisions and handing it in before the end of the school day.

Multiple Choice

Experienced AP English instructors most often report that students struggle with multiple-choice questions because the students do not spend enough time reading the passages—and that's because they are so worried about the number of questions that have to be answered in the 1-hour time limit. Here are a few suggestions that may prove helpful when approaching multiple choice:

▸ Read and engage with varied types of nonfiction.

▸ Model the techniques of annotation. (See Chapter 5, pp. 76–79.)

▸ Practice the skills for reading multiple-choice stems.

▸ Practice the strategies for answering multiple-choice questions. (See Chapter 4, pp. 47–49.)

▸ Don't try to do everything at once.

  ▷ Try one text and choose a limited number of multiple-choice questions.

  ▷ Work with one type of multiple-choice question at a time. (See Chapter 4, p. 44.)

  ▷ Plan the multiple-choice activity for a specific day and time, such as every other Monday for the first half of the period.

Your first resource for multiple-choice questions that apply to all AP English Language units and formats is the AP Classroom. Here you will find both multiple-choice questions and explanations of correct choices. There is no need to reinvent the wheel.

Activities for the Multiple-Choice Questions

Using the multiple-choice format, you can create activities related to rhetorical analysis and the writing process. The following are two activities that have been proved to be quite successful. Both are student-centered.

Activity 1: Game   Students are given a text with accompanying multiple-choice questions without being given the correct answer. Students are assigned a question and asked to determine the correct choice and defend it. This activity can be changed into a game using one multiple-choice passage and its questions. AP instructor Matt Brisbin sets up this game as follows:

▶ Place students into four groups and assign each group a letter: A, B, C, D. Students will read the passage and decide if their letter is the correct answer.

▶ If students believe their letter is the correct answer, they stand up. If they're incorrect, they lose points. If they stand up and it is their letter, they gain points. If they don't stand up at all, their score stays the same. (Each group starts with 10 points so they have something to lose from the beginning.)

▶ The score is kept for the allotted period of time, and the winning group is declared when the time expires. You choose the prize. After groups have discussed passages and decided on answers, you can lead the group through the questions.

Activity 2: Practice   Choose one passage with a specific goal in mind. You make the decision of whether this will be an individual, small-group, or whole-class presentation. (This is not a graded activity.)

▶ Timing the activity: number of questions + 2 = minutes for reading and questions. (This is always adjustable based on the length/difficulty of the text.)

▶ Students read and annotate the text. (You may decide to have the students read the stems before reading the text. This may provide a kind of "heads-up" prior to reading.)

▶ Students answer the multiple-choice questions. You can identify what type of question each question is; this allows you and the students to see which types are causing any difficulty.

▶ Cite the correct answers and invite the students to discuss what was easy for them, what was difficult and why, and what questions they might have.

QUESTIONS

Asking students the right questions is an important part of the teacher's tool box. At the end of this teaching manual, you'll find questions you can use to help students understand both rhetorical analysis and argument.

STEP 3

Evaluate Your Students' Progress

The best way to evaluate student progress is to develop units that incorporate elements of the skills needed for the exam as presented in the CED for AP English Language. This plan also allows the teacher to incorporate these approaches with specific sections of *5 Steps to a 5*. While each of the following recommendations fall under an approach for the course, a reference is given in parentheses that shows where this approach fits contextually in *5 Steps to a 5*. This advice focuses on opportunities for teachers to reinforce lessons offered throughout the text. The placements of the recommendations are merely suggestions; the timing and extent of teacher integration of these recommendations would naturally be based on the needs of students and the rhythms of the class. *Note: 5 Steps to a 5* is available online in the Cross-Platform Prep Course. See the back cover of this book for instructions on accessing it.

The recommendations include the following:

The Arc of the Course (Chapters 1 and 2)

While some elements of discrete knowledge (such as learning terms related to rhetoric) are valuable in preparation for the exam, the AP English Language exam is primarily skill-based. Therefore, the teacher should look for students to have numerous encounters with varied texts (focused on nonfiction) so that the structures, ideas, and techniques within them can be analyzed. Students should have numerous encounters with texts from earlier time periods. The greater exposure provided over time through discussion and analysis, the better equipped students will be to handle this material on the exam.

Approaches to the Units (Chapter 2)

While the need for test prep is duly acknowledged, the reviews, diagnostics, and practice exams work better as integrated elements within specific units. A timed essay as the culmination of a unit offers both AP practice and an opportunity for students to crystallize their ideas about a type of prompt. Furthermore, a unit and chapter can incorporate texts specifically related to rhetorical analysis, or argument, or synthesis. Test prep can be drudgery. By integrating the multiple-choice passages and essays into the course units, the bludgeonings from one test after another just before the actual AP exam can be avoided.

Essay Approaches (Chapters 5–10)

Teachers can use the activities in these steps to help develop students' knowledge and skills related to rhetorical analysis, argument, and synthesis. A strong foundation of rhetorical techniques and how to apply them will make students better equipped to handle these essays. Furthermore, lessons and practices in annotating texts will help students gain a better grasp of how to develop responses and a line of reasoning.

Multiple-Choice Approaches (Chapter 4)

Before students move on to the "Explanations of Answers" on page 64, teachers should have students review their incorrect answers in the multiple-choice section of the diagnostic exam. First, teachers might want to go over the most challenging of the multiple-choice passages, discussing what made a particular choice right for each question of the passage. This modeling will lead to students returning to the other passages and their wrong answers. With the correct answers given to them, the students should look to explain briefly in writing (a sentence or two) why a particular answer is correct. To incentivize greater commitment from students in this assignment, teachers can offer either points back on an exam or extra credit. Clearly, for this approach to work, students cannot look at the answer explanations provided on pages 63–66 until they have completed the correction assignment.

The Thesis Statement (Chapter 8, p. 158)

As the chart on page 158 indicates, a clear, strong, sophisticated thesis statement not only will give students the first point on the rubric, but also will establish a direction so that students can go about collecting the additional 4 points that can be gained through evidence and commentary. Therefore, teachers will serve their students well by constantly presenting opportunities for them to compose thesis statements in spoken or written form. The openings of excerpts and full-length texts often offer possibilities for students to draft thesis statements. Teachers can help students hone their skills by encouraging them to go beyond simple arguments. Students should be aware of the warnings and limitations (even contradictions) embedded in the passage. When choosing material for student practice, look for passages that have undercurrents that may temper or undermine a seemingly apparent argument.

Annotation (Chapter 5, pp. 76–79, and Chapter 6)

After students have carefully read pages 76–79, teachers might give another passage to annotate as a small-group exercise. This annotation followed by a thesis statement, or if time permits, an entire introduction, advances student growth without committing to completing an entire essay.

Reinforcement in annotation should be considered. Large-group, small-group, and independent responses can all be employed. Small-group work followed by a larger-group discussion (which would benefit from some modeling) should serve to build confidence and comfort with the material and the concomitant annotation.

Annotation should not be limited to the primary texts. Teachers can ask students to highlight and make notes in the margins for both the student samples on pages 96 and 97. The annotation will increase the likelihood of students absorbing the lessons and skills of these samples rather than simply reading and forgetting them. Larger-group sharing, following the independent annotation, would further enhance the lessons. Teachers can use the same approach for Chapter 5, for both the student essays.

AP Classroom

If you or another AP English Language instructor has created a College Board–approved syllabus, then you and your students have access to the AP Classroom, which is a dedicated online platform designed to support AP teachers and students. The platform offers a variety of powerful resources and tools that provide yearlong support to teachers and enable students to receive meaningful feedback on their progress

STEP 4

Get Students Ready to Take the AP Exam

They have also practiced, at least once in each unit, specific types of multiple-choice questions related to selected, brief texts. In the final weeks before the exam, students should receive increased in-class exposure to both the essays and the multiple-choice questions for the exam.

As a rule, students should begin their direct preparation of the AP English Language exam approximately 2 to 3 weeks prior to the May date. Depending on the teacher's approach or other mitigating circumstances, review and prep for the exam might include activities completed individually, in small groups, or with the full class. For example, the review for the exam could include:

▶ A full practice exam as presented in the *5 Steps to a 5* (Practice Exams 1 and/or 2). Given the time constraints of a class period, the multiple-choice section and the essays should be allotted a full period each, or more if needed.

▶ Concentration on each section of the exam separately.

▶ Review of previous exams.

▶ AP Classroom practice.

STEP 5

Become a Better Teacher Every Year

The AP English Language course focuses on the development and revision of evidence-based analytic and argumentative writing, the rhetorical analysis of nonfiction texts, and the decisions writers make as they compose and revise. The first-time teacher of the course should be primarily committed to introducing students to the multilayered process of rhetorical analysis, argument, and synthesis. In addition, that teacher should look to draw on nonfiction from a broad variety of authors, time periods, subjects, and cultures.

Building on the basics of the course, teachers should look to add more texts and activities that can strengthen and enrich the core skills and goals of the course. Each new year is an opportunity to explore additional works and activities with students that will broaden the nature of analysis and argument. Finally, the teachers should look for new ways to help students hone their crafts as writers and readers as they move beyond what a text says to what an author does to present and enrich that claim to an audience.

A variety of curriculum development workshops, conferences, professional organizations, videos, and institutes are available to AP English Language instructors throughout the year. Here are some suggestions:

- Check AP Central (http://apcentral.college board.com/apc/public/courses/teachers _corner/2123.html) for the listings of College Board–sponsored workshops and summer institutes.

- Join the AP Central English Teacher Discussion Group (https://apcommunity .collegeboard.org/web/apenglish/home).

- Consider joining these Facebook groups (by invitation) for AP English Language teachers:

  ▷ AP Language and Composition Teachers (https://www.facebook.com/ groups/335905713208037)

  ▷ AP Language and Composition Resource Group for Teachers (https://www .facebook.com/groups/2567237349 40746)

Additional Resources for Teachers

Literally thousands of websites are, in some way, related to the study of college-level English. Here is a list of resources that were selected because they are most relevant to the AP English Language and Composition exam. *Note:* These websites were live at the time this book was revised. However, it is possible that the URL for a particular site may have changed or ceased operation.

- Because this is an Advanced Placement exam you are preparing for, go to the source as your first choice: http://apcentral.collegeboard .com.

- Dogpile (https://www.dogpile.com) is a good search engine that finds topics via categories and other search engines.

- BGSU Firelands Writing Lab (https://www .firelands.bgsu.edu/tlc/writing-lab.html) is chock-full of useful information.

- Purdue On-Line Writing Lab, otherwise known as OWL (https://owl.purdue.edu/ writinglab/the_writing_lab_at_purdue.html), is a helpful online writing center with a huge set of links.

- A+ Research & Writing (http://www.ipl.org/ div/aplus/) is a comprehensive guide to writing research papers.

- American Rhetoric (https://www .americanrhetoric.com) has political speeches and speeches from movies.

- Grammar Bytes (http://chompchomp.com) provides terms, exercises, tips, and rules from a primate with attitude!

- Two useful sites that provide help with rhetorical and literary terms are:

  ▷ AP Language and Composition Glossary of Literary and Rhetorical Devices (https:// yale.learningu.org/download/f10e0a0e -1866-4958-9058-11e84f35ad24/H2976 _APEngLangGlossary.pdf)

  ▷ Glossary of Rhetorical Terms (https://mcl .as.uky.edu/glossary-rhetorical-terms)

- Arts & Letters Daily (https://www.aldaily .com/) provides access to the world of arts and letters—including newspapers, literary magazines, and blogs.

- The Electric Typewriter (https://tetw.org/ Greats) offers excellent short articles and essays, long reads, and journalism—examples of interesting nonfiction writing by famous authors.

▸ AP Classroom Tutorial Series (https://www
.youtube.com/results?search_query=AP
+Classroom+tutorial+series) hosts free, live
sessions on YouTube that provide complete
in-depth looks at the resources and supports
available in the AP Classroom.

▸ Owens Community College Writing Center,
"Sentence Variety" (https://www.owens.edu/
media/writing/sentvar.pdf), has activities to
create variety and interest in students' writing.

▸ The Garden of English (https://www.the
gardenofenglish.com/) has instructional
videos for students and teachers, as well as
resource pages for teachers.

▸ CommonLit (https://www.commonlit.org/
en) is a searchable catalog of texts paired
with guiding questions, multiple-choice
questions, and discussion questions. The
site scores student multiple-choice questions
and provides exemplars for student-written
responses.

▸ Angie Kratzer (https://angiekratzer.com/)
writes curriculum materials so that teachers can
spend their time and energy on differentiation
and feedback, not the reinvention of the wheel.

▸ Coach Hall Writes (https://www.youtube
.com/c/CoachHallWrites) has instructional
videos to help guide teachers and students
through different components of the AP
English Language and Composition course.

▸ The *New York Times* Learning Network
(https://www.nytimes.com/section/learning)
has resources for student writing and teacher
lesson plans based on current events. It also
publishes teacher and student content with
multimedia resources for cross-curricular
learning.

AP English Language Teachers Tool Box

In the tool box you will find a list of basic
questions for your students to help them
understand rhetorical analysis and argument,
followed by a list of recommended resources for
AP English Language and Composition.

Basic Questions

**Basic Questions for Rhetorical Analysis
(Chapters 5 and 8)**   There are many ways
to address the process of rhetorical analysis.
The first is to make certain to carefully review
the information presented in the AP English
Language CED. Coupled with the CED
overview, you could ask the following questions:

▸ What is the rhetorical situation?

▸ Who is the author/speaker?

▸ What is his or her intention in speaking?

▸ Who is the audience?

▸ What is the content of the message?

▸ What is the form in which it is conveyed?

▸ How do form and content correspond?

▸ Does the message/speech/text succeed in
fulfilling the author's or speaker's intentions?

▸ What does the nature of the communication
reveal about the culture that produced it?

Or you could apply the tried-and-true AP Language acronym SOAPStone, asking "who is?"/"what is?" in reference to the:

- *S*peaker
- *O*ccasion
- *A*udience
- *P*urpose
- *S*ubject
- *T*one

Basic Questions for Argument (Chapters 6 and 9)   As with the basic questions for rhetorical analysis, make certain to carefully review the information presented in the AP English Language CED. You could couple the CED overview with the following questions:

- Is there a clearly developed thesis?
- Are facts distinguished from opinions?
- Are opinions supported and qualified?
- Does the speaker develop a logical argument and avoid fallacies in reasoning?
- Is support for facts tested, reliable, and authoritative?
- Does the speaker confuse *or* not confuse appeals to logic and emotion?
- Are opposing views represented in a fair and undistorted way?
- Does the argument reflect a sense of audience?
- Does the argument reflect an identifiable voice and point of view?
- Does the argument reflect the image of a speaker with identifiable qualities (honesty, sincerity, authority, intelligence, etc.)?

Texts Recommended for AP English Language and Composition

- *Saturday Night*, by Susan Orlean. A *quinceañeras* story
- *The Library Book*, by Susan Orlean. Story of the burning and rebuilding of the Los Angeles Public Library
- *All Over but the Shoutin'*, by Rick Bragg. Personal narrative
- *Thousand Pieces of Gold*, by Ruthanne Lum McCunn. Personal narrative
- *Give War a Chance*, by P. J. O'Rourke. Argumentation
- *Monster*, by Sanyika Shakur (aka Monster Kody Scott). Personal narrative
- *Voice Lessons*, by Nancy Dean. Lessons in tone, diction, and syntax
- *Rhetorical Grammar*, by Martha Kolln. Syntactical strategies for writers
- *Song Dogs*, by Colum McCann. Memoir, descriptive writing, rich in similes and visual imagery
- *Blue Highways*, *PrairyErth*, and *River-Horse*, by William Least Heat-Moon. Personal narratives, description, place
- *Pilgrim at Tinker Creek*, *The Living*, and *The Writing Life*, by Annie Dillard. Personal narratives, essays
- *Blue Pastures*, by Mary Oliver. Place, narratives
- "A Hanging" and "Shooting an Elephant," by George Orwell. Structure, narration, tone, attitude
- *In Pharaoh's Army*, by Tobias Wolff. Narrative, voice
- *All but My Life*, by Gerda W. Klein. Narrative, description, voice

▸ *Into Thin Air*, by Jon Krakauer. Narrative, description

▸ *The Perfect Storm*, by Sebastian Junger. Narrative, mood, tone, description

▸ *In the Heart of the Sea*, by Nathaniel Philbrick. Narrative, description

▸ *Still Life with Rice*, by Helie Lee. Memoir, personal narrative, voice

▸ *Reading Lolita in Tehran*, by Azar Nafisi. A must for all who teach literature

▸ *If It Bleeds, It Leads: An Anatomy of Television News*, by Matthew R. Kerbel. Media literacy/persuasion

▸ *Amusing Ourselves to Death*, by Neil Postman. Essays/readings on modern culture

▸ *Reading Like a Writer*, by Francine Prose. A must for those who teach both writing and literature; great teaching tool

▸ *The Bookseller of Kabul*, by Åsne Seierstad. Nonfiction; even better than *The Kite Runner*

▸ *Fast Food Nation*, by Eric Schlosser. The dark side of the all-American meal

▸ *Nickel and Dimed*, by Barbara Ehrenreich. On not getting by in America

▸ *My Year of Meats*, by Ruth L. Ozeki. Comical-satirical novel about two women on opposite sides of the globe dealing with issues important to everyday life

▸ *Freakonomics*, by Steven D. Levitt and Stephen J. Dubner. Explores the "hidden side" of everything

▸ *Tipping Point*, by Malcolm Gladwell. Tries to explain and describe "the moment of critical mass, the threshold, the boiling point" in life

▸ *Three Cups of Tea*, by Greg Mortenson. Story of one man's mission to promote peace, one school at a time